W9-BXO-194

JERUSALEM
PRAYER TEAM
✡

John,

I love you — Thank you
for being my partner

Happy Holidays!

Mike and Carolyn

DR. MICHAEL D. EVANS

Son, I Love You

MIKE EVANS

#1 *NEW YORK TIMES* BESTSELLING AUTHOR

Son, I Love You

(Strangled by His Father and Left for Dead)

TimeWorthy
BOOKS

P.O. Box 30000, Phoenix, AZ 85046

Son, I Love You

Copyright 2017 by Time Worthy Books
P. O. Box 30000
Phoenix, AZ 85046

Design: Peter Gloege | LOOK Design Studio

Hardcover:	978-1-62961-144-0
Paperback:	978-1-62961-143-3
Canada:	978-1-62961-145-7

All rights reserved. No portion of this book may be reproduced, stored in a
retrieval system, or transmitted in any form or by any means—electronic,
mechanical, photocopy, recording, or any other—except for brief quotations
in printed reviews, without the prior permission of the publisher.

This book is dedicated to
my beloved wife, Carolyn.

She is the most selfless person I know
and my best friend. Carolyn told me
that the greatest evidence Jesus Christ
is real on earth is my life.

> Christians kill Jews.
>
> Christians hate Jews.
>
> The Pope, Billy Graham,
>
> and Adolf Hitler
>
> were all Christians.
>
> Jesus died.
>
> Don't dig him up.
>
> —JEANIE LEVINE EVANS

The story begins in March 1913,

in the Pale of Settlement.

CHAPTER

1

A cool breeze swept through the treetops as Michla stood outside the tiny wooden post office. In one hand she held the letter, its words scrawled in Schleman's unmistakable Cyrillic script. In her other was the money that had accompanied it—well-worn currency from the United States, smoothed flat from the long journey the letter had taken from New York to the village of Naroulia where she lived. Almost two hundred dollars in total. She'd never seen even a single dollar from the United States and had no way of knowing how much it was really worth. She only knew it was enough to pay for passage on a ship to the United States for her and her two sons.

"America," she whispered, as a sense of sadness welled up inside. "It is finally time to go."

After two years, filled with long nights yearning for the time when she and Schleman would once again be reunited and equally long days wishing for her sons to be once again with their father, at last the day had arrived when they could begin the journey and complete their dream of being together again. Of living in a country that offered them safety and a bright future for their children. And now she found the moment wasn't at all what she'd expected.

She was glad that she and Schleman would be together again, as a husband and wife should be. And equally glad that their sons would be with their father. But getting all of them together again as a family would come at an expense. One beyond the cost of passage on a ship or the anxiety of settling in a new land.

From the time of her birth until the day the letter arrived from Schleman, Michla had lived in the Gomel and Minsk regions of Belarus, which then was part of the Russian Empire. Now the prospect of leaving Russia and traveling to America, of going beyond the familiar confines of the region, of leaving the only home she'd known, left her nostalgic, anxious, and already homesick.

Not so much a longing for the place, perhaps, as for the memories. Of growing up in Mazyr, forty miles to the northwest, the town where she was born. And of Vishnyeva, still farther to the north, where her parents lived. She'd been separated from them, too, but they were only a few hours away by train. If she went to America, she might never see them again. Returning would be impossible for her. Or for any of them. They would become Americans, through and through, with no possibility of living in Russia again.

Not that living in America will be a bad thing, she thought as she tucked the letter and money back into the envelope. *There's certainly nothing here for us now.*

Since the death of Tsar Alexander III, life had become unbearable for Jews in the Russian Empire. Not only were economic conditions deplorable but persecution and sporadic waves of ethnic cleansing made life treacherous. Even in Michla's native Belarus, roaming bands of Russians attacked them, indiscriminately dragging Jews from their homes and shops and from the streets. Sometimes beating them. Sometimes killing them. Sometimes burning their homes. And all of it with the approval of the current tsar, Nicholas II.

Three days later, Michla took the boys, Nochem and Mottle, on the train and traveled north, toward Vishnyeva. If she was going to America—and she most certainly was—she could not leave without telling her parents. More than that, she would need their help.

As the train passed through Mazyr, she remembered the day she and Schleman married. It was a wonderful day and it seemed the entire town had turned out for the ceremony. They danced and sang and laughed all day and into the night. And the thought of that night brought a smile to her face. Schleman had been so nervous. She would have been, too, if she'd stopped to think about what would happen after everyone was gone and they were alone in the bedroom. But she pushed it from her mind and only thought about it when the moment came, and then she wasn't nervous but excited. He, apparently, had been thinking of it all day and as the evening grew late kept telling their cousins, Simon Cohen and Shura Guzman, who were playing the violin and providing the music, to play yet one more song. And he continued to swing her around and insist on one more dance, laughing and singing with the music the entire time. Later she learned just how anxious he had been about the married things they would do when they were alone.

It seemed like such a long time ago and memories of the years they'd been together filled her mind, but as the train continued north past Mazyr her thoughts moved on to her childhood and growing up with Bella, her sister, in their father's house. They played and laughed together, and they dreamed together, too. At first of marrying and living the life of a wife and mother. Then of moving beyond the Pale of Settlement—the region of the Russian Empire, including Belarus, where Jews were allowed legally to reside—of attending the Bestuzhev Courses in St. Petersburg, the highest schooling offered for Russian women. Michla was certain neither of them really believed that dream would come true, but they never spoke of their doubts, only of their optimism and hope that one day they would be educated and equipped for a life beyond the confines of Russian limitations. And now that life was opening before her. Not in St. Petersburg and not in Russia, but in America where—

Just then, Nochem spoke up. "I'm hungry."

Michla opened an oversized bag made of heavy fabric and pulled out a small loaf of bread. She pinched off a piece and handed it to him, then gave some to Mottle. They leaned against her, one seated on either side, and slowly chewed the bread. She was hungry, too, but she would wait before eating. It wasn't that far to where they were going. Not today. On the trip to America, that would be different. But for now she could last a day without food.

Late that afternoon they arrived on the outskirts of Vishnyeva, a town of modest size located halfway between Minsk and Vilnius. The train slowed as it clattered gently past a stockyard and tannery, then along rows of houses that lined the dirt streets on either side of the tracks. As Michla let her eyes scan over the settlement, she again saw what she'd always noticed about it—that all of the structures were made of wood, unpainted and weathered to a gray hue that gave the place a bleak appearance, as if the town were forever trapped in the overcast twilight of winter, even on a pleasant summer day.

In a few minutes the station came into view, and as the train slowed along the platform Michla saw her father, Mikael. He made his way down the platform, timing his steps to the speed of the train, reaching a point opposite the door to their car when the train came to a stop.

His payot—the magnificent dark curls hanging from his temples—protruded from beneath his black broad-brimmed hat and dangled past his ears to his jaw. His beard fell across the collar of his jacket and tumbled toward his chest. *He looks like a rabbi,* she thought. And indeed he was.

As chief rabbi at the synagogue near the center of town, Mikael was responsible for the care and direction of the region's largest congregation. He'd held that position since not long after Michla and Schleman had married.

With Mikael that day was Zvi Meltzer, the cantor rabbi—the *chazzan*—who acted as Mikael's assistant, helping with services at the synagogue. In his official duties, he led the congregation in worship, guiding them in the prayers and readings. Unofficially, he was Mikael's best friend.

Her sons in tow, Michla made her way up the aisle to the door of the train car and down the steps to the platform. Mikael stepped forward to greet her. Michla collapsed against him, her head resting on his chest, her arms wrapped around his waist. "Oh, Papa," she sighed. "I have missed you."

He gave her a hug. "And I have missed you."

After a moment, Mikael pulled away and knelt beside her, taking the boys in his arms. "You two have grown a meter since I saw you."

"You say that all the time," Nochem giggled.

"And each time I say it," Mikael laughed, "it becomes truer than before."

Michla greeted Rabbi Meltzer, then they slowly walked up the platform, through the station building, and around to a horse-drawn wagon that was parked on the street side. Rabbi Meltzer put her bag in back and helped her up to the seat while Mikael lifted his grandsons and set them in the wagon. Then Rabbi Meltzer got in with the boys, Mikael sat on the seat with Michla, and they started toward the house.

The day they arrived was market day, when farmers from the surrounding countryside came to town to sell their produce and livestock. Baskets filled with vegetables and cages of chickens lined the street near the train station. Interspersed were pots full of wonderful things to eat and tables covered with quilts and clothes made by the people who lived in town. The crowd was large and the sound of it rose around them, all but drowning out the plodding clop of the horse's hooves and the rusted creak of the wagon wheels turning beneath them.

Although she'd never lived there, the town had always felt like home to her and now, as she absorbed the sights and sounds of it once more, the same sense of sadness she'd felt that day at the post office welled up inside her. *This may be the last time I see this town. The last time I see their faces or hear their voices. And the last time I smell the aroma of their presence.* A lump formed in her throat but she swallowed hard, slipped her arm in the crook of Mikael's elbow, and leaned against his shoulder.

✦ ✦ ✦

Late that evening, after the boys were asleep, Michla sat at the dining table with Mikael and Goldy, her mother. Michla reached into her pocket and took out the letter, then handed it to her father. "This is why I came to see you."

Goldy reached across the table and gave Michla's arm a squeeze. "I knew there must be more to it than merely a visit. And whatever it is, you did the right thing coming to us."

Mikael read the letter, then handed it to Goldy. Tears filled her eyes as she scanned over it. "I prayed this day would never come," she whispered softly. "And I prayed it would come quickly." She laid the letter on the table and wiped her eyes.

Mikael gestured to the letter. "And he sent you the money?"

"Yes, I have it in a safe place." Michla looked over at him. "He thinks it should be more than enough for the trip."

Mikael nodded. "It should be."

"But where do I begin? Where do I buy the tickets for the ship? And what ship do we take?"

"Relax," Goldy patted her arm once more. "One thing at a time."

"You can't purchase tickets until you get to the ship's office," Mikael explained. "So you will have to wait to buy them until you get to Libau."

Michla frowned. "Libau?"

"Yes."

"In Latvia?"

"Yes."

"Why not Riga?"

"You must go to Libau. Just as Schleman did."

"But why Libau?"

"The authorities in Libau are...more sympathetic."

"Oh." Michla looked away with a worried expression. "That is a long way," she said softly.

Mikael noticed the look in her eye and heard the concern in her voice. "I will go with you." He made the offer without checking first with Goldy.

"But we can't make it in a day."

"No, we can't," Mikael conceded. "But we can stay with Semyon Ginsberg and his wife. I will make the arrangements."

"They are in Lithuania. I thought we were going to Latvia."

"We must go through Lithuania first. To get to Latvia." He smiled at her. "I will help you. Don't worry. You will see."

"You will write and make the arrangements?"

"Certainly he will," Goldy replied. She cast a glance in his direction as she turned to Michla. "He will travel with you and the boys as far as Libau. It will be fun."

Michla nodded with a wan smile. "Perhaps you could come to America with us? Both of you?"

Mikael shook his head. "No. Our place is here. We must care for our people."

Michla couldn't help but notice the sadness in her mother's eyes. As if she knew something terrible awaited them. Something horrible and unspeakable. Something inescapable.

Their fate, Michla mused silently. *She knows their fate already.*

Schleman had warned her of what was coming. "The Germans will return. And the end for those of us who remain will be worse than any our people have ever known."

She hadn't understood him then, and even now she wasn't sure what he meant. But her mother knew. And if her mother knew, so also did her father, though he never spoke about it. Never said *anything* about the Russians or the Germans or anyone else. He was careful, she realized. Cautious. As were many his age.

Sitting at the table that night with her parents, a foreboding sense of doom settled over Michla. The threat Schleman had warned her about—whatever that threat might be—was real. And it was not merely a threat to her parents or to her or to those who remained in the region. It was a threat to her children. Nochem and Mottle were in danger. Serious danger. She didn't know what it was. She didn't know how things would happen. But she knew that whatever was going to happen, it was going to be even more real than any of them could imagine. And with that realization came the urge to flee right then. To get up from the table, take her children, and go.

"Perhaps we should go tonight," she suggested.

"Not now," Mikael replied. "We must make arrangements."

"The Ginsbergs will not give us a place to sleep if we arrive unexpected?"

"It is not them we are concerned about."

"Then who?"

"The Bulak-Balakhowich."

Michla frowned. "The volunteers? I have never heard of them."

"Not merely volunteers," Mikael replied. "But the Bulak-Balakhowich. A volunteer army."

"You never know who might be watching," Goldy added. "You must not arouse suspicions."

"Watching?" Michla asked, still not understanding. "People are watching us?"

"It will be fine," Mikael said with a smile. "We will go in a few weeks. After I have made the arrangements. Then we will go. When all is in order."

"That will be soon enough?"

He nodded. "Yes. It will be soon enough."

✦ ✦ ✦

Three weeks later, Michla traveled by train with her father and her sons northward across Belarus and into Lithuania. The border crossing went without a problem, their papers permitted it without restriction, and they spent the night at Vilnius with the Ginsbergs.

The following day, they continued north to Klaipeda, a town on the coast of the Baltic Sea. Neither Michla nor her sons had ever seen the sea, and the sight of it, with its seemingly unending expanse, made her realize how enormous their adventure was.

"It's so big," she said as she stared out at the waves.

"And that is not even the Atlantic," Mikael noted.

"I know," Michla sighed, though she hadn't thought of it until then.

"Don't worry," Mikael said. "A journey is taken one step at a time. Not all at once. You only have to do what's next."

"And what is next?"

"We wait...for nighttime."

They rested that evening at the home of Esther Kopel, an elderly woman who lived alone in an apartment above a butcher's shop. Michla had never met her before, but Esther seemed to know Mikael very well and she doted on Nochem and Mottle with chocolate babka and rugelach.

That night, they traveled by truck to Būtingė, a rural community just south of the Latvian border. A slender gray-haired man met them there, hid them, and then took them into Latvia. They traveled beneath the load of a freight wagon that carried stacks of lumber, the timbers cut and arranged to form a hollow cavity in the center of the load with just enough room for Mikael, Michla, and her sons.

It was late the next day when they arrived at Libau. All the ships' offices were closed. Mikael found a room in a boardinghouse where they could have dinner and spend the night. The room had only one bed, which Mikael insisted Michla and her sons should share.

"And where will you sleep?" she asked.

"Over here," Mikael grinned, pointing to an overstuffed chair in the corner.

"You cannot sleep all night sitting in a chair."

"I have done it many times before," he insisted. "And besides, I will return home to my bed."

"The ship will not have beds?"

"Not like the one you will sleep on tonight."

The following day they went to the office of the Russian American Line, a shipping line that was part of the East Asiatic Company. Mikael insisted it was the best. "They make a trip to New York almost every week," he explained. "And not one of their ships has had any trouble."

Trouble. Michla hadn't thought about trouble at sea. Ships sometimes had trouble. Boilers exploded. Engines failed. And icebergs. She'd known about all of these. She just hadn't thought of them. Or maybe she didn't want to think about them. And anyway, there was nothing she could do about it. She had to go to New York, and travel by ship was the only way.

After examining her papers—a birth certificate and immunization card—the clerk at the shipping office issued Michla tickets for passage to New York on the *SS Czar*. It had arrived two days before and was preparing for departure the next morning.

The clerk nodded to Nochem and Mottle. "You may board now, if you like. We have a full complement of passengers for this trip and if you wait until tomorrow you will stand in line all day."

"Thank you," Mikael replied. "We need to return for their luggage."

"The crew will be there all day." The clerk paused to scribble a note, then handed it to him. "This is the location of the *Czar*. Simply show up at that berth."

Michla looked over at Mikael. "What about Schleman?"

Mikael had a puzzled look. "What about him?"

"How will he know to meet us?"

"I will send a message to him."

Michla looked perplexed. "You can do that?"

"Yes, I will send a message to him in New York. He will be waiting for you."

"He will know where to find us?"

Mikael smiled reassuringly. "He will know."

With travel set, Michla, Mikael, and the boys returned to the boardinghouse to collect their luggage, then loaded it onto a livery wagon for the trip across town to the docks.

Two blocks up the street, they stopped at a bakery and purchased three loaves of bread, then returned to the wagon and continued on their way. Tears filled Michla's eyes as they wound through the busy streets.

"This is really happening?" she asked.

Mikael nodded. "You are about to be on your way to New York."

"I am scared." Michla leaned against him as tears streamed down her face. "Really scared."

"You will be fine," Mikael patted her shoulder. "You will board the ship now. That will give you an opportunity to get settled before the ship gets full. Then you and the boys can eat the bread for dinner. But make certain you save some of it for tomorrow. The ship will feed you at least one meal, but not until after you are under way."

"You make it sound so simple."

"It is simple, actually. It only seems more."

"Board the ship. I can do that."

"Yes. You can do the rest, too, but you needn't think about it now."

"The rest?"

"Getting settled in America. Schleman has been there two years already. He will know what to do."

"All I have to do is board the ship?"

"Right. After that, the rest is simply enduring the crossing."

Michla wiped her eyes on the backs of her hands. "Enduring?" she asked with a worried look.

"You will be at sea," Mikael explained. "Every day will be the same."

"You mean we will get bored."

"Nochem and Mottle will."

"And I?"

"You are their mother." He grinned. "A parent's life is never boring."

Before long they arrived at the dock and located the berth where the *Czar* was moored. A porter took their luggage aboard and stored it, then returned with a receipt and handed it to her. Mikael paid him for his help.

He turned to face her. "Well, I guess this is it."

"I miss you already." Michla rested her head on his chest.

"I know." He put his arms around her shoulders. "But this is the right thing to do. And it is what you must do. You cannot remain here."

"But what about you and Mama?"

"Our end was chosen when I became a rabbi."

"Surely, they need rabbis in America."

"No doubt, they need many rabbis in America. But my congregation is in Vishnyeva." He squeezed her tighter. "Yours is in New York."

Michla looked up at him and for the first time in her life saw tears in his eyes. She brushed them away with her fingertips, then buried her face against him and wrapped her arms around his waist.

They stood there a moment, holding on to each other, both of them knowing this was the last time they would be together, then he whispered to her, "I love you."

"I love you, Papa." Michla's body shook as she sobbed. "I don't want to let go of you."

"I know, but it is time for you to go. And Nochem and Mottle need your attention."

Absorbed in her own anguish, Michla had lost track of time and realized she hadn't any idea where her boys might be. She jerked around to check, her eyes wide and alert with fear. Almost at once, she caught sight of them standing a short distance down the dock, tossing pebbles into the water.

"They are safe." Mikael answered the question he knew was on her heart. "I have kept an eye on them."

And that, Michla knew, was the one thing she would miss most. The watchful eye of her father. She would be far away from him now. First on board the ship, then at sea, and finally—too finally it seemed—in America.

Michla gave him one last hug, gathered up her heavy handbag, and called for Nochem and Mottle. Together, they started up the gangway, the boys in front, Michla urging them forward.

On the ship's main deck, she turned toward the dock, located Mikael standing right where she'd left him, and gave him a wave. He waved in return and she lingered there a moment, then turned and started down the steps toward the steerage-class quarters.

CHAPTER 2

As the ship got under way, Michla pushed aside whatever sense of sadness she had about leaving her parents—and Belarus. Instead, she focused her attention on helping Nochem and Mottle settle into life aboard the *SS Czar*.

The ship, designed for thirteen hundred passengers, was loaded for that trip with over fifteen hundred. Packed into the steerage berths and crammed into every available space on the open deck, there was scant room for anyone to mill about.

For passengers like Michla, with bunks in the steerage section below deck, the days were spent lounging in their quarters, a dormitory-style section with rows of bunk beds in the bow of the ship.

Though protected from the elements, the section was stuffy and the air stale. Occasionally, for a break, they made their way up to the deck where they stood at the rail and watched the sea, its passing all but unnoticeable except for the wake. For most of the journey, however, they were confined to the area below.

At night, they lay on their bunks and listened to the groans and babble of their fellow passengers as they tossed and turned in their sleep. Aside from that, Michla found the initial days and nights mostly filled with long periods of boredom, punctuated only by meals, which for steerage passengers were sparse and not particularly appealing.

As they became more accustomed to the ship and the routine of the day, Nochem and Mottle ventured out to explore the halls and passageways, occasionally encountering the ire of porters and officers.

One bright spot for them all was Celia Kobrin and her son, Ryhor, who shared a bunk not far from their own. Like them, Celia was making the trip to New York to reunite with her husband, Ryhor's father, and she was from Belarus. Over the course of the first week, the two found plenty to talk about and soon filled the long daylight hours with rambling conversation.

Aside from that, the voyage across the Atlantic was smooth and uneventful. The ship met with fair weather most of the way and reached New York Harbor on March 4, 1913. Passengers who were able manned the rail as tugboats guided the ship around the tip of Manhattan. They stood gazing in awe at the city, then gasped out loud as the Statue of Liberty came into view. Michla and the boys were two rows back from the edge and watched from between passengers.

Rather than tying up at a wharf or pier, the *Czar* dropped anchor a little way out from Ellis Island and a lighter—a large, flat barge powered by the harbor current and an oarsman who stood at one end—took passengers from the ship to the dock at the island. Guards directed them into the main building, where they were assigned to bunk beds. Michla had a bottom bunk of her own. Nochem and Mottle shared the one above.

The following day, around midmorning, they were herded into a great hall that was lined with rows and rows of seats. Tables stood at one end with clerks seated behind them. The clerks had stacks of records before them and one by one they called passengers to the tables, reviewed their documents, scanned down long lists of names, and made notations, presumably from the answers they were given by the passengers, most of whom looked as scared and bewildered as Michla felt.

When it was Michla's turn, a young male clerk called her forward and, speaking nearly perfect Russian, began a litany of questions. Where was she born? How old was she? Was she a criminal? A prostitute? From what port had she embarked? Why had she come to America? The clerk seemed to take note of her answers, scribbling on the paper as she spoke, then noted Nochem and Mottle before directing her back to her seat.

Late that afternoon, Schleman appeared, and the clerk called Michla back to the table. "What is your relationship to her?" the clerk asked.

"She is my wife," Schleman said in English.

"She has two small boys with her."

"They are my sons."

"You are their father?"

"Yes," Schleman beamed. "I am their father."

"Very well." The clerk glanced up at Michla. "You may go."

Michla looked over at Schleman, suddenly unsure what had just transpired. Schleman took her in his arms, kissed her lightly on the lips, and gestured for the boys to follow. "We must go."

On the ferry ride from Ellis Island to Manhattan, Michla stood next to Schleman at the railing and leaned her head on his shoulder. "I have missed you."

Schleman put his arm around her. "And I have missed you."

"We will be alone tonight?"

Schleman looked away. "I do not think so," he sighed.

"Why not?"

"There isn't much room in Esther's apartment."

She looked up at him. "But you said we could stay there."

"Yes," he nodded. "But still there isn't much...privacy."

Tears filled Michla's eyes. "I feel very sad."

"Why?"

She lifted her head from his shoulder and gestured to the skyline. "It is all so...different."

"I felt the same way when I first arrived." He squeezed her closer. "But it gets better. Things work out here. You'll see."

When they arrived at the Battery pier, on the lower end of Manhattan, Schleman and Michla gathered their luggage from the ferry and led the boys off the boat to the pier.

Michla felt bewildered. "How will we get to Esther's?"

Schleman glanced around as if searching, then his eyes lit up. "This way," he smiled. "I have a treat for us."

A black delivery truck with a sign reading *Hennig's Grocery* was parked at the curb and as they approached the driver stepped out. "Samuel," he called, waving his hand and smiling.

"Hey!" Schleman called. "You found a parking space."

"I told you, I'm good with the truck."

"See," Schleman said. "Isn't this great? Izzy will take us over to Brooklyn in the truck from the store."

Michla looked askance at him. "Samuel?"

"Come," Schleman whispered tersely. "Don't make a scene. It's just a name."

They made their way to the truck, and Izzy opened the door for them. Michla and the boys climbed onto the seat, then Schleman helped load the luggage into the back. When the bags were in place, Schleman set the boys behind the seat and climbed in next to Michla.

Izzy started the engine, put the truck in gear, and eased away from the curb.

Michla looked over at Schleman. "You changed your name?"

"I had to," Schleman replied.

"Why?"

"No one could pronounce Schleman. I said Schleman Lewin and they kept writing my name as Louis Schleman. They couldn't get it right, so I changed it."

She had a disapproving look. "*They* couldn't get it right."

"Yeah."

"So *you* changed it."

"This is America," he protested. "It is not Mazyr."

"And that is it? Just like that? You are now Samuel Lewin?"

"Levine."

"What?"

"Levine. That is our name now. Levine. Not Lewin."

"Oh. So you changed *your* name and *ours*?"

"Yes," Schleman sighed. "I changed your name. And I changed Nochem and Mottle's, too."

Michla's eyes opened wide. "You changed *my* name?"

"Yes."

"So, what is *my* name now?"

"Mollie."

"Mollie?" The name sounded funny to her. "Why Mollie?"

"Because Americans will never understand Michla Lewin. They'll think you're a man."

She had an amused expression. "Why would they think I'm a man? Can they not see I am a woman?"

"Michael is a man's name in English," Schleman explained. "They'll think your name is Michael Ewing."

They sat in silence a moment and then she said in a matter-of-fact tone, "Mollie."

"Yes. Mollie Levine."

"And you are Samuel."

"Yes. Samuel Levine."

"And the boys?"

"Nochem is Nathan and Mottle is Max."

"Nathan and Max."

"Yes."

Mollie shook her head. "I will never understand America."[1]

"You've only been here two days."

She nodded slowly. "And already my name has been changed."

"You should thank Izzy for giving us a ride. That way we don't have to ride the subway or walk."

Michla looked confused. "The subway?"

"A train that runs underground."

"Under the ground?" Nochem gasped. Mottle giggled.

"Yes, I will show you. Maybe not tomorrow, but you will see."

33

Mollie turned in Izzy's direction. "We are very grateful, Izzy."

"And you are very welcome," Izzy replied. "And if it helps any, I was as confused as you when I first arrived."

"And when was that?" Mollie asked.

"Three years ago. But even now I sometimes don't respond to my American name."

"And what was your name before you came to America?"

"Isidore was always my first name. But my last name used to be Geremeck."

"And what is it now?"

"Goldberg."

"And that is easier?"

"It is for Americans," Izzy replied.

Mollie shook her head. "I don't know," she sighed. "I don't know."

✦ ✦ ✦

Since arriving in New York, Schleman, now known as Samuel, had lived at the home of his sister, Esther Feigelman and her husband, Aaron. He had found work as a carpenter and, even after paying for his share of the rent and food, managed to save the money he sent to Mollie. But living with his sister, however convenient it might have been when there was only him to worry about, quickly became unmanageable after Mollie and their sons arrived. The tiny apartment was just too small for an additional adult and two small children.

Though they likely didn't know it, Schleman and Michla Lewin were part of a wave of Jewish immigration to the United States from Eastern Europe during the first half of the twentieth century. From 1900 to 1924 almost two million Jews came to the United States, from Eastern Europe. By 1930, the Jewish population in the U.S. grew to 3.5 percent, most of whom lived in or around major northeastern cities. And not just New York or Boston.

In western Massachusetts, the city of Springfield had become one of New England's major centers for Jewish immigrants. Arriving in significant numbers during the nineteenth century, by the early twentieth century Springfield had a thriving community of some ten thousand or more Jews.

Jews first came to Springfield as peddlers, making the trek out from Boston or Providence to sell their wares to farmers in the countryside. As Springfield moved from an agricultural to an industrial economy, succeeding generations turned the peddling business into a thriving mercantile center.

On a broader scale, Springfield was a city with a history of innovation that placed it at the forefront of some of the nation's most significant achievements. It was home to the country's first national armory, which produced the country's first musket, introduced the technique of mass-produced interchangeable parts, and accounted for most of the major small arms used by the US military through the 1960s. In addition, Springfield was home to Merriam-Webster, the first steam-powered car, the first gasoline-powered automobile, the first motorcycle, and the place where James Naismith invented the game of basketball.

When Michla arrived, the Springfield Armory was undergoing a massive expansion and renovation, which required many skilled and unskilled workers. As a carpenter, Samuel might easily have found a job at any of several locations. But regardless of the specific reason, not long after Mollie arrived, she and Samuel moved with their sons to Springfield, Massachusetts.

Most Jews in Springfield settled in the North End. Samuel and Mollie did likewise, making their home in a modest house on Ferry Street, squarely in the heart of Springfield's Jewish community.

With shops lining both sides of the street, along with vendor carts and wagons parked at the curb, the neighborhood had the look, feel, and smell of a typical Jewish village back in Russia. It was an area in which Mollie felt right at home. Far more than she had in Brooklyn during her brief stay in the crowded tenement building where Samuel had lived when she arrived.

Mollie found established Jewish congregations. The city's first synagogue, Beth Israel, a congregation comprised mostly of Lithuanians, was located on Grays Avenue, south of Ferry Street. Not long after the congregation's building was constructed, a group of men split off to form their own synagogue, known as B'nai Jacob. In 1900, a group broke from Beth Israel to form Kesser Israel, a Hassidic congregation that met on Ferry Street. In 1911, B'nai Israel formed, which met on Sharon Street. In addition, a number of other congregations gathered with the intent of forming synagogues but were never officially recognized.

Judging from the lives her children led, Mollie was a practicing Jew. Instructing them in the details of those traditions and instilling in them the necessity of their observance was important to her, a fact that became readily observable in the lives of her children and in succeeding generations.

In Springfield, Mollie gave birth to a son, Michael, who was born on January 1, 1914. Their first daughter, Ginger, was born February 25, 1915, followed by a second, Jennie, on November 17, 1917.

In 1921, they had a third daughter, Sarah, but by 1930 she was a patient at a state facility in Belchertown, northeast of Springfield. Later, she was transferred to Letchworth Village, a state psychiatric facility in Thiells, New York. Records of her life are sparse, particularly about the condition that led to her institutionalization, but she lived to be at least eighteen years old. After that, she disappeared into obscurity and apparently died while residing at Letchworth.

On November 1, 1921, Mollie died at Springfield Hospital from complications with a pregnancy for yet another daughter. Nathan was fourteen. Max was twelve. Though no doubt devastated by the loss of their mother, they nevertheless persevered, exhibiting the same kind of determination she'd shown in crossing the Atlantic to give them a chance at a life far freer than they would've known in Russia.

Max developed an interest in business at an early age. As a teenager, he attended Springfield High School of Commerce, a public school founded in 1910 by Carlos Bent Ellis. Designed for students interested in a business career, its curriculum focused on skills needed to flourish in a business environment and suited Max perfectly.

Three years after Mollie died, Samuel married Lena Menard. Shortly after that, her adult brothers came to live with them. Too many adults in the house proved as unsettling for Nathan and Max as the arrangement in Brooklyn had for their mother. Not long after Samuel and Lena married, Nathan and Max moved to New York, where they lived in Brooklyn with their aunt Bella Sachs—Mollie's sister.

When the United States entered World War II, Nathan was working in the textile industry. He left that job, enlisted in the army, and was stationed in Canada at Goose Bay, where he worked as an aeronautical instrument technician.

After the war, he returned to the textile business and married Byrdie Feinstein. They had one child—a daughter named Marcy.

Not long after he and Byrdie married, Nathan was transferred to Dalton, Georgia, where he managed a factory for his employer. He lived there the remainder of his life and died on February 3, 1977. He was seventy years old.

Max married Frieda Shapiro and went to work in the food-service industry. They had three children: Terrance, Marc, and Steve. In 1946, Max, along with Hy Epstein, founded Milady Food Products, a company at the forefront of the frozen-food industry. They specialized in the manufacture and distribution of frozen blintzes and potato pancakes. When not working, Max served on the board of directors for several charities and was active at his synagogue. He died on July 13, 1964. The following year, Milady Foods was purchased by Pet Milk.

Michael, the youngest son, married Mildred Engleman. The following year, they moved to Brooklyn. Samuel and Lena moved to Brooklyn also. Lena died there in 1955.

Samuel married for a third time to a woman named Rose and lived until 1970. He died in Brooklyn and was buried at Beth David Cemetery in Elmont, New York.

When other members of the family left Springfield for New York, Jennie and Ginger stayed behind. By then they were in their early twenties. They boarded with Eli and Dora Beron. Eli was a fruit and vegetable peddler. Dora was a homemaker.

Jennie worked as a winder for an electronics manufacturer. Ginger worked as a folder for a corrugated box manufacturer. Later, Jennie worked at a restaurant in the Indian Orchard section of Springfield. She was working there during World War II when she caught sight of a handsome army engineer named Robert Evans. He was just back from the war in Europe, awaiting deployment to the Pacific Theater.

Attracted to each other at first sight, they had a whirlwind romance and, like many of that era, married during the brief interval before he shipped out.

After the war, they remained in Springfield and had seven children: Sherry, Michael, Robert Jr., James, Sheila, Bonnie, and Daniel. And that's where I come in. Jennie was my mother. Robert was my father.

CHAPTER
3

If my mother's family was steeped in the Jewish-American experience, my father's family was equally a product of the American South. The Gothic South, to be more particular. That strange blend of Protestant revivalism, Appalachian superstition, and sordid anger—all of it fueled by alcohol, most often in the form of illegal moonshine. They were the kind of people one might find in a William Faulkner novel.

My father's family consisted of two clans—Evans on one side, Crosby on the other. Tough, hard men. Farmers one and all, they worked day in and day out in the vain attempt to make a living from unproductive, unforgiving ground. When they weren't farming, they were logging, snaking pine trees out of the dense forests that filled the counties where they lived. It was the kind of life that can sap a man of strength and purpose and bring out the worst in him—which it did. An angry, sullen, vindictive kind of worst, which they visited upon the bodies, souls, and minds of the women unfortunate enough to have married them.

The women, for their part, mostly endured in silence, birthing children, preparing meals, and just getting by. Daily they bore the marks on their bodies of the brutal agony heaped on them by nature, by life, and by the men who lorded it over them.

Like many of their neighbors, the Crosbys were prisoners of the misery that gripped rural Alabama from the mid-nineteenth century until the end of World War II. Their story goes something like this:

In December 1831, Drucilla Butler was born in North Carolina. About that same time, Jim Crosby was born in Georgia. Andrew Jackson was the US president. John C. Calhoun was vice president. The big news that year involved a slave rebellion in Virginia, led by Nat Turner, which resulted in fifty-five deaths.

Drucilla Butler grew to be a woman of marrying age and, by some series of unknown events, married a man named Huggins and moved to Arkansas. They had two children together. Then, by circumstances as mysterious as those that took her from her native North Carolina, she left Arkansas with her children and moved to Alabama. No record exists of how her marriage to Huggins ended or why she made the move.

In the meantime, Jim Crosby moved from Georgia to Alabama. Somewhere along the way, Jim and Drucilla met. Not long after that, they married and moved to Jim's farm, where they lived with the two children from her prior marriage.

In 1853, Drucilla gave birth to a son, whom she and Jim named Bill. Five years later, in 1858, they purchased an eighty-acre farm in Covington County, Alabama, from the US Land Office. The property was located halfway between the towns of Opp and Florala.

About that same time, Eleazar Kirksey married Annie Jane Lee. Annie Jane was from South Carolina. Kirksey was from somewhere else. They moved to Alabama, settled in Covington County, and by 1854 had four children. One of them was a daughter named Mary Jane.

When the Civil War broke out, Eleazar enlisted with the Thirty-Seventh Regiment of Alabama volunteers, a unit in the Confederate army. Apparently, army life didn't suit him well. He was wounded, tried for desertion, found guilty, and sent home. A few years later, he died from wounds received during the war.

Eventually, Bill Crosby and Mary Jane Kirksey married and moved into a house just down the road from Bill's parents. They had eight children, the seventh of whom was born on March 5, 1891—a daughter they named Minnie.

On June 2, 1907, Minnie married James Wise. The service was held in the home of Minnie's parents. She was sixteen years old.

No one knows what happened to James Wise or their marriage, but four years later, Minnie was married again, this time to her third cousin, Countz Rigdon. The ceremony was held in the home of one S. F. Hairbuck. No one knows anything about Mr. Hairbuck, either, but we have a few details about the young couple.

Countz, it seems, was an oxen driver. Oxen were used to snake logs through the woods to a collection point—a railroad spur or road where they could be transported to a nearby sawmill, of which the region had many. A slight man, Countz stood five feet six inches tall and weighed 125 pounds. Ox drivers usually walked beside the animals, making it a physically demanding job. Minnie was of the same height and weighed one hundred forty pounds.

We'll come back to the Crosbys in a moment, but first we need to talk about the other half of Dad's family. His father's side. The Evans clan.

✦ ✦ ✦

Near the middle of the nineteenth century, John Evans was born in Pennsylvania. At more or less the same time, Falby Barrett was born in Alabama. No one knows for sure why or how they met, but in 1885 they married and moved to Brewton, a lumber and logging town near the Alabama–Florida line. In 1892, Falby gave birth to their son, Will.

In April of 1917, the United States entered World War I. To support the war effort, Congress passed the Selective Service Act, which required all men between the ages of twenty-one and thirty-one to register for the draft. The first national registration day was set for June 5, 1917.

On that day, Will Evans appeared before the Covington County draft board and asked for a deferment, arguing that he had to care for his mother. Apparently, he was her sole source of support, which suggests Will's father was no longer alive.

The request for deferment was denied and on July 25, 1918, Will was inducted into the US Army and sent to Camp Hancock in Augusta, Georgia. His stay in the army proved brief, and as far as anyone knows he was never sent overseas. The war ended on November 11, 1918, less than four months after he was inducted. Shortly after that, he was released from service and sent home.

Six months later, on May 30, 1919, Will Evans married Minnie Crosby. This was his only marriage. It was Minnie's third. No one seems to know what happened to Countz, her cousin and second husband. There's no record of a divorce and no record of his death.

The wedding ceremony took place at Florala. Will was a farmer working rented land. I think they probably rented all their lives and ended with about as much as they began. The marriage certificate noted that Will was five feet ten inches tall and weighed 158 pounds. Minnie was five feet six and had slimmed down to 130 pounds.

By today's standards, five feet ten inches isn't all that tall, but proportionally he towered over her—a physical advantage he employed with devastating effect, ruling her with an iron fist—literally.

Will and Minnie had seven children: Clifton, Robert, Raymond, Thelma, Willie Lee, Harold, and Harlan. Robert was my dad. He was born in March of 1920 at the Evans farm, a hardscrabble plot of rented ground in Florala. Calling it a farm lent it more dignity than it deserved. It was an inhospitable place both to humans and row crops.

March of that year was much cooler than normal, with frost and traces of snow all the way to the coast. It was blustery, too, and later in the month a string of tornados ripped through the northern half of the state—part of a weather system that became known as the Palm Sunday Tornados. Rather an uncanny likeness to the life Dad would live.

Though his name was Robert, everyone called him Bob—at least to his face. Behind his back they called him Wally, after the name of a cartoon character. He learned early from the hand of my grandfather, Will, that disobedience—real or perceived— brought swift retribution. A slap, a fist, the pop of a whip. Will Evans, who had learned the power of a punch from his father, was an abusive man who ultimately passed that curse along to his children. Through his son, he attempted to pass it to me.

As a seven-year-old boy, Dad was forced to plow rows of peanuts and cotton with a mule, working all day long in the hot Alabama sun.

Barely tall enough to reach the crosspiece on the plow stock, he spent most of his time and energy trying to hang on as the animal dragged him down one row and up the next.

All the while, his father sat in the cool shade of an oak tree that stood near the edge of the field. Tobacco juice dribbling down his chin. One hand grasping a long length of rope. The other holding a jug of white-lightning whiskey, which he sipped at regular intervals.

When Dad slowed his pace or the mule stopped, Will slowly rose from his resting place, fed out the rope, and walked just far enough into the field to reach Dad with the end of it. Twirling it like a whip, he unleashed the rope with a snap across Dad's sweat-soaked back. While Dad writhed in agony, Will hauled in the rope, then set it in motion again, popping the mule on the flank to urge it forward.

With boy and mule moving again, Will settled back in the shade, took another sip of whiskey, and stared out across the field, waiting for the next opportunity to unleash his anger on beast and boy. Dad and the mule did their best to please him, but it was a pointless attempt. Will was an un-pleasable man.

One evening after plowing all day Dad went to a nearby pond to catch fish for dinner. It was peaceful by the water and he stayed there as long as he could without risking a beating for coming home too late. It was almost dark when he started back, so he took a path through the swamp to shorten the trip. In the dim gray of twilight, his foot struck something soft and when he looked down he saw he'd stumbled across the body of a black man. The man was dead and there was a rope tied around his neck. Although frightened at the sight of a dead man, Dad knew his father hated blacks and thought he might have been responsible for the man's death, so he decided to keep quiet.

Later that evening, after they'd eaten the fish and everyone was relaxing from the hard day, he overheard his father talking about a black man who had been found dead in the swamp. "He was caught sleeping with a white woman," Will said. The tone of his voice suggested the man had deserved to die. There must have been many conversations like that because those racial attitudes were deeply ingrained in Dad. I don't remember a time in my life when he wasn't like that.

As one might expect, the harsh nature of their relationship created emotional distance between Dad and his father. That distance later manifested itself in physical separation as well.

By contrast, Dad and his mother, Minnie, were very close. She was a devout Christian and took Dad and his siblings to church every Sunday. Sometimes they attended a church that met in a member's home, rather than a separate church building, but wherever they met, Minnie made sure her children never missed a Sunday.

Will was not a Christian and had no use for church, Bible study, or anything else of a religious nature. He knew how to pile on the ridicule, though, and dished it out when Minnie and the children returned home from a meeting, berating them for the waste of time and the ridiculousness of faith. I'm sure it offended Minnie but she never stopped believing. And her children never stopped attending services, either, though they had a twisted and corrupt view of what true faith in God actually meant.

As I mentioned earlier, Minnie's maiden name was Crosby. She sang all the time and insisted she was related to the singer Bing Crosby. When I asked why she sang so much, Dad replied, "She was in love with Jesus and sang despite the hell she was going through with that old man."

Jim Crosby, Minnie's grandfather, died at a rather early age, but Drucilla lived to be 104 years old. She was buried at New Hope Church Cemetery. Her death certificate said she died of food poisoning and old age—a lethal combination, no doubt.

Their son, Bill—Minnie's father—died in 1932 while a patient at Bryce Hospital in Tuscaloosa, Alabama.[2] He was buried in the hospital cemetery. His wife, Mary Jane, died the following year and was buried at Mount Hope Cemetery in Florala.

In 1940, Phalby Evans passed away. She was Will's mother and Dad's grandmother. She was buried at Pondtown Cemetery. The year she died, Dad worked for the Civilian Conservation Corps "digging gravel." He never talked about her and I never met her. She was gone before I was born.

The Civilian Conservation Corps where Dad worked was a public relief program that operated from 1933 to 1942. It was part of the New

Deal—the government's attempt to put people back to work during the Great Depression. They had a camp in the Blue Springs Wildlife Management Area not far from where Dad lived. I suspect his time there was the beginning of his fascination with construction and earth-moving equipment, though the equipment at that camp was probably little more than a pick and a shovel.

Minnie, Dad's mother and my grandmother, died in 1968. I spoke at her funeral. Her daughter, who was not a Christian, told me afterward that when Minnie had gone to bed the night before, she said, "This is it. I'll be dead before morning. Jesus is coming to get me and tomorrow I'll be with him." The next morning, the daughter went in to see about Minnie and discovered she really had died in the night. The daughter told me that when she approached Minnie's bed she felt a presence in the room. "Like angels were with her. I didn't believe in much of anything before that," she said. "Now I do."

We buried Minnie at the Union Baptist Church Cemetery in Slocomb. Dad attended the service. It was one of the few times I ever saw my father cry.

Will, my grandfather and Minnie's husband, died in 1972. Dad refused to attend his funeral. "He beat my mother mercilessly," he said. "I want nothing to do with him." Which was ironic considering all of the things Dad did to us and to *our* mother.

I didn't attend Will's funeral either. In fact, although he was my grandfather, I never met the man. They buried him next to Minnie at the Union Baptist Cemetery. I hope that somewhere between his last breath and the moment his body expired he found the same peace she did.

✦ ✦ ✦

That was my father's family and the environment in which he grew up. A family rife with contradictions as glaring as the ones we saw in his life later on, as his children. A childhood steeped in the Bible and in traditional preaching, yet laced with superstition and moonshine. A mother who reflected the gospel in almost every way. A father who was a bitter, angry racist. It was his family context and the context of the community in which they lived.

Dad was born nine years before the Great Depression officially arrived. Across the United States, the unemployment rate rose as high as twenty-five percent. Gross Domestic Product dropped by fifteen percent. Crop prices plummeted. People in the rural South used to say that they didn't know there was a Great Depression until they looked around and saw that everyone else was as poor as they were. That's a tired cliché but in Dad's case it provided a rather accurate picture of the economic condition in rural Alabama.

One could easily attribute the anger evident in Dad's father and grandfather to deep-seated frustration born of the hardships of a rural, agricultural life that had changed very little since the eighteenth century. A life formed from an unending stream of days spent laboring under the hot southern sun. Rising before sunup. Following a team of mules across a dusty field until the shank of the evening. Then collapsing at home in a cabin lit by a tallow candle or a kerosene lamp—with no electricity and no running water—only to rise the next morning and do it all over again. Day in and day out. Over and over. Spring, summer, and fall. And even in winter, to spend the day felling timber in the southern piney woods, then snaking the logs out with a mule or oxen.

It was a life no one dreamed of giving their offspring, yet each of them passed that life on to their children—along with the abuse, addiction, and anger that hardened into generational curses. Dad did his best to pass that curse to us, too.

✦ ✦ ✦

That was the past my parents brought with them when they married. A Protestant father and a Jewish mother. Perhaps more to the point, a cosmopolitan mother from the Northeast and a bigoted, racist father from the Deep South.

In spite of opposition from my father, our mother did her best to maintain her Jewish identity. Her Jewish heritage was evident to anyone who entered our home. From the food we ate—lox and bagels and gefilte fish on special occasions—to the menorahs she displayed during the Jewish holy days. Occasionally, she made trips to Brooklyn to attend bar mitzvahs and Passover seders in the homes of her brothers. When we were young and still lived at home, my siblings and I accompanied her on those trips. I remember those occasions as times when she was particularly happy. We all were. She because she could slip back into her identity as a Jew; us because we were free of our father for the day.

My father wanted a Christian home. Not one where a true, inward spiritual life was pursued but one that bore the outward trappings of what he thought a Christian family ought to look like—an imitation, as it were, not the real thing—so we always celebrated Christmas and Easter with as much visible evidence as possible.

As one might expect, the tension between the two led to conflict. A battle, actually, between two people and two faiths. A battle that was fraught with contradiction on both sides.

I remember Pastor David Flower, the preacher at the church we attended, came to our house one day. He didn't visit often but when he did he seemed totally taken by Dad. "Brother Bob, so great to see you," he'd say, as if Dad were the greatest person he'd ever known. And then they'd share a brief conversation notable for the overuse of acceptable but trite Christian clichés.

On this particular instance, my father was in his underwear, drinking Jack Daniel's and popping what he called goofballs—a form of sedative he'd been given while serving in the Pacific during the war.[3] The army's solution to intolerance for the extreme heat and constant fear of dying. He took them to get through the war and continued to take them afterward whenever he got nervous.

That day when Pastor Flower came to see him, Dad and some of his friends were in the basement playing cards for money. He had a bar down there and a rifle range at one end. On weekends his friends came over, got drunk, and shot guns. That's what they were doing when Pastor Flower arrived.

When someone shouted down the steps to tell him the preacher was coming, Dad pushed the cards and money into a drawer and called for Mom to bring his pants. She brought the pants to him and he handed her the ever-present bottle of Jack Daniel's.

"Put this in the cabinet," he ordered. "And don't let anyone see it." Sometimes, if time allowed, he sucked on a lemon to hide the odor of alcohol. I don't remember whether he did on that occasion or not, though it wouldn't surprise me. He was the consummate hypocrite— and a redneck one at that.

With the evidence of his real character out of sight, Dad went upstairs to visit with Pastor Flower. As their conversation settled into its usual rhythm, we children hid in our rooms or headed out the back door. We knew what would follow if we were around when Pastor Flower was gone. As I said, Dad believed in the outward signs of Christianity, a belief that didn't involve him putting aside alcohol, pills, foul language, or carousing with other women, but which *did* involve beating us regularly.

Pastor Flower's visits made the contradictions in his life inescapably apparent—an awareness that brought with it the associated guilt. He exorcised his guilt by flailing our bodies with an extension cord, broom handle, or anything else readily at hand. Like my grandfather, my father had a violent temper, which he often vented and not just against us.

One day, he saw a neighbor hit our German Shepherd with a baseball bat. Our dog had attacked the neighbor's dog. Dad flew into a rage, stormed from the house, and punched the man three times in the face. The force of the blows broke the guy's nose. Blood dripped from his chin. Dad screamed, "If you ever lift that bat against our dog again, I'll use it on you instead of my fists!"

And during one of those drunken weekend card games he became angry with our mother and slapped her so hard she was knocked almost unconscious. A friend who happened to see it called the police and when the officers arrived, Dad beat both of them. They staggered back to their cars, and Dad thought he'd won the day, but that time things didn't turn out so well for him. Not long after the first officers left, four more arrived. They beat Dad with their nightsticks, then carried him off to jail.

But I'm getting ahead of myself. Mother and Dad married during World War II. While they were finding their way together, tragedy struck Mother's family in Belarus. You need to know about that because what happened over there affected her and, in turn, all of us.

CHAPTER
4

When Mollie and her sons emigrated from Belarus in 1913 to rejoin Samuel in New York, they left behind a large extended family that was unable to make the trip. For the first few years after she was gone, life for those who remained in Mazyr and Vishnyeva was much the same as it always had been. But beginning with the Revolution of 1917, which brought an end to the Russian Empire and swept the Communists to power, Jews throughout Russia were subjected to new and far more devastating pogroms. That unrest continued until 1922 and resulted in the deaths of some 25,000 Jews in Belarus alone.

As if that were not enough, in 1939, the German army moved eastward into Poland, an act noted by historians as the beginning of

World War II. Two years later, in 1941, Germany unleashed its military might on the Soviet Union and advanced into portions of Poland then under the control of Soviet forces. In very quick order, they seized control of Belarus.

Mazyr, the town where Michla was born and the place where she and Schleman were married, came under German occupation on August 22, 1941. At the time the Germans arrived, the town was almost entirely Jewish. To solidify control over the region and to purge it from so-called non-Arians, German army units executed many of Mazyr's citizens.

In the face of widespread atrocities, those who survived the first wave in the slaughter attempted to escape. Others did their best to hide, while some simply gave up and committed suicide.

In the fall, a ghetto was established for the Jews in the region. Before winter, fifteen hundred of them had been forced to live there. During the week of January 7, 1942, they were executed. Gunned down in ritualistic murder. Women, children, and the elderly first, then the others. The Germans sang and celebrated as they shot them. After the ghetto was emptied, another seven hundred Jews were identified, captured, and drowned in the Pripyat River.

Not all Jews were content to sit and wait for whatever end was coming. Instead, they attempted to escape, fleeing into the surrounding forest. German soldiers, relentless in their pursuit, searched for them diligently, turning that, too, into sport, chasing them with dogs like they were hunting foxes. They celebrated as the dogs attacked their prey, then stood by and laughed as the captured Jews cried out in agony. Many of those who died were my relatives and even now the thought of what happened to them is unspeakably painful.

As the German army continued northward, Vishnyeva came quickly under their control. Mikael and Goldy Katzenelson, my great-grandparents, were there when the Germans arrived. Rather than flee, they chose to stay with their people. As rabbi of one of the town's most important synagogues, Mikael felt his place was there, in town, with those he'd spent his adult life serving. Zvi Meltzer, the cantor rabbi, stayed, too.

German soldiers rounded up as many Jews as they could find, then forced them into the synagogue, nailed the doors shut, and set the building on fire. My great-grandparents perished in the flames, along with Meltzer and more than two thousand of their fellow Jews.

During the German occupation, people reported seeing a young soldier walking down the street with the head of a Jewish baby impaled on the bayonet of his rifle. He was singing as he walked.

Others reported that Jews were buried alive, noting they could see the ground moving for days as people struggled to free themselves. Others witnessed a woman who was tied to a pole. German soldiers used her for target practice, throwing knives at her until she died from her wounds.

I'm not sure when my mother learned of what happened to Mikael, his wife, Goldy, and the people of Vishnyeva, but from what she said about events there, I believe news of their death reached her during the war. Certainly long before any of her children were born. She first told me about it when I was still a young boy; the way she did it made a lasting impression on me.

Like most children in America, I spent Saturday mornings watching cartoons on television. Our little black-and-white set was typical for its time—more snow than picture—but I could still enjoy *Howdy Doody* and *The Lone Ranger*. One Saturday, when the cartoon programs ended, a Billy Graham broadcast came on the same channel. With nothing else to do that day, I sat in my chair and watched it.

Mom heard the program and darted across the room. "Never watch this again!" she screamed as she charged toward the television, grabbed the knob, and turned it off. "The pope, Billy Graham, and Adolf Hitler were all Christians," she railed. "Christians kill Jews. Christians hate Jews. Jesus died. Don't dig him up."

Then she told me about Mikael and Goldy Katzenelson, the wooden synagogue in Vishnyeva where Mikael served as chief rabbi, and the day the Germans burned them alive in the building.

As I grew older she repeated that story, especially when we became the subject of anti-Semitism ourselves. Like the time our house was spray-painted with the words *Jew- witch*. Or the times eggs and tomatoes were thrown at us as we made our way home from the

A&P grocery store. Or the time I was beaten for being a "kike." Though the discrimination we received was nothing like what our relatives had endured in Belarus, those were challenging times for me, and my mother encouraged me by reminding me of what happened to my great-grandparents.

Until she learned that Mikael and Goldy had died and the circumstances of their death, the Holocaust had been something impersonal. Not that she was unaware of it or did not see it for the horror that it was, but until the day she learned of what happened, the Holocaust was something that happened to others in a part of the world far removed from her life in Springfield. Learning that her grandparents had been murdered by the Germans brought those events much closer to home and made the Holocaust a very personal matter for her. Perhaps far too much so.

When I was born, my mother named me Michael, after Mikael, my great-grandfather. It's a Hebrew name that means "Who is like God?" An archangel by that name appears in the biblical books of Daniel, Jude, and Revelation, variously described as the prince of the people of Israel and one who takes on the role of their protector.[4] As a child, I had no idea how significant that name would be for me, or how deeply into the role of a protector of Israel I would be led.

CHAPTER
5

To say that my father was a hard and angry man would be to state the obvious. When angered, his blue eyes turned to ice and his voice to steel, especially when he'd been sipping Jack Daniel's and popping pills. Even when sober, he ruled our household with a rod of iron, but when he was drunk he reached for a coat hanger, a belt, or an electric extension cord—whatever was handy—and used it to inflict pain on us. He called it punishment, but it was mostly just pain. An inexplicable venting of his own frustration. A release of dark and evil emotion from which he derived a lurid sense of satisfaction.

I'm not sure how old I was when his abuse of us began, but the first incident I remember was from a time when I was four years old.

The morning began like any other, but not long into the day, something set Dad off. As we looked on, he stomped around the house, yelling and screaming at my mother, growing angrier and angrier with every step, every shout, every passing moment. In the midst of that, he took a swing at her and struck her with the back of his hand against her jaw. It made a sickening sound, and the force of the blow sent Mom to the floor.

Terrified at what I'd heard and seen, I ran from the house and raced up the sidewalk toward the park. I had gone there often with my older sister, Sherry, and it was the one place in our neighborhood that I knew how to reach on my own. So with tears streaming down my cheeks, I ran up the street in that direction, doing my best to get as far from Dad as my little legs would take me.

My dash from the house gave me a head start, and I ran as fast as I could, but all the way up the sidewalk I was certain I could hear the heavy thud of my father's boots coming right behind me. I ignored the sound, afraid to look back until I neared the entrance to the park, then I could stand the suspense no more and glanced over my shoulder to check.

To my relief there was no one behind me, but as I turned back to face the direction I was going, I ran headlong into a group of senior citizens on an outing from a local nursing home. Their sudden appearance startled me and I stumbled. A nurse accompanying the group took hold of my shoulder to keep me from falling.

"Hi, little guy!" she said with a concerned look. "Are you running from the bogeyman?" She knelt beside me and took out a handkerchief. "Don't worry; you're safe here with us," she assured me as she wiped my face. When she'd dried my cheeks she offered me a bag of breadcrumbs. "Do you want to help me feed the pigeons?"

She was trying to be nice to me, but I was so scared my father would come after me that I pulled away and screamed, "I don't want to feed the stupid pigeons!" Then I threw down the breadcrumbs, whirled around, and continued running up the sidewalk, through the park, all the way to the street on the opposite side. That's where my older sister, Sherry, and a police officer later found me wandering up and down the street.

Sherry was worried the policeman would become suspicious of what had happened, so she explained, "Our mother slipped in the kitchen, and when Dad reached out to help her, she fell to the floor." She glanced in my direction. "He thought Dad hit Mom and it scared him."

I suppose the officer believed her. Or maybe he just didn't want to get involved. In any case, he slipped me a piece of peppermint candy, and I agreed they could take me home.

We rode in the officer's patrol car and all the way Sherry kept repeating the story she'd told earlier—that Mom had slipped and fallen. I was equally sure that Dad had hit her, but quickly grew tired of the argument. Instead, my four-year-old mind was on the piece of peppermint candy I clutched in my hand.

I've often wondered if God put that group of elderly people and their nurse in my way to keep me from harm. And sent Sherry to find me with the policeman's help. Even back then it wasn't safe for a four-year-old to be loose on the street alone. Not in Springfield.

Now, looking back on my life, I can see many ways God protected me as a teenager and adult. But I wonder sometimes if that protection didn't begin way back then, when I was a little boy, long before I made any overt profession of faith in Him.

✦ ✦ ✦

When I was six years old we lived in a small low-income apartment in the city's housing project. The space was one of many that had been made available to military veterans returning from the war. As with many public housing facilities, it kept the rain off our heads, but that was about all it had to offer.

Everyone who lived there was, like us, poor. Most of them—men and women alike—were angry and bitter, too, and all of them struggled to make it, living from day to day both financially and emotionally. Many of the men, like Dad, who had been soldiers in the war, suffered from battle fatigue—what we know today as Post-traumatic Stress Disorder. My dad sometimes awakened in the night screaming like a madman. That's why he took those pills—the goofballs—to hold back the fear that plagued him back then and for most of his adult life.

Like I said, the apartment in the Projects provided a roof over our heads, but it wasn't much of a place to raise young children. I remember very early one morning, while it was still dark, we were awakened by the flashing lights and the wail of an ambulance siren. All of us rushed to the windows to see what was happening but all we could see were the lights from outside. Later that day, we learned the man who lived in the apartment across the street from us had hanged himself.

There was a lot of hopelessness and despair in the Projects, but there were also rays of hope, too. One of those came in the form of Mrs. Cignonee, though it took me a while to appreciate just how good and kind she really was. She was a member of Evangelical Covenant Church, located several miles from where we lived, and had a heart for helping people in tough situations.

We first met Mrs. Cignonee one afternoon in the summer when she knocked on the door of our apartment. I was about five years old. When Mom opened the door I saw a lady who, to my young mind, appeared to be about a hundred years old. In reality, she was probably only in her forties, but having no concept of age or time I was certain she was older than anyone I'd ever seen. And on top of that she reminded me of the wicked witch from *The Wizard of Oz*.

Mrs. Cignonee smiled at us and in her hand I saw a bright red piece of construction paper. She gave it to Mom and said, "This is an invitation for your children to attend our Vacation Bible School."

Mom glanced at the paper with a puzzled frown. She'd never heard of Vacation Bible School and neither had we. Mrs. Cignonee quickly explained—a week-long program for the children with fun and games. "I'm sure they'll have a great time."

When Mom hesitated over the obvious religious nature of the program, Mrs. Cignonee added, "Think of it this way. The children will have a fun time and it will give you a few hours for yourself without them underfoot."

The part about time for herself appealed to Mom but there were other problems, too. "It sounds nice, but I have no way to get them to the church," she explained. "We only have one car and my husband uses it for work."

"I'll pick them up and bring them home," Mrs. Cignonee replied. "You won't have to worry about a thing."

In spite of her feelings about Christianity, Mom agreed to let us attend. I think the need for time alone won her over.

When Mrs. Cignonee left and Mom closed the door, I ran to my room and hid my shoes. I only had the one pair and they were worn out. They'd rubbed a blister on my heel during the previous school year and the blister turned into an abscess. Recovering from it kept me home from kindergarten for two months and forced me to repeat the level the next year. Vacation Bible School sounded like school to me and I didn't want a repeat of that experience. Besides, I didn't want to go anywhere with *that* strange old lady. In spite of her kind smile and winsome way, I couldn't get past how much she reminded me of that wicked witch.

As determined as I was not to attend, Mom was equally resolute that I would. So, after a spanking and more than one scolding, I located the missing shoes and we set off with Mrs. Cignonee for Vacation Bible School the following week.

The experience at the church wasn't as bad as I had expected and actually proved enjoyable, though I was reluctant to admit it. I enjoyed the games, Bible stories, songs, and snacks. Especially the snacks. They had lots of snacks.

That Vacation Bible School was where I first heard hymns like "'Tis So Sweet to Trust in Jesus" and "Trust and Obey." The words from that latter song, "Trust and obey, for there's no other way to be happy in Jesus but to trust and obey," repeated in my mind throughout the summer and has remained with me for the rest of my life. As a five-year-old, I had no idea what the words meant, but the sweet and happy part appealed to me on several levels.

Every morning when we arrived at the church the people who ran the Vacation Bible School—the teachers, volunteers, and pastor—patted me on the head and told me how happy they were that I had come and how glad they were to see me. They told me that Jesus loved and saved me, too. But having no concept of what that meant, I was left confused and bewildered. So, like any confused five-year-old, I smarted off.

"Yes, I know Jesus saves," I quipped, "and so does the bank." It was a one-liner I'd heard in the Projects and was the first thing that popped into my mind.

When they persisted in telling me how much Jesus loved me, I retorted, "Jesus doesn't love me. Everyone says I am a Jew and I cruci-fied Him." I didn't know what *those* words meant, either, but I'd heard them often enough that I remembered them and thought they might mean something to the people at the church.

They weren't put off by that, either, and as the conversation contin-ued, I added, "My mom says Jesus died and I should not dig Him up."

They exchanged knowing looks and concerned sighs, but no one told me I had to leave, so we kept coming every day that week. Eventually, they learned how to avoid an argument with me, and things settled into a daily rhythm.

Mrs. Cignonee never gave up on us, either. Throughout my early childhood she sacrificed time and money to reach out in love to us. I was battered and bruised, both physically and emotionally, and so beset with fear that I couldn't lift my head to look her in the eyes. And on top of that, I stuttered with almost every sentence. Still, she continued to visit us long after that summer Vacation Bible School ended. Her involvement in our lives sowed the first seeds of the gospel in my life—the genuine gospel, not the twisted version my father tried to give us.

CHAPTER
6

As I mentioned earlier, my father enjoyed gambling and often gathered with his friends on weekends to play cards. The church we attended was opposed to playing card games, especially games that were played for money, but the example my father set—attending church on Sunday after drinking and gambling on Saturday—was far more powerful than anything anyone said about the topic.

In spite of the way he treated us, and the horror his anger brought to our lives, I found myself, as a young child, drawn toward some of the things he did. Even though I resisted the worst parts of him with as much determination as a child could muster, there still was a certain sense of inevitability about my life. The kind of natural inclination a son might have toward the things his father valued as an attempt to win the father's approval. In my case, it was the hope that the beatings would stop.

Drinking held little attraction for me. However, I had my first encounter with gambling when I was seven years old. A group of friends from the neighborhood suggested we play. I was eager to participate.

Being young, we had little money, so we played for pennies. Although we knew our fathers gambled we weren't sure how they would react to our taking it up, so we held our game in the woods about five minutes away from where we lived. Everything was going fine until one of the older boys said, "Let's play strip poker."

Most of us kids had played poker many times, especially us older ones, but I had never played the strip version before and lost most of the hands. Every time I lost, I had to take off an article of clothing. Before long I lost everything except my underwear. Then I lost those, too.

As I peeled off my undershorts, the other boys snatched up my clothing and ran away, leaving me naked in the woods with no clothes to wear. I can still hear the sound of their laughter as they disappeared through the trees.

Alone, scared, and naked, I had to find a way to get home without being seen. The situation posed few options so I waited until dark, then broke off two branches from a sapling to use as cover. Holding one in front of me and one behind, I hurried through the woods to the street and ran home as fast as I could, cutting through yards and darting behind houses to stay out of sight as much as possible, hoping with every step that no one would see me.

Thankfully, the front door was unlocked, the porch light was off, and none of my family was in sight. I dropped the branches near the front door, darted inside, and ran up the stairs to my room. That was my last game of strip poker.

One Saturday morning, Sherry and I were left home alone. She decided to make toast and loaded two slices in the toaster. When it was ready she attempted to remove the slices using a dinner knife. In doing so, she touched the wires inside the toaster. Instantly, electricity shot through her body. I knew from the look on her face that she was in trouble but as I ran toward her, she screamed, "Don't pull the plug! Don't pull the plug!"

What she said left me confused but I knew enough to know how to stop the electrical current and yanked the cord from the outlet anyway. She collapsed unconscious on the kitchen floor, and I called the telephone operator for help. A few minutes later an ambulance arrived and the attendants revived her. They gave her oxygen and worked with her until she was conscious again, but I had saved her life.

✦ ✦ ✦

As I grew older, Dad drank more and became even angrier than before. With that, the abuse escalated as he lashed out more and more against Mom and all of us—me in particular. Those were days when I didn't think I would survive the fists, coat hangers, and extension cords that came my way.

Not only that, but Dad's reaction became increasingly unpredictable. It was impossible to know what might set him off or which way he would react. No matter how carefully I tiptoed around, no matter how cautiously I responded to his questions or comments, I never knew when he would erupt in violence against me.

About the time I turned seven, we moved away from the public housing facility to a house at 77 Pasco Road. A two-story structure, it had three bedrooms, a living room, and a dining room separate from the kitchen. Far larger than the apartment where we'd been living.

Not long after we were settled in the house, Dad decided it was time to take control of our spiritual training. His brother Cliff had recently announced that he'd found Jesus, then nearly beat his son to death in the barn with a bullwhip. I hoped Dad hadn't gotten saved like that.

Friday night was date night for Dad. Not for Dad and Mom—just Dad. He came in from work and took a bath, then shaved and doused himself with Old Spice while singing a chorus or two from "Ghost Riders in the Sky" or "Rawhide." When he was finished, he slipped on his best shirt and pants and left the house for the Twilight Café, a restaurant and bar uptown in the Old Orchard section of the city where we lived.

At the Twilight, he spent evenings checking out the women who hung out there. In the course of the night, one drink would lead to another and before long he would be more than a little intoxicated. Most Friday nights, I think he might have bedded one of the women from the bar, and by the time he staggered home he was too drunk to be out in public.

Dad's trips to the bar might have been fun for him, but those were nights of fear for us. Most of us were in bed when he returned but I slept *under* my bed. Not so far under that I couldn't see the glow of the hall light as it seeped into the room, and not quite far enough to risk a spider that might be hiding in a corner, but far enough to be out of sight if he happened to come into the room. Like an ostrich hiding its head in the sand, I thought Dad couldn't find me there—as if that made any difference.

We dreaded to hear the front door open and slam shut on Friday night when Dad finally made his way home from working all week out of town. He would shout, "Line 'em up!" In a rage, he pulled me from under my bed, rounded up my siblings, and systematically beat us. Not a spanking. Not a whipping. He beat us. An action he justified by arguing we must have committed some infraction, even if he didn't know what it was. "Spare the rod and spoil the child," he'd repeat over and over again. He had no real understanding of what that meant but thought it supported his beating us. So we got Saturday-night beatings like most kids got Saturday-night baths.

As the oldest boy, I was usually first in line for Dad's wrath. That was bad enough, but what frightened me most was the way he looked at my sisters. One day Sherry was sunning in her swimsuit in the backyard. Dad and one of his brothers were staring at her when Dad leaned over and said softly, "Boy, wouldn't you like those long legs wrapped around you?" I discovered later that he was more depraved than I could imagine.

Regardless of what transpired on Saturday, on Sunday morning he rousted us from bed and demanded that we dress for Sunday school and the morning church service. Once dressed, he would line us up in the living room and give each of us a nickel or dime for the offering plate. Then he would drive us to the church, all the while screaming things like, "Stop kicking my seat!"

When we arrived, he marched us inside Bethany Assembly of God Church and seated us on the front pew. Reverend Flower was the pastor. His father was one of the founders of the denomination.[5]

Everyone called Dad "Brother Bob" and made over him as if he were one of the giants of the faith. We never said anything to let them know otherwise, but the contradiction between what he said at church on Sunday and how he lived the other six days of the week left us with no respect for him.

When it was time for Sunday school to begin, Dad sent us off to our various classes. At first we did as we were told, dutifully making our way to the appropriate classrooms and enduring the lessons until time for worship service. But somewhere in all of that, I came up with the brilliant idea—I thought—to pool our offering money and sneak down the street to the Dunkin' Donuts shop. Combining our money usually gave us just enough for a Coca-Cola and a chocolate-covered donut. Each Sunday we were courageous enough to try it we savored every bite of our sweet treat, then raced back to the church before anyone noticed we were gone. The fact that I am alive today is proof that our dad never discovered our deception. We always returned in time to hear the sermon, but I never really listened. Most Sundays I spent the time daydreaming.

One Sunday Brother Flower, as Dad called him, preached on the importance of family devotions. As we sat on the pew next to Dad, my mind wandered to the backyard ball game we might play with the neighborhood kids once we got home. Lost in thought, I didn't hear Reverend Flower challenge every parent to begin a family Bible study that very day. I'm sure he had no idea what was about to transpire at our house.

On the way home from church, Dad announced that after lunch we would have devotions. Having failed to listen to the sermon, none of us kids had a clue what that word meant.

When he repeated his plan during our regular Sunday meal of

fried chicken, our mother gave him a disapproving look. She, being Jewish, never attended church and only begrudgingly went along with Dad's attempts to educate us in the faith. Incensed by her reaction, Dad jumped up like a raging bear and slapped her plate from the table. It crashed to the floor and broke into a dozen pieces. As we sat in stunned silence he screamed, "I am the head of this house!" No one wanted to challenge him on that point.

After lunch, Dad threw back a few shots of whiskey and popped a pill or two, then set about implementing the pastor's challenge. From his seat in his favorite chair, he yelled for us kids to form a circle on the floor in the living room in front of him.

Once we were in place, he pushed himself up from the chair and wobbled across the room to retrieve his *Thompson Chain-Reference* Bible from the bookshelf. He tucked it under his arm and picked up an electrical extension cord, then started back to his chair. When he was seated again, he thrust the Bible toward me.

I took the Bible from him and glanced down at it. In my heart I knew this was not going to turn out well for me. He was going to tell me to read aloud a passage of Scripture and, being more nervous than normal, I was going to stutter even more than usual. I knew it was coming—a self-fulfilling prophecy about to be fulfilled in the worst possible way—and the thought of it made me all the more apprehensive.

As I stood there, waiting for his command, one of my brothers asked in a nonchalant tone, "What's a devotion?"

Dad paused long enough to take a sip from his glass of whiskey, then snorted, "You're going to read the Bible, and then we're going to pray."

There. He'd said it. We were going to read aloud from the Bible. I cringed at the thought of it.

At school I struggled through the ridicule of fellow classmates when the teacher called on me in class. She did her best to help me, but at home I was on my own. When I stuttered at home, Dad's name of choice for me was "Moron!"

I was lost in worry and thought when I heard him shout, "MORON! Read John 3:16."

Having regularly traded time in Sunday school class for a trip to Dunkin' Donuts, I was not familiar with the books of the Bible. As he glared at me, I flipped through *Palms*, an Old Testament book, trying to locate the Gospel of John, which was in the New Testament.

"Where in Palms is the book of John?" I asked, mistaking the word *psalm* for *palm*.

"It's *Psalms*, you moron!" Dad screamed. "Not *Palms*. And it's not in the Old Testament!"

As I struggled to find the correct place, Dad demanded, "Who is the first woman in the New Testament?"

"M-Mary M-magazine," I replied.

"No!" he screamed again. "Her name is Mary Magdalene, you moron! It's Magdalene, not magazine!" When he shouted at me, I looked up at him and saw his eyes had that all-too-familiar hooded gaze, like I imagined a cobra might appear as it prepared to strike. He looked like that when he was thoroughly intoxicated, and I knew trouble wasn't far off.

Finally I found the New Testament, located the book of John, and attempted to read. As I struggled to get out first one word and then another, my father screamed again, "Moron! Can't you get anything right? Just read the @#!# scripture."

As I tried harder to squeeze out the next word, the extension cord slapped across my back. It stung, even through the fabric of my shirt, and in the same instant the heavy plug on the end struck the side of my head. I staggered back, doing my best to get out of the way, when he leapt from his chair, crazy with rage, and took hold of me by the arm.

"Bend over!" he shouted.

Suspecting that the compulsory devotional exercise might end in violence, I had slipped a piece of cardboard into my pants before coming down to the living room. As he held me by the arm, he drew back the cord and aimed it at my backside. As his arm came forward, the cord struck the seat of my pants and made a *thwap* sound as it contacted the cardboard.

Dad's eyes opened wide in a look of surprise but the expression on his face quickly turned to anger. He flung me onto the floor, yanked down my pants and shorts, and lashed my bare buttocks with the cord. Then he drew it back again and again, striking me over and over until my flesh was raw. All the while, my siblings sat quietly on the floor, frozen in place with fear, knowing that they were likely to be on the receiving end of the cord next.

Finally out of breath, Dad collapsed back in his chair. I pulled up my pants and stood there staring at him, my buttocks too sore to let me sit.

"Read," he growled, gesturing to me with the hand that still held the cord.

Someone picked up the Bible from the floor and handed it to me. Though racked with pain and totally frustrated, I tried again to read the scripture. But the more I tried, the worse I stuttered.

With an angry sneer, Dad snatched the Bible from my hands. "If you can't read it, you moron, your brother can." Jimmy took it and started to read, but although he didn't stutter he was so terrified of the extension cord that he could barely whisper the words.

Each of my siblings took a turn with the Bible, but each attempt fell short of what Dad expected. As the afternoon wore on, he became angrier and angrier, screaming at us and lashing out again and again with the extension cord, striking each of us as we passed the Bible around and did our best to read the passages he'd selected.

The more we read, the more Dad screamed at us. The more he screamed, the more he drank and the more he drank, the more frightened we all became—and we hadn't even gotten to the prayer part yet.

Then, just as suddenly as it began, Dad let the cord slip from his hand and drop to the floor. He snatched the Bible from the grasp of the last reader and rose from his place in the chair.

Stunned by the sudden, inexplicable development, we sat motionless on the floor as Dad lumbered across the room and disappeared into the kitchen. A moment later we heard the back door swing open, then bang closed.

For a moment we remained where we were, motionless on the floor. Too scared to move, too scared to remain, and uncertain what to do next. Then, as if on command, we jumped up from the floor all at once and scurried off to our individual hiding places.

That was our first and only attempt at family devotions. While we lived at home we continued to attend church on Sundays. Dad would have it no other way, and none of us wanted to risk the consequences of defying him. But most of my siblings vowed that when they were able to decide for themselves, they would never set foot in church again. Sadly, as adults, they kept that vow, and I am certain our father's Sunday-afternoon attempt at family devotions was a big part of the reason why.

CHAPTER
7

Life in our home at 77 Pasco Road was dysfunctional, even on good days. More than once our mother would say, "This place is a nuthouse. If the story is every told about what goes on around here, it will be a bestseller." My siblings and I thought of it as a torture chamber, but Mom's point was well taken.

One difficulty in talking about our situation lay in the fact that, even if we told the neighbors what happened inside our house—and from time to time we did tell our friends—no one would believe us because no one wanted to believe us. They didn't want to know about the things we endured—not really. I mean, knowing intellectually that bad things happen to children is one thing; hearing it from the kid next door is quite another. The people on our street didn't want to know about our abuse at a level like that.

On the other hand, I'm sure most of the neighbors heard Dad screaming at our mother or at one of us kids. And I don't know how they could have avoided hearing us scream while he beat us. But if they admitted he might actually be doing those things to us, they would be compelled to intervene. And they'd be forced to confront the darker things that were happening in their own lives and with their own families. Though no one ever admitted it, the people who lived near us were as afraid of our father and his temper as we were. So we all lived a double life. My siblings and I did our best to act and appear normal in public despite the horrible violence we endured in private. And our neighbors did their best to act as if we were a typical New England family.

As bad as things were at home, it wasn't the only place where we encountered abuse. Springfield has a history of ethnic and racial conflict—first between the Puritans and Irish, then later between everyone and the Jews—as waves of immigrants made their way from Boston to western Massachusetts. The initial trouble occurred much earlier, in the eighteenth and nineteenth centuries, and in the early twentieth century when our ancestors arrived. Even so, we still were subjected to acts of anti-Semitic discrimination and violence some forty years later.

How anyone found out about Mom's background remains a

question. I suppose a few might have decided she was Jewish from her physical appearance, although there were significant groups of people in Springfield who came from Eastern European countries who had a similar appearance and were not Jewish. And some—particularly the Friday-night crowd at the Twilight Café—might have overheard our father talking about her. He sometimes referred to her as "my old lady, the Jew with the big nose." But however they learned we were Jewish, it proved to be a trial for all of us, particularly for me.

As the oldest boy in the family it was my job to accompany our mother to the local A&P grocery store on Fridays after school. As we walked home, teenagers from the community sometimes drove past us screaming from the windows of their cars, "Jew-witch!" On other occasions they threw tomatoes and eggs at us while yelling, "Christ killer!" Often their derisive comments were peppered with profanity.

As a student in elementary school, I was labeled a *kike* by people my own age. At first I didn't know what that word meant and for a long time thought they were saying "kite." I doubt they knew what it meant, either, and were merely repeating words and labels they'd heard at home. But as I entered junior high, things got worse. I was beaten on more than one occasion by some of the same kids who'd earlier labeled me a kike. While they pummeled me with their fists they shouted at me, as the teenagers had done before on the street, accusing me of being a "Christ killer."

Childhood is often portrayed as a time of innocence and children are sometimes thought of as the embodiment of untrammeled purity. In reality, children can be as cruel as adults and once the kids in my class started on me, they never let up.

By the time I was old enough to attend kindergarten, stuttering was an obvious and embarrassing problem for me. Some of the kids from our street seemed to accept me in spite of it but the kids at school, especially the ones who didn't know me very well, weren't so graceful. They mocked my speech pattern and laughed in my face. It was terribly demoralizing but I didn't know how to make the stuttering go away.

At home my father ridiculed me, too, which further reinforced the treatment I received at school and compounded the growing sense of doubt, fear, and self-abasement it and his physical abuse instilled in me. Even Mom, who was the one source of hope in our lives, seemed unmoved by my predicament. And my trouble at school didn't stop with speech problems.

For most of my childhood, I was seriously underweight. Mom did her best to provide us with good meals, but the constant physical and emotional abuse took its toll on me and I developed stomach ulcers at an early age. Abdominal pain from the ulcers made eating difficult which, together with growth spurts and normal activity, made it impossible for me to gain weight.

Kids at school regularly laughed at how skinny I was and made fun of me because of it. After one too many skinny jokes, I started wearing two pairs of pants and three undershirts during the school year. I thought the extra layers of clothing would make me appear heavier than I actually was. It didn't really work like I thought it would.

The abuse I received at home and the ridicule I received at school left me in constant fear of my life. By the time I was ten years old, I was convinced I'd never live to reach adulthood. I was certain the beatings we received from our father—which seemed to steadily escalate in intensity—would one day get so bad that he'd kill me.

One day in the fifth grade our teacher, Mr. Maurice, asked us, "What do you want to be when you grow up?"

At first no one spoke up as Mr. Maurice's eyes scanned the room, searching for someone to respond. I hid in the back row, refusing to raise my hand to answer his questions or offer a comment. That day I hunkered down even farther, hoping he wouldn't notice me.

One by one, others in the class warmed to his question and they related their dreams to be a teacher, doctor, lawyer, nurse, fireman, or actress. I didn't have an answer like that and didn't want to endure the added torment of stuttering my way through the answer I had. So I sat with my eyes focused on the floor and tried to think of something else.

At some point in that exercise I became aware that Mr. Maurice's voice was louder as he repeated the question. Then I saw his shoes beside my desk and looked up to see he had stopped in the aisle next to me. I was sweating profusely because of the extra clothing I wore and because I was nervous at the now all-too-real likelihood I'd be forced to speak up.

"Michael Evans," he said. "Answer my question. What do you want to be when you grow up?"

"T-t-twenty," I said, giving him my best answer.

As I expected, the kids in the room laughed, but Mr. Maurice raised his hand in a gesture for silence, and they quickly stopped.

"What did you say?" he asked with a puzzled frown.

"Twenty," I repeated. "I-I-I w-want t-to be t-t-twenty."

"No, you misunderstood me." He tried to explain. "Don't you want to be a lawyer, or a teacher? Maybe a policeman?"

"N-n-no," I stuttered. "I j-just want t-t-to be t-t-twenty."

Mr. Maurice looked confused. The class burst into laughter again and I started to cry. My classmates had no idea how big that goal was for me—how impossible it seemed or the obstacles that stood in my way. I understood the question Mr. Maurice had asked, but I didn't have the emotional energy to dream of things like being a lawyer or a doctor. All of my energy was burned up dodging, then enduring, the power of my father's right hand as he slapped me, hit me, and whipped me like an animal. Living to the age of twenty seemed like a big enough dream to me.

✦ ✦ ✦

When we reached junior high we were required to take gym class, which meant time in the locker room, putting on shorts and a t-shirt before participating in physical activity. My legs and back were always bruised from the beatings my father gave me, which made undressing in the locker room not only embarrassing but also a risky endeavor. Someone might see the marks on my body and become concerned enough to actually do something. That would almost certainly generate an official investigation from someone—school administrators, welfare officers, perhaps even the police, who already knew a little about our family situation. I was sure my father would wriggle out of any official inquiry into our home life and equally convinced that I would pay a heavy price for it afterward.

I did my best to avoid detection, but eventually our gym teacher noticed the bruises on my legs and back and notified school officials. They visited our house on two different occasions and their appearance at our door struck almost as much fear in me as our father. Thankfully, both times they came he was away at work.

Instead of telling the truth and pleading with the officials to intervene, I lied about how I had received my injuries. Had I done anything else, I would have faced my father's wrath when he came home.

After those visits, I skipped school when the bruises were severe and waited for them to heal before returning. It was easier to take discipline from the principal over unexplained absences than to take an extra beating at home.

By the time I entered seventh grade, fear was the defining focus of my life and affected every aspect of my personality. When I walked down the street or stood in the hall at school, when I sat in church with my father or shopped with my mother, I did so with my head down, my eyes focused on the ground, or the floor, or the sidewalk, unable to look anyone in the eye because of fear. I didn't really suffer from low self-esteem; rather, I suffered from *no* self-esteem. I was afraid of the dark, of spiders and rats, of policemen, heights, life, and death. I was afraid of girls and of people in general. But mostly I was afraid of my father. Deeply, terribly, appallingly afraid of my father.

Even at that young age he had convinced me that I really was a moron. My mind, numb from the incessant belittling and devoid of creativity, took the notion of my worthlessness and ran with it, projecting that personal assessment on to every aspect of my being—physically, emotionally, intellectually, and spiritually. I was convinced that I had nothing to offer, that my father didn't love me, that God didn't love me and had reserved a place in hell for morons like me.

One of the most vivid instances of how bad things were—how the intensity of his abuse grew—came as the result of a pocketknife I found in the snow when I was eight years old.

Back then most young boys dreamed of having their very own knife. Knives were useful for many things we thought were essential—like whittling aimlessly on a stick or carving our initials into an unsuspecting tree or fence post—and as a sign that we'd arrived at the brink of manhood.

One day on the way home from school I saw a knife lying in the snow. It was brand-new and still as shiny as the moment it'd been taken from the box. My dream had come true! I snatched it up, shoved it into my pocket, and swaggered home. I couldn't wait to show Dad what some careless owner had dropped. I knew he would at last be proud of me.

At dinner that night, I pulled my prized treasure from my pocket and with a big smile displayed the knife for Dad to see and admire. But instead of the affirmation I'd hoped for, he grabbed the knife from my hand and snarled, "Where'd you steal this, Moron?"

My heart dropped and my gaze fell to the floor. "I d-d-didn't s-s-steal it," I stuttered.

Dad rose from the table so abruptly his chair tipped over behind him and crashed to the floor. "Don't lie to me." His voice had a steely edge. "God hates liars and so do I!" His face was twisted with rage and he balled his fists as if to hit me. "For the last time," he roared. "Where did you get that knife? Tell me the truth now or I will beat the s@#t out of you, Moron!"

"I-I f-f-f-ound it in the snow," I stuttered, on the verge of tears.

"Look me in the eye!" he roared, grabbing me by the chin and lifting my head to force me to look at him. "You stole that knife and now you're lying to me. I'm going to teach you what happens when you lie to me!"

By then I was hysterical with fear. I jumped up from my chair and screamed, "I d-d-idn't s-s-teal it! I found it on the s-sidewalk in the snow." I moved behind my chair, positioning it between us while I considered my options. "S-someone must have dropped it," I continued "just before I walked by."

His voice was deadly calm and in his eyes I saw a hint of laughter. "Don't even think about running from me."

That's exactly what I was thinking about and exactly what I did. I was almost to the kitchen before he grabbed hold of my arm. With little effort, he dragged me through the kitchen and down the steps into the basement.

When we reached the bottom of the stairs, he rummaged around on a shelf until he found an extension cord, then doubled it over and began swinging it wildly, striking every place on my body that he could reach. I jumped and twisted this way and that in an effort to avoid the burning lash of the cord, but he kept swinging it, slapping it against my neck, back, legs, and arms. And as he did, I continued to protest my innocence, "I-I'm n-n-ot l-lying!"

"You stupid moron," he screamed in response. "I'll beat you until you pee your pants, then I'll beat you for peeing!"

After only a few swings, the force of the cord ripped through my shirt, and blood began to seep from the welts that formed on my back and arms. I screamed and begged him not to hit me, but he kept going until I could no longer cry out and hung limp from his grasp.

Then, as suddenly as his rage had erupted, it ceased—just like it had on the afternoon he'd insisted on having family devotions—and I thought the worst was over. But to my surprise and utter terror, he didn't let go of me. Instead, he flung open the door to the canning cellar—a windowless pantry carved into one wall of the basement—and heaved me inside. I landed with a thud on the floor and he slammed the door shut, then clicked the lock in place.

A moment later I heard the sound of his footsteps as he started up the stairs toward the kitchen. An instant later the lights went off and I was alone in the dark—totally, completely alone in darkness that was darker than a thousand nights. I opened my eyes as wide as they could go in an attempt to force them to adjust, to find a sliver of light seeping through a crack in the door or the gap at the floor, but no matter how hard I tried I saw only the empty void of pitch-black nothingness.

Although my legs were wobbly and unsteady from the beating, I struggled to my feet and stumbled forward in the direction of the door, thinking maybe I could force it open. In the process, I walked straight into a curtain of spider webs. They draped over my head and shoulders and I thrashed about, waving my arms and hands in a desperate attempt to brush them away.

In the midst of that, I felt something crawling through my hair.

Spiders! There were spiders in my hair! Fear struck at my soul and I brushed all the more frantically. I hopped around in the dark, slapping at my head, trying to get them off me, hoping not to touch them, all at the same time.

When it seemed the spiders were gone I noticed my pants were damp. One sniff of the air told me I was wet with urine. Dad was right. He did beat me until I wet my pants. My shoulder was damp, too, and when I reached up to touch it I felt the warm, sticky feel of blood as it seeped through the rips in my shirt.

And that's when I heard the scratching sound of rats and froze in horror. My heart pounded at the thought of their teeth gnawing at my flesh. No doubt they knew I was human, but they would find the smell of urine and blood too tempting to resist. They'd come for me. I knew it as surely as I'd ever known anything. They'd come for me and by morning I'd be dead. Gnawed to death by a swarming pack of rats.

One thought tumbled onto the next as panic rose inside me. I wanted to get out, to slam my shoulder against the door again and again until I broke it to pieces, but when I tried to move I found myself paralyzed, unable to do anything to affect my own release.

Panic gave way to resignation and I stood there, listening to the silence. Then, in the stillness of that moment, I heard a sound on the other side of the cellar door. Not the sound of rats but of a human. *At last, someone has come to let me out.* Hope sprang up where panic had ruled. Mom, my brother, Sherry...someone had come to find me.

Just as quickly as those thoughts arose, others were right behind them, telling me that the sound I'd heard was Dad returning to finish the job he'd started with the cord. This was it. I was going to die, right there in the basement, that very night.

Then came a whisper, "Mike, it's me, Jim."

Jim was my best friend. Unbeknownst to me, he'd been watching from outside through the basement window. When Dad left me in the canning cellar and went upstairs to the kitchen, Jim squeezed through the window and came to let me out. He took me to his house and got me cleaned up.

Later, when I returned home, Dad was passed out on the bed in his bedroom. Mom hardly noticed as I came through the door. And no one asked where I'd been or what happened. So far as I can remember, no one ever said a word about the incident.

✦ ✦ ✦

Throughout my childhood death seemed always at hand. Not so much from the bullying I received at school or the racial harassment from people in the community. That was demeaning and emotionally traumatic but I didn't really think of it as life-threatening—at least not physically threatening. The abuse we received from Dad was another matter. The way he treated us posed a direct threat to our safety and well-being and as time went by raised the question of whether we would physically survive.

There were other times in my childhood when my life was in danger. More than once I had the thought that death was searching for an opportunity to take me out. Several times I thought I really was gone, but each time something or someone intervened to keep me alive.

Like the time when I was ten years old and at a lake in a park near our house. I heard the scream of a little boy and, having become well-acquainted with fear, knew in an instant someone was in trouble. When I looked up to see what the trouble might be I saw a little boy some distance from shore, flailing his arms frantically as if he was drowning.

Without a moment's hesitation, I jumped into the water and swam out to him. By the time I reached him, the water was way over my head. I had no training in swimmer rescue so I moved up close to him while I tried to figure out what to do next.

Overcome with panic, the little boy grabbed at me with both hands. I tried to fend him off but he succeeded in taking hold of my head. Then, in a desperate attempt to save himself, he pushed down on me with all his weight as if to climb out of the water. He wasn't very big and a trained lifeguard could have easily handled him, but I wasn't a lifeguard and I wasn't all that strong, either. Instead, the force of his effort and the weight of his body pushed me under the water with him on top of me, still trying to climb out.

Now I was the one who panicked. The bottom of the lake was far below my feet. There was no way I could use it to push myself away. The air in my lungs was running low, too, and I had to concentrate to keep from breathing in the water that surrounded me.

By then, the work of swimming out to him and then of extricating myself from his grasp had left my muscles spent. Now I was in trouble, too.

Just when desperation seemed ready to overwhelm me and all hope was lost, a hand reached down through the water, took hold of me, and lifted me up to the surface. An adult had seen us and jumped into the water to save us.

Another time, my brother Bobby and I were at Sullivan's Pond. It was winter and the pond was iced over. We thought it was solid enough to hold us and gave it a test near the shore. It seemed good enough so we ventured farther out.

Suddenly, the ice gave way and Bobby went into the water. I knew he couldn't last long in the frigid water so I jumped in to save him. He was younger and lighter and I succeeded in hoisting him to safety, but when I tried to lift myself from the water, the ice around me cracked away. The more I tried, the more it cracked until my body was numb with cold.

Once again—just when all seemed lost—a hand took hold of my shoulder and lifted me to safety on the ice. This time, however, when I looked around to see who it was that helped me, there was no one in sight. Bobby didn't see my rescuer, either.[6]

CHAPTER
8

Despite the beatings, the intimidation, and the terror of living with an abusive parent, we enjoyed some fun times, too. They weren't the moments that defined us like the beatings and berating did, but they were a welcome relief from the terror that ruled our lives.

Fall brought cooler weather and with it came showers of leaves. From mid-October until the end of November our yard was covered with them. Raking them was one of our assigned tasks, but that also presented an opportunity for fun. I enjoyed raking them into a huge pile, then diving into the pile, burrowing to the bottom, and hiding myself away for a short while.

One of my prized possessions was a BB rifle and I enjoyed prowling around the backyard, imagining myself as a hunter. One time I actually fired a shot that hit a squirrel, though I don't remember whether or not I killed one.

On weekends we occasionally went to a movie at the Grand Theater. We usually went with a crowd of kids and all sat together. When the lights dimmed and the movie started, we amused ourselves by throwing popcorn at unsuspecting moviegoers.

Television was an escape for us and we watched the Lone Ranger rescue the downtrodden with his silver bullets and saw Superman save the day, his cape trailing in the wind behind him. Roy Rogers rescued Dale Evans from the bad guys, and Gene Autry sang his way through the Old West on his horse, Champion.

Sometimes on Saturday nights Dad would sit us in front of the television, adjust the rabbit ears to sharpen the picture, and then we'd watch *The Twilight Zone*. He found the show thoroughly entertaining. We found it thoroughly frightening, though in an entertaining manner.

The moment the show ended, Dad would jump from his chair and race up the stairs yelling, "Last one out has to turn off all the lights."

Invariably, we all made it to the stairs at the same time, then pushed and shoved for position in order to avoid being the last one in the room. The others usually beat me to the choicest positions around the television, which meant I had to watch from a spot that was farthest from the stairs. As a result, I often got stuck with turning out the lights. That meant I had to climb the stairs alone and in the dark. Most of the time, I made that trek certain that monsters from the *The Twilight Zone* were lurking behind me, ready to grab me at any moment.

During one period of my life, my friends and I made a game of shoplifting from the stores uptown. We entered the store as quietly as possible, trying not to draw attention to ourselves, then stuffed our pockets full of merchandise from the shelves. The point of the game was to see who could make it out with the most stuff. Whoever took the most also got the things everyone else took.

One summer, someone got the idea that we should vandalize cars in the A&P parking lot. I'm not sure why we thought that was a good idea—our mothers all shopped there and everyone who worked in the store knew us. Still, it seemed like fun so we put on our baseball shoes, the kind with metal cleats, and ran up and down every car in the lot—scratching and marring the paint from hood to trunk.

On Halloween night we worked our way up the street, going from house to house lighting stink bombs and positioning them on the molding above the front door. Then someone rang the doorbell while the rest of us ran away yelling, "Trick or treat!" Naturally, someone came out to see about the commotion and when they did, the force of opening the door jarred the stink bomb loose. As it rolled around on the porch, smoke and odor from the bomb wafted into the house.

Not all of our fun was malicious, though. One day after seeing the movie *Mary Poppins* I decided that with the help of Mom's umbrella I, too, could fly. I climbed onto the roof of the garage, opened the umbrella, and jumped. Unfortunately, the umbrella didn't generate as much lift as I thought and I fell straight to the ground. I landed on a pile of leaves, which broke my fall, and I escaped without physical injury—just my pride.

Yankee, my German Shepard, was amused. He barked and ran around in circles while I gasped for breath.

Mom's umbrella, however, was a different matter. Pressure from the rush of air created as I left the garage roof was more than it could handle. The force of it bent the spines backward, rendering the umbrella useless. Rather than own up to what I'd done, I folded it back in place and sneaked it inside. If she ever noticed she didn't say anything.

At home, we ate the same meals each week. Friday night was hot dogs and beans. Saturday was lasagna. Sunday was fried chicken. The food was good, but there was always a twist that ruined an otherwise enjoyable time.

For one thing, Mom and Dad fought a lot at mealtime. He would become enraged about something, pick up his plate and hurl it to the floor, splattering food everywhere. Then he would knock her out of her chair while my siblings and I cowered, our eyes downcast, hoping to escape his wrath. We did escape it sometimes, but on other occasions his anger was turned against us, too. The good in our lives, what little of it there was, was tainted by the things that haunted Dad, always perverting and corrupting even the hope of laughter that crept into our otherwise bleak existence.

When I was a young child and we lived in the Projects, Dad worked for others as an employee. Our parents struggled to make ends meet, which is how we ended up in public housing. It offered them the cheapest apartment possible. While we lived there, Dad went into business for himself. He did the same thing as before—operating a bulldozer and other heavy equipment—he just did it for himself instead of as someone else's employee. Money was still a problem but things were generally better than before, though my folks never attained the financial stability they sought.

In spite of our financial issues, Dad always found money for the things that interested him. He bet on horse races and from time to time took sports bets as a bookie. He found money to purchase a boat, dozens of guns, and pay for a hunting lease, but he never had any money for his children.

When I was ten, I cried on Easter Sunday because the other kids made fun of the way I dressed. My pants had holes in them and splatters of paint dotted my shirt. Dad saw that I was upset and asked, "What's the matter with *you*?"

I told him what the other kids had said and he replied, "Boy, shut up. If you want new clothes, get a job and buy them."

It was a cruel thing to say to a ten-year-old, but that's exactly what I did—I got a job. Being so young, the jobs available were mostly menial, but I took what I could find. My first job was as a paper boy. Springfield had three daily newspapers and I delivered them all. In the spring and summer I mowed lawns and even worked for a time picking tobacco. Not many people know that Massachusetts and neighboring Connecticut are home to a number of large tobacco farms.

By the time I was sixteen, I had three jobs: working construction, bagging groceries, and waxing floors. Working with the floor crew kept me busy all night on Fridays and Saturdays. Those jobs paid much better than mowing lawns and delivering newspapers, but as my earnings increased so did my empathy for my siblings, who had nothing. I spent most of the money on them.

In the summer I worked full time and saved to buy my dream car—a 1957 Chevy Bel Air convertible. By the time I was fifteen I'd saved enough to buy one, but being too young to obtain a driver's license, all I could do was drive it up and down the driveway.

One Friday Dad caught me smoking in the car with the top down and the music blaring. He leaned over the door and asked, "Boy, you like to smoke?"

"No, it's just my first pack." He and Mom were chain-smokers. I didn't think they would mind.

He had an amused look. "Tomorrow will be smoke day."

At ten the next morning, he ushered me out to the back steps and handed me a big Cuban cigar. "Light it up," he ordered.

I struck a match and took a puff thinking this was odd—a father and son smoking together—but I enjoyed what appeared to be positive attention from him, so I lit up the cigar and took a puff.

"Keep going," he demanded. "Take another puff." I took a drag on the cigar and exhaled. "Do it again," he insisted. "Keep going."

If I flagged, he nudged me and insisted I continue smoking. Puff after puff at a fast pace, not taking time to savor the aroma or note the taste. Just puff, puff, puff. Every five minutes or so, I leaned over the side of the steps and vomited. When I finished the first one, he handed me another. I had never been so sick in my life, but I never smoked again, either.

CHAPTER
9

Even though Mom was Jewish, she made no effort to take us to a synagogue or introduce us to Jewish tradition and practices. Nor did we celebrate the High Holy days. We did, however, eat some of the traditional Jewish foods. Mostly things like lox and bagels, matzo ball soup, gefilte fish, and challah bread, which were things she remembered and enjoyed from her childhood.

Sometimes on Friday nights, when Dad left for the Twilight Café, she took out her menorah and lit the candles. She had a mezuzah, too—a small parchment inscribed with verses from the Torah—which fit neatly into a decorative case. It was designed to be affixed to the doorpost of the house, but she didn't dare put it on ours. Dad had no use for Jewish traditions and rituals.

Dad's attitude toward all things Jewish was well known. Everyone in the family knew he was mean, angry, and prejudiced. They also knew he was a drunk, routinely unfaithful to our mother, and that he covered it all with an overtly Christian rhetoric—which, in their eyes, made him all the more a bigot and hypocrite.

In spite of all that, our Aunt Ginger was determined that my siblings and I should be exposed to and educated about the Jewish side of our family. She didn't have the constant association with us that Dad and Mom did, but she made sure we were introduced to traditional Jewish events and celebrations. She also made sure we met our extended family—descendants of Mollie and Samuel Levine—most of whom lived in New York. She and her husband, Art, took us there on several occasions. The most memorable times with that side of the family were when we celebrated Passover at our uncle's home and a weekend when we attended our cousin's bar mitzvah.

Ginger and Art also took us to a Yankees baseball game once. Ginger was a big Yankees fan. Art cheered for the Boston Red Sox.

Through Aunt Ginger we learned that Passover was a night of remembrance of God's grace and mercy toward His people when, thousands of years earlier, He saved Israel from the death angel. It was a solemn occasion with everyone seated around a single table and began with our uncle pouring each of the adults a glass of red wine.

I watched, hoping he'd fill my glass with wine, too, but the children were served grape juice.

When the glasses were filled, we leaned to the left like kings and queens and said the *Kiddush*—an ancient Hebrew prayer. Having never attended Hebrew class, I didn't understand the words but did my best to follow along.

"Blessed are You, Lord our God, King of the universe, Who creates the fruit of the vine. Amen."

"Blessed are You, Lord our God, King of the universe, Who chose us from all the nations, and elevated us above all tongues, and sanctified us with His commandments. And You gave us, Lord our God, with love, Sabbaths for rest, festivals for happiness, holidays for joy, and this day, the Festival of Matzos, the time of our freedom, a holy convocation, a remembrance of the Exodus from Egypt. Because You chose us, and sanctified us from all the nations, and gave us Your holy festivals in happiness and in joy, You have given us as a heritage. Blessed are You, God, Who sanctifies Israel and the holiday seasons. Amen."

"Blessed are You, Lord our God, King of the universe, Who has kept us alive and sustained us and brought us to this season. Amen."

After the prayer, we washed our hands by pouring water over them. Three times over the right hand and three times over the left. I'd heard about the Passover but never about the washing.

Next came the small pieces of potato, which were already on our plates. I watched the others, trying to determine what to do with it. Aunt Ginger, sensing my confusion, leaned close to me and whispered, "Dip the potato in the salt water." She gestured toward a small dish that sat near my plate. As I dipped the potato in it she said, "Now take a tiny bite."

While I swallowed she added, "This is to remember the tears the Jews cried when Pharaoh was so mean to them in Egypt."

Before I'd finished all of the potato, my uncle began another prayer, and everyone joined in. "Blessed are you, Lord our God, King of the universe, Who creates the fruit of the land."

A beautiful plate sat at the center of the table with a lid over it. When we'd finished the prayer, my uncle lifted the lid to reveal the matzah—squares of unleavened flatbread—that rested on the plate. He removed a piece of it and broke it in half. Then someone took the broken piece away to hide it.

"When we are finished," he said, "the children will search for the matzah. Whoever finds it will get a wonderful gift." Right then, I was determined to find it.

Then a cousin asked, "What makes this night so different from all other nights?" I thought it was an excellent question and had been wondering the same thing myself. Not that I didn't know about Passover from the Bible; I'd picked up enough from attending church with Dad to know the basics. But the question I had was what made it so special that they marked it with a special ceremony. I didn't realize the question was part of the ritual.

Four people spoke up with an answer. "On all nights we need not dip even once," the first person said. "On this night we dip twice."

The next said, "On all nights we can eat any kind of bread. Tonight we only eat matzah."

Another said, "On all nights we eat any kind of vegetable. On this night we eat bitter herbs."

And the last to speak said, "On all nights we eat sitting up. Tonight we all recline."

While the answers were given, our glasses were refilled and when the drinks were finished we washed our hands yet again. As we did, we prayed again, too. "Blessed are you, Lord our God, King of the universe, Who has sanctified us with His commandments, and commanded us to wash our hands."

With our hands ceremonially clean, we each received a slice of matzah. This was followed by another prayer, then came the parsley—the bitter herb. Using the matzah, we made a sandwich with the parsley and a leaf of romaine lettuce. While we chewed we recited another prayer.

With the ceremony finished at last, we were served a traditional meal. I don't remember all of the dishes. I just remember that we never ate like that at our house and I stuffed myself until I couldn't hold another bite.

As we finished eating, the children were sent away to find the hidden matzah. One of our cousins located it and returned to the table carrying it triumphantly. As a prize, he received a ten-dollar bill. My eyes were wide with wonder at the sight of it and I vowed to watch more closely next time to see which way the person went when they left the table to hide it.

Having stuffed ourselves with dinner and found the hidden matzah, I assumed the evening was done. But we were called back to the table and our glasses were filled yet again. Then we ate desert—the hidden portion of matzah that our cousin had found. Afterward we were poured a fourth glass and I noticed my uncle, who did the pouring, stepped to the front door and opened it wide. I whispered to Aunt Ginger, "What is he doing?"

"He is welcoming the prophet Elijah," she replied. "We welcome him on Passover because he is the one who will come before the Messiah. He is the symbol of hope for all of us."

Around the table, the men and women began to sing, this time in English. I understood the words clearly as they praised God for His great works and miracles on behalf of the Jewish people. When they finished the song, we drank the fourth glass and as we downed the last drops, everyone shouted, "Next year in Jerusalem! We want Messiah now!"

That was the first of many Passover Seders for me, but at the time I'd never witnessed anything like it and I marveled at how wonderful it was to be Jewish. And to be together at the table with my family without anyone screaming in anger or fighting.

✦ ✦ ✦

The bar mitzvah we attended was for our cousin Mark—Uncle Max's son and Aunt Ginger's nephew. It was an important event in his life and in the life of our family, and Aunt Ginger wanted us there. Before that, though, she took us uptown to buy new clothes and shoes. Ours were too worn and ill-fitting for such a grand occasion.

On the ride down to Brooklyn, Aunt Ginger explained the significance of what we were about to witness. Mark had completed a number of assigned tasks. He'd read the Torah aloud from the podium, then led the congregation in prayer during weekly Shabbat services. That was enough to impress me. I was sure I would never be able to speak in public like that. But Mark had done more than that. He'd also written and delivered a speech about the Torah to the congregation. And he had planned and executed a charitable act to raise money for the temple.

All of that denoted Mark's entry into adulthood, at least in terms of Jewish tradition. The ceremony we would attend was designed as a celebration of that fact, a rite of passage that marked the beginning of a lifetime of study and serious participation in the Jewish community.

The ceremony turned out to be far more solemn than I'd imagined and, unlike the Passover Seder, it was an event that included people from outside our family. We made it through to the end, though, without embarrassing our aunt. Then the real fun began as we joined our family for a huge buffet dinner. Never in our lives had we seen so much food in one place. The typical indulgent aunt, Ginger turned us loose to eat as much as we wanted.

Like most good things in our life, the weekend came to an end in more ways than one. Aunt Ginger and Uncle Art took us home and we arrived back in Springfield late on Saturday night.

We were trying to be quiet as we eased the front door open but we had been telling jokes in the car on the way home and were in a giggling mood. As we came inside the house, someone said something funny and we burst into laughter. At the sound of it, Dad appeared at the top of the steps, wearing nothing but his underwear. "Shut up!" he shouted.

"We were just having fun," Art said, trying to smooth over the moment. "Come down and help us bring everything inside."

Like a raging bull, Dad flew down the stairs, cocked his fist, and hit Uncle Art in the face. The force of the punch broke Art's nose and blood seemed to flow in every direction. He staggered backward, crashed through the screen door, and collapsed in agony on the front porch. Everyone was screaming as Uncle Art fell backward through the screen door. Dad burst through what was left of the door frame and continued to beat my uncle, blacking his eyes, and inflicting cuts and bruises.

Aunt Ginger screamed for Dad to stop as she tried to stanch the flow of blood. We children stood at the bottom of the stairs, not moving a muscle.

Finally Dad muttered something under his breath and turned back to enter the house. As he disappeared upstairs, we carried our things up to the bedroom and turned in for the night. The glow from our wonderful weekend had been dimmed but not quenched. I lay in bed that night and relived every wonderful bite of food, occasionally reaching down to touch my new shoes that lay beside me on the floor.

Ginger and Art didn't come around for a while after that, but somehow her love for us was greater than her disgust for Dad. The next time I saw her, I said, "I'm sorry for what Dad did to Uncle Art."

"Oh, honey," she cooed, "it's not your fault. Robert should have never married, or had children. He's just not the kind of person who cares for others."

The last time I saw Aunt Ginger, she was ninety-one. It was football season and she was watching the New York Giants on television in her tiny apartment. "Oh, honey," she said, "please come back in three hours. My Giants are on right now."

Even then she knew the statistics for every player on the Giants roster. And the New York Yankees. And for her favorite hockey team, the New York Rangers. She had been a Yankees season ticket holder so long that when she died, her name was announced during a game.

I did as she asked and came back after the ball game ended. When we talked she said, "I have some advice for you."

"What's that?" I asked, eager to hear what she had to say.

"Never date anyone when you're ninety-one—they die off way too quick."

When I asked how many men she was dating, she answered, "Three, but Jimmy just dumped me."

"He dumped you?"

"Yeah. He found out I was ninety-one. I told him I was eighty-nine, but he found out the truth. He said he had a rule never to date women over ninety." That was Ginger. Always quick-witted and determined to find the best in life, no matter what obstacles opposed her. She did her best to help us find it, too.

When it was time to leave, I gave Ginger flowers and kissed her good-bye. A few months later she became ill and not long after that she died. I was honored to speak at her funeral.

CHAPTER
10

Studies indicate that in the United States, at least five children die every day as a result of child abuse. According to advocacy groups, a report of child abuse is made every ten seconds. People who received six or more incidents of abuse as a child have a life expectancy that is two decades shorter than those who report experiencing none.[7] Those statistics alone make my survival to the age of eleven a miracle. Herbert Ward was right when he once said, "Child abuse casts a shadow the length of a lifetime."[8]

Without a miracle, I likely would have become just like my father—prejudiced, bigoted, and angry. And there is a very strong likelihood I would have died before I reached my goal of attaining the age of twenty. A death most likely inflicted by my father's hand. Or perhaps by my own.

Every angry encounter with his fist, his belt, and his boot seemed worse than the one before. Every beating, I thought at the time, was the worst of my life until the next one came. But nothing that had happened before prepared me for what was about to occur.

That Friday night began like any other. Dad came home from work, showered in the bathroom upstairs, and shaved while singing verses from his favorite songs. When he was finished in the bathroom, he changed into clean clothes and headed for the Twilight Café.

After he was gone, we ate dinner and played in the street until bath time. Once we were bathed and ready for bed, we sat in the living room and watched television. Two of my favorite shows, *The Adventures of Rin Tin Tin* followed by *Walt Disney Presents*, were broadcast on Friday nights and I loved watching them. For an hour or two while those shows were on, the good guys always won, the dog saved the day, and wishes really did come true.

Long before Dad was due to stagger back from the bar, Mom hurried us off to bed. She hoped that we'd be sound asleep when he arrived and that she could coax him upstairs without creating a scene. That almost never worked out and the night usually ended with them in a fight. It never worked for me, either, as I found it impossible to sleep through Dad's ranting and raving.

That particular Friday night I heard the front door slam shut and knew there would be trouble. "Jean," he roared. "Come here. Now!"

Nothing about that was unusual. Dad would often come home in an angry, drunken stupor and shove Mom into a chair near the bottom of the stairs, then take out his frustration on her with his fists.

That night followed the typical pattern and as things heated up downstairs I rolled onto my stomach and covered my head with the pillow. I pulled it tight against my ears and tried to block out the angry screams coming from the kitchen and the sickening thud of his fist against her flesh.

About two-thirty in the morning, during a lull in the mayhem, I eased from the bed and crept out to the bannister at the top of the stairs. But just as I settled into place, Dad started again. I dropped to the floor and sat there with my arms wrapped around my shoulders, tears rolling down my cheeks, listening to Mom whimper as Dad continued to beat her.

"You Jew-whore!" he shouted. "Tell me about that bastard moron upstairs who thinks he's my son. You know he's not mine! He can't be. I went off to the army and you whored around while I was gone. Spread your legs for a big-nosed Jew. Tell me the truth! Who was it that gave you that bastard moron for a son?"

With every sentence, I heard the slap of his hand against her face. He was a big, strong guy. I'd felt his slap before and though from the sound I heard that night his palm was open, the impact of it was almost as bad as being hit by his fist.

Dad continued to yell at her, demanding to know about an affair she'd supposedly had with a Jewish man. Suggesting over and over that the moron upstairs—me—was the result of that liaison.

And that's when it hit me. All this was my fault! He was beating my mother because of me. He thought I belonged to some other man, and I hung my head in shame.

My eleven-year-old mind concluded that certainly I was a bad person to make my dad hit her because of me. I hated myself as much as my father hated me and wished I had never been born.

Mom protested her innocence, but a night of whiskey and pills had deadened Dad's senses. He was convinced he was right—in his mind he was always right—and usually there was no way to persuade him otherwise.

The next blow brought the sound of a chair crashing to the floor. I moved down the stairs far enough to see that Mom lay on the kitchen tile, curled in a fetal position, sobbing. As Dad lifted his hand to strike her again, I could take it no longer.

"Stop it!" I shouted. "Stop it."

Dad whirled around, his eyes ablaze as he stared at me. The sound of my voice was unexpected and for a moment caught him off guard. But just as quickly, he recovered and started toward me.

I stood paralyzed at the top of the stairs. He grabbed me by my shirt and began swinging his fists wildly as he battered my body. I raised my arms in self-defense and caught many of the blows on my forearms. I later found out that the force of the blows was so powerful that I had suffered hairline fractures to both arms.

As he hit at me, I tried to back away until I ran out of space, then he grabbed hold of me with both hands and lifted me over his head as high as he could reach. I hung there, suspended in the air, my feet dangling above the floor as he glared at me.

"Moron Jew," he seethed between his clenched teeth. "You're gonna regret the day you were born."

As he held me in that position with one hand, his other hand closed around the front of my neck, his fingers pressing against my skin, slowly choking off the air. Fury rose higher in him and I could see in his eyes nothing but cold, murderous intent. He shook me from side to side and swung me back and forth like a pendulum, all the while squeezing my throat even tighter than before.

Desperate to free myself, if even for a moment just to take a breath, I kicked at him and grabbed at his hands to pull his fingers away. But the more I fought, the tighter his grip became and choked off the air to my lungs completely. No longer able to resist, my body went lip and I began to lose consciousness, certain my life was about to end.

At the last moment, he released his grip and let me drop. I hit the floor with a thud and collapsed in a broken heap. Still desperate to get away, I crawled toward the bedroom, hoping to reach my favorite hiding place beneath the bed, gasping for breath all the way, only faintly aware of my surroundings.

My stomach muscles tightened in an involuntary spasm and I vomited, emptying the contents of my stomach down my chest and onto the floor. And in the midst of that, I finally passed out, my body spent and drained of energy.

Sometime later I awoke to find I was still lying on the floor, curled in a fetal position. My face was caked with dried vomit and the front of my pajamas was stained brown with it. Muscles in my neck, back, and arms ached with fatigue.

After a moment to take a mental inventory of my limbs and assure myself that I was still fully intact, I tried to push up to a standing position. As I did, the room started spinning and I collapsed again to the floor.

Lying there next to the bed, I closed my eyes and clenched my fists in agony that was both physical and emotional. Once again, tears filled my eyes and I bumped my fists against my thighs. "Why was I born?" I sobbed. "Why? Why? Why?!"

My words sounded like a prayer, but at the time I didn't really believe in God, or Jesus, or anything else religious. I'd been attending church most of my life and from what I'd seen, church had more to do with a person's education than anything else. People who were educated and successful were Episcopalian. Those of average intelligence were Baptist. And those who were just plain stupid were Pentecostal.

That was attributable partly to the people I knew and partly to my father—he was a Pentecostal, at least in name. I'd also concluded that even if God existed He didn't care about me. If He did, He would have intervened to stop the abuse long before.

All I knew was my father's warped version of Christianity, the basic tenets of which involved booze on Friday, beatings on Saturday, and church on Sunday. He had never once given me a single word of affirmation. Not once had I heard him say, "I love you." Never a gesture of friendship. To him, whiskey was his friend, I was his moron, and after years of physical and emotional torture, I came to see no purpose for my life. My father hated me for who I was, and my mother and I suffered because of it.

After lying on the floor for what seemed like a long time, I managed to drag myself onto the bed and sat atop the covers with my legs drawn up in front of me, knees against my chest, ankles pressed against the backs of my thighs. Then I leaned forward, rested my head on my knees, and closed my eyes.

As I sat there thinking of all that had happened that night, I whispered again the question I'd asked while I lay on the floor. "Why was I born?"

Just as quickly as those words left my lips, the room was flooded with light so bright it blinded me. Fear struck deep in my soul and I was sure Dad had come back to finish the job he'd started earlier—as I'd imagined before when I was locked in the canning cellar. Only this time there was no one to intervene. No one to save me. He was going to beat me and choke me and I was going to die.

Running was useless and I had little energy left to fight back. Instead, I closed my eyes tightly shut to escape what seemed to me to be a spotlight. I rocked back and forth, whining from deep in my throat in a high-pitched moaning whimper not unlike that of an injured dog, waiting for the sound of Dad's voice, for the grasp of his hand in my hair as he lifted me from the floor. Waiting for the pain in my jaw as he hit me with his fist and in my side as he kicked me again and again.

After a moment or two I heard nothing but silence. The only sound in the room was the one coming from me, and realization of this struck me as odd. If my father had been there he would have been screaming and cursing long before then.

Slowly, carefully I opened my eyes and glanced around as imperceptibly as possible, hoping to see an empty room. Instead of Dad's angry face, I saw two hands stretched out toward me. The palms were open and in the center of each wrist was an ugly scar. I had seen those scars many times before in Sunday school literature illustrations that were supposed to represent the nail scars of Jesus.

Could this really be Jesus? And if so, did I dare look beyond the hands to the face? For an instant I wondered if I was crazy even to entertain that possibility. I'd heard adults talking about people in psychiatric hospitals who sometimes claimed to hear God's voice.

Others claimed to have seen Him in person. Was I one of those? Had Dad finally broken me completely? Was I crazy?

Curious about what was really happening, I opened my eyes wider and raised my head a little to peek through my fingers. As I lifted my gaze to look, I was filled with the most comforting, exhilarating sense of warmth I'd ever felt in my life. Deep, healing warmth that touched the innermost part of my soul and brought both a sense of peace and of power. And for a moment I thought I must surely be dead and somehow transported to heaven.

As minutes ticked by, I slowly raised my head higher and allowed my eyes to follow past the hands and up the arms. That's when I saw an individual standing in my room that I knew in my heart was the Lord Jesus Christ. He was surrounded by light and robed in the most brilliantly white garment imaginable. Whiter than fresh snow. Whiter than the clouds that floated across a sun-filled sky. Whiter than anything I had ever seen. And draped across His body from His shoulder to His waist was a deep purple cloth, more purple than the heavens at sunset.

As I lifted my head still higher I saw His bearded face and instantly my focus was drawn to His eyes. They were smiling, happy eyes filled with every color of the rainbow. Looking at them was like peering into an illuminated bowl filled with the world's most highly prized jewels and I felt as if I could see through them all the way to heaven.

Sitting there, mesmerized by His smile and eyes that drew me into their depths, He reached toward me and rested one of those nail-scarred hands lightly atop my head. Then He spoke to me with words I had never heard before—words that were salve to my wounded heart and starved spirit.

"Son," he began. It was the first time anyone had ever called me that. Certainly never so gently and with such love and respect as He'd shown. Love and respect for me! I felt my heart melt.

Then He continued with, "I love you." In an instant I felt as if I'd escaped a death sentence. Someone loved me. Not the general proposition that God is love, but the statement that He loved *me*. Those two statements alone could have sustained me for the rest of my life, but He continued.

"I have a great plan for your life." He knew me! I was His son—a son whom He loved. And He had a plan for my life.

Very few people had ever noticed me in a positive way. Aunt Ginger occasionally. Mom once in a while. But Dad only noticed me when he was angry and then only to punish and brutalize me. The kids at school only noticed me in order to make fun of me. And the guys in the neighborhood only paid attention to me when we were vandalizing someone's property, or playing tricks on the people who lived near us, or when they wanted to play tricks on me.

But Jesus—the Lord of the universe—had His eye on me. And not only that, He had things for me to do. Not just an errand to run or a chore to complete. He had a plan for my entire life. God had something for me—Michael Evans—to do. Something that only I could accomplish.

As I thought about those words, inexplicable joy consumed me and tears trickled down my face. Not the tears of fear and pain, but of overwhelming release and relief. Of finding the promise of a calling and a purpose. Of at last finding my way to the point of beginning for something much bigger than myself.

Eventually I realized that the light had departed from the bedroom, but the overwhelming warmth remained in my soul and in my spirit. Jesus might have been gone from my room but not from my heart, not from me.

As I sat there, thinking of all that had happened, I found myself compelled to offer something in return. So I promised I would serve God, would keep myself sexually pure, and would not take His name in vain. Those were the three biggest things I thought I could offer Him and I was more than willing to give them to Him.

Though physically battered, bruised, and broken, I eventually drifted off to sleep. When I awoke the next morning, I stretched my arms and legs and remembered the beating I had endured the night before. At first, I thought it had been a nightmare, then I remembered the visitation from Jesus and a smile spread over my face.

Tentatively I stretched my arms again, expecting the usual pain and stiffness that followed from Dad's abuse, but to my amazement there was no pain. The night before, my arms had been too sore to move. Now they swung freely without any pain.

Still smiling at the thought of all that had happened, I rolled out of bed and made my way down the hall to the bathroom. No one else was awake so I slipped inside and closed the door quietly behind me. Carefully, I stood before the mirror at the sink, peeled away my pajama top, and took an inventory of the aftermath from the beating.

My arms and shoulders were bruised and already there were purple-and-black imprints on my neck from where my father's fingers and hands had squeezed so tightly against my throat. Suddenly the reality of what he had tried to do became starkly real and overwhelming. Then I remembered Jesus had laid His hand on my head the night before and the memory of the tenderness with which He'd approached me rose in my mind. All over again, the love that had flowed from Him through me the night before returned as I stood in the bathroom. And then His words came rushing back. *I* was His son. He loved *me*. And had a plan for *my* life!

I knew God had called me to the ministry, but I also knew it could not be accomplished while I lived at 77 Pascoe Road. I promised Him that I would enter the ministry when I was twenty years old. And that is exactly what happened.

✦ ✦ ✦

Right then and there I wanted to tell someone, but I didn't dare. Mom would have been horrified to learn that I had given my life to Jesus. Many times she'd told me that if I ever became a Christian she would consider me dead and have a funeral for me.

"If you murder someone," she would say, "or become a drug addict or a homosexual, it would not give me as much heartbreak and grief as if you accepted Jesus." I'm not certain she actually meant it, but she said it to me and I didn't feel free to talk to her about what had happened.

Though Dad claimed to be a Christian, he would've thought I was lying. To him, anything good that ever happened to us kids was either a lie or the result of a lie—and that always meant a beating. I'd had enough beatings for no cause at all and didn't care to invite another of my own volition.

At the same time, I didn't want anyone to challenge my moment of hope—to tell me that things could not have happened as I described them or that what I'd seen wasn't really Jesus. So, rather than talk about what had happened, I kept my experiences to myself. But I still was convinced that I had to do something to earn God's love and as I grew older that sense of owing Him something only grew. The only love I'd ever known was that of the scant, conditional approval I'd seen others earn. That understanding ran deep in me, much deeper than I realized at the time. So rather than talk about what had happened, I added to the promises I'd already made to God and told Him that if He could wait until I was twenty—the age I'd told my fifth-grade teacher was my dream—that I would spend the remainder of my life telling everyone the story of how He had intervened on my behalf.

As the days wore on, though, I realized that Jesus had made other changes in my life—changes that became obvious to me and should have been obvious to others. Changes that had the potential of forcing me to talk about what had happened, whether I wanted to or not.

The initial and most obvious change involved my speech impediment. It had simply vanished. As a lifelong pattern of behavior, it had become so ingrained in me that at first I hadn't noticed when it left, but eventually someone pointed out to me that I no longer stuttered. I was astounded and every time I opened my mouth to speak, the words that came out—smooth, consistent, and uninterrupted—bore witness to my spirit that God really had visited me that night and really had acted on my behalf.

At the same time, my stomach stopped hurting. For most of my life, I'd endured painful stomach cramps—the result of ulcers that developed in response to the stress of worrying about when the next beating might occur. After that night in the bedroom, the stomach cramps stopped.

And not long after I realized my speech and stomach problems had vanished, I noticed that I was no longer plagued by fear. Instead of walking with my eyes staring down at my ragged sneakers, I now walked with my head up. I looked people in the eyes without fear of rejection or ridicule and carried with an air of confident rectitude.

Those changes—the cessation of stuttering and stomach pain and the manner in which I handled myself—were open and obvious. For several days I waited for Mom or Dad to notice, but they never said a word about it. I was utterly amazed. My life had been dramatically transformed, both internally and externally, and yet no one in my family—neither my parents nor my siblings—offered any comment at all. But that was the way things were in our house. Our parents were physically present—often painfully so—but when it came to actual, positive emotional presence, they were far away.

Though I had been transformed on many levels, some things in my life remained the same. The emotional storms that ravaged our family raged on. Dad continued to frequent the Twilight Café on Friday nights, abuse our mother when he returned, and line us up on Saturdays for a merciless beating. But inside, Jesus had calmed my body and infused my spirit with His power. The tumult continued, but getting through it and surviving to the age of twenty now seemed a distinct possibility.

CHAPTER
11

As I grew older, the physical abuse lessened but the verbal abuse never abated. When Dad was at home, he verbally assaulted me with an unrelenting barrage of put-downs and slurs that often included profanity and his favorite epithet—moron Jew.

In 1963, I turned sixteen. By then I had endured as much from Dad as I cared to take. Getting away from our house on Pasco Road became my number one priority. During the summer and later into the fall, I began searching for opportunities to extricate myself from the dysfunction and insanity that had become the normal routine in our family.

That November, we watched and listened in shocked silence at school as televised news reports from Dallas, Texas, told us that

President Kennedy had been assassinated. The Kennedys were from Massachusetts and although we didn't know them personally—we lived a life far removed from theirs—they seemed like one of our own. For us, President Kennedy's death was as much a personal matter as political or historic.

In the days surrounding that event and in the weeks that followed, Americans everywhere felt a renewed sense of patriotism. I was no less affected than anyone else and in the aftermath of President Kennedy's death, I decided to join the army, both as an expression of devotion to our country and as a means by which I could leave home. I'd been considering military service as an option already and the president's death made the decision all the more palatable. With conflict heating up in Vietnam and American troops still subject to skirmishes in Korea, the opportunity seemed tailor-made for me. As strange as it may seem, a war somewhere, anywhere, was a welcome opportunity to escape the war at home.

When I discussed my plans with Jim, my best friend, he agreed with my decision and was eager to enlist, too. I first went to the Marine Corps office and tried to enlist. I was rejected because I had failed the physical due to insufficient weight. After talking about it further, Jim and I decided to join the army on the buddy system—a popular program we'd heard about that supposedly allowed friends to serve together. We assumed we'd be assigned to the same unit and sent to the same location.

A few days later, we made our way to the local recruiter's office and announced our desire to enlist. We wanted to join the Eighty-Second Airborne, though I don't think either of us really knew what that meant. I'm sure we never noticed the irony of that choice. The Eighty-Second was a parachute division; I was afraid of heights.

The recruiter was delighted to see us and administered an aptitude test on that first visit. I'd long since given up attending high school and held a full-time job. Somehow, though, I managed to achieve a passing score on the written portion. Passing the physical exam proved more problematic.

Although I was tall for my age, I still was thin and terribly underweight. I'd been eating much better since the stomach pain was gone but my overall size hadn't caught up with my height. When the recruiter weighed me he glanced down at the scales and shook his head. "Boy, you're too skinny. For your height, you need to weigh at least one hundred thirty-two pounds."

I was crushed, and I think he was disappointed, too. Jim and I were eager young men of prime military age. He was as eager to have us as we were to join. Still, they had rules.

"Go home and try eating bananas," he said finally. "Maybe that'll fatten you up enough to get you into the army."

The suggestion sounded strange. I had never heard of eating bananas as a way of gaining weight but I was intent on enlisting and did as I was told. For weeks after that I ate bananas every day. As many as my stomach could tolerate. But though I stuffed myself with that and everything else I could hold, I failed to gain an ounce. Day after day I stepped onto the scale at the drug store, only to look down and see the needle stuck on one hundred eleven.

Determined to solve the weight problem, I resorted to other measures and made a trip uptown to Ryan's Sporting Goods. After looking through the store's shelves, I located five-pound weights that appeared useable and bought four of them. Later at home I devised a method of strapping the weights to my thighs using a couple of belts.

Later that week, I returned to the recruiter's office with the weights in place. I was worried they would slip down my legs and took small steps in an attempt to prevent that from happening. It felt awkward, and I'm sure it looked awkward, too, but I made it through the initial interview and when the recruiter told me to strip to my shorts, I stepped into the restroom and adjusted them just to be sure.

Wearing nothing but boxer shorts I walked back to the room and as I did, sure enough, the weights shifted on my legs. Only, the shift was toward the inside. Pain shot through my body and I was on the verge of tears—both from the physical pain and the angst of being discovered—but no one seemed to notice my predicament. So I continued across the room and stepped onto the scale.

"Boy," the recruiter said with a grin, "I can't believe that banana trick really worked! You are exactly one hundred thirty-two pounds."

I stepped off the scales as quickly as possible, afraid he might change his mind. Then he patted me on the back and said, "You're in, but you're too young."

"Too young? I'm sixteen."

"Yeah," he replied, "but you have to be seventeen years old to sign up on your own. Otherwise, you need your parents' permission. Come back on your seventeenth birthday and we'll send you off. You'll be in the army." That was one of the proudest days of my life. I was going to the army.

After I dressed, I asked about getting my parents' permission to join right then. The recruiter gave me a form, then said, "Tell me, do you have any idea where you'd like to be stationed?" Most of those in the recruiting office that day expressed a desire to be posted to Europe or Hawaii. Not me!

A map hung on the wall of the office and I studied it a moment, trying to determine the point farthest from Springfield. Pushpins marked the location of places where US troops were stationed. "There," I said, pointing to a spot in South Korea. "I want to be stationed right there."

Although the Korean War had officially ended in 1953, the United States still had troops stationed in South Korea along the demilitarized zone to deter the North Koreans from slipping across the border. As best I could tell, it was the farthest point on the map from Springfield and the farthest away from my father.

I pointed again toward the map. "There. That's where I want to go. South Korea."

"Good," he nodded. "We'll see what we can do about that."

The following Saturday, while Dad was watching television, I slipped up beside him and held out the papers. "Would you sign this paper so a recruiter can come by and talk to you about me going into the army?"

He gulped down one of his goofball pills and chased it with a swig of whiskey, then burst into laughter. "You? In the army?"

"Yes, sir," I answered, determined not to let him ruin my opportunity.

"You'll never make it," he roared. "They don't take morons!" Then he snatched the papers from my hand and signed them.

I had lied to him; my dad could hardly read. The document was not a consent form that allowed a recruiter to come for a visit. It was a form giving his permission for me to join the army. I felt guilty over having deceived him, but I was desperate to get out of the house, and after all he'd done to me and my siblings, I felt it was my due. A justification, yes, but I wasn't about to confess it to him. Not then.

A few days later, Jim and I returned the consent forms to the recruiter and enlisted in the army. We planned to go through boot camp together and hoped to be assigned to the same location afterward.

Our departure date was scheduled for later that summer, but after we were signed up and committed to join it seemed that time stood still. I thought the day for us to leave would never come.

When that day finally did arrive, Mom prepared lunch for me, just in case—two bologna sandwiches, a banana, and a candy bar stuffed into a brown paper sack. We were only going as far as Fort Dix, New Jersey, but she was a mother and I was her son, so she made a lunch for me. I thought of it as her way of blessing me. She knew that once I left I was never coming back.

Dad took a different approach. As I left the house, he followed me outside and stood on the porch shouting at the top of his voice, "You're garbage, you moron! You'll be in the stockade in six months." He said more—most of it too profane to repeat—but it was the opposite of a blessing. I'm sure he, too, knew I was never returning but rather than sending me off with a smile he continued to abuse me, right up to the moment I disappeared on my way up the sidewalk.

✦ ✦ ✦

Pete Seeger, a twentieth-century American musician, once said, "Education is what you get when you read the fine print. Experience is what you get when you don't." I'm not sure reading the fine print would have made much difference. I was determined to get away from my dad, and the army offered the best opportunity available to me.

My introduction to basic training—both as education and experience—began the moment Jim and I stepped off the bus and joined a group of raw recruits at Fort Dix. As we stepped onto the paved parking lot, looking bewildered and puzzled, a sergeant shouted, "Welcome, girls!"

A puzzled frown wrinkled my forehead. *What is he talking about? We'd come there to learn how to fight and he was calling us girls?* For all of my experiences to that point, I remained a naïve literalist. I would soon learn what he meant by that term.

After about ten weeks of boot camp, I had a growth spurt. Now being the tallest person in the group, one of the sergeants who was standing a few feet away noticed me immediately. I saw his eyes lock on to me and instinctively clutched my duffel bag under my arm, anticipating the unexpected. The sergeant walked over to me, got right in my face, and barked, "Do you think you're Superman?"

His breath was stale and I didn't care to have anyone stand that close to me, but instead of telling him how I really felt, I said, "No, sir," in the most confident voice I could muster.

"Don't call me sir," he snarled. "I'm a sergeant." He circled me as he talked and when he came back around, he looked me in the eye and said, "You *do* think you're Superman. I don't believe it. Superman, right here with us." He seemed to smile and I thought the moment would pass without further trouble, but just as quickly as he'd smiled, the smile vanished and he was right back in my face. "Get on one leg, soldier, and hop around with that duffel bag on your back, yelling, 'I'm Superman! I'm Superman!'"

Humiliated, I did as I was told. While the others were hustled off, I was left hopping around the parking lot. That didn't last too long and I caught up with them later, but my muscles ached that night as I dropped into bed. In the space of a few weeks I'd become certain that my home life had prepared me to endure anything.

Things didn't get any better the next morning, either. A sergeant entered our barracks well before sunrise. He must have had a head-splitting hangover and a bad attitude. All of which he attempted to cure by kicking our bunks and shouting in a loud voice, "On your feet, ladies. Let's go! Let's go! Let's go!"

When I didn't move quickly enough he kicked the end of my bunk and shouted even louder, "Get outta that bed, maggot!" For a moment I saw a reflection of my father yelling at us and calling us names. Overcoming that automatic response was a challenge but it helped when I noticed that he talked to everyone that way, not just me, and realized it was simply part of the drill instructor's training philosophy.

In spite of the treatment I'd endured at home, the six weeks of boot camp were difficult. For one thing, the harassment from our drill instructors never let up and members of our platoon soon picked up on it, dishing out harassment to each other. Having been the victim of that kind of treatment as a child, I did my best to avoid it, but many in our unit seemed to relish the practice of needling and belittling each other.

At seventeen years old, I still was growing, which became obvious from the way my uniform fit. Only halfway through training, my arms stuck out beyond the cuff of my shirt, and my legs protruded beyond the hem of my pants. I asked for new uniforms and pointed out the ill-fitting nature of the ones I'd been issued, but, much to my chagrin, the sergeants turned me down, forcing me to wear the same clothes I had been issued when I arrived on base. My fellow trainees soon noticed my appearance and saw it as a point of humor. Not long after that, someone gave me the nickname Donald Duck, which I bore the remainder of our time at Fort Dix. It was humorous, I supposed, in an army sort of way, but the way they treated me brought back memories from my classroom days at school in Springfield, which was emotionally painful. I tried not to show it—after only a few weeks I'd learned that in the army, displays of emotion were viewed as weakness—but it was painful all the same.

In addition to that, I found I had a poor sense of rhythm, which made marching in time with everyone else a very difficult task. Our sergeants stayed after me constantly when we drilled, walking beside me, barking in my ear in an attempt to force me to do it the correct way. More often than not, I failed to keep up. Soon everyone was frustrated with my performance and picked up where the instructor left off with needling and derisive comments.

Even Jim—my best friend—my only friend—mocked me for being out of step and I was terrified he would turn on me, too. But when I confronted him about it he grinned, "Lighten up, man. Don't take it personally."

"But it *is* personal," I insisted.

"I know, but don't take it that way," Jim advised. "If you stop taking it personal, they'll stop harassing you and move on to someone else. Have a sense of humor about it."

That was easy for Jim to say, and much easier for him to do than it was for me, but it sounded like good advice so I took it and tried to view each day from a humorous perspective. It was a challenge for me to do that. We didn't have much humor in our family and I didn't grow up viewing life from that perspective. I was too busy just trying to survive. But in boot camp I tried to follow his advice and, for the most part, it helped.

Although boot camp included plenty of verbal abuse, the physical abuse I had endured at my father's hand was replaced with ten-mile hikes—complete with loaded pack. Or drills spent crawling across an obstacle course with live bullets flying overhead. All of it during long days and short nights. But in my free time—what little there was of it—I was able to slip away for a few moments alone, without fear of incurring anyone's anger. That was a refreshing change for me.

Somewhere in all of that, I realized that the drill instructors were trying to break down our individuality—something I'd spent my life trying to preserve. They were also attempting to eliminate any resistance to taking orders. I'd come to deplore taking orders from my father and saw his attempts at breaking me as attempts to end my life. Getting over that took some effort and gradually I came to see that our instructors had but one goal—to mold us into a united, obedient, disciplined force, but I didn't like it and for the most part found boot camp to be more difficult than I'd imagined.

CHAPTER
12

When Jim and I enlisted, we thought we would serve together for our entire tour of duty. We completed basic training together, but that's when the buddy system we thought the army had agreed to came to an end. Jim was accepted into the Eighty-Second Airborne and sent to North Carolina for advanced training. We were angry and felt betrayed but there was little we could do about it. Again, the fine print caught up with us as we were informed the buddy system only worked when the needs of the army permitted. Otherwise, they could do with us as they pleased—which they did not hesitate to do.[9]

I was left in limbo while waiting for the papers I had been told would arrive in the mail. I went back to Fort Dix, climbed through a window, found an empty bunk and went to sleep.

The following day, the sergeant saw me and didn't know who I was. After some investigation, I discovered that my papers had been lost. The sergeant revealed that had I not returned, no one would have known. I had to hang around until a new set of papers had been created for me. I was then ordered to report to Fort Sam Houston in San Antonio, Texas, for training as a medical technician—a medic.

Although I was aggravated about being sent somewhere without Jim, the medical training at Fort Sam Houston proved interesting. I was trained for work in a hospital, rather than on the battlefield, and once I put my initial disappointment behind me, I realized that helping injured soldiers and civilians could be a rewarding experience.

While in San Antonio, I had more free time than in basic training. To fill that time productively, I began studying for the General Education Development test (GED). I had never finished high school but had learned a lot in the meantime. Obtaining a certification that showed I'd received the equivalent of a high school education seemed important.

When I completed medical training, I was posted to a base in South Korea, just as I'd requested from the recruiter back in Springfield when Jim and I enlisted for service. Jim was sent to Vietnam.

At the time, the war in Vietnam held the world's attention, but serving in Korea during the mid-1960s wasn't without risk. The first week there I was standing near the guard shack talking to one of the soldiers on duty. A Buddhist monk approached us, walking slowly up the road, but I didn't pay him much attention. We often saw them walking along the road near our base and this guy seemed legitimate to me. His head was shaved and he wore a saffron robe, just as all the others.

As the monk came nearer, my radio crackled and a moment later a guard on the lookout tower shouted at me, "Evans! Stand down."

"What for?" I asked, amused at the excitement in his voice.

"I'm taking out that fake Commie monk."

"Take him out? Are you crazy?" I protested, suddenly aware he really meant to do it. "The guy's just a Buddhist monk."

"No, he's not," the guard retorted. "He's a North Korean. Get out of the way."

"How do you know he's not a monk?"

"He's got a cigarette in his mouth. Buddhists don't smoke. Step back!" he barked.

That was more discussion than our boot camp drill instructors would have allowed and it seemed like the guard was overreacting. But just to be safe, I took a step back and got out of the way. As I did, the guard opened fire.

Instantly, the monk's body exploded, sending shrapnel in every direction. Thankfully none of us were wounded, but in the moments that followed we learned the monk had dynamite strapped around his waist. A subsequent investigation showed he was headed for the guard post where I'd been standing, intending to blow it up and take all of us with him. That was my introduction to the horrors of war—even though our location wasn't considered a threat on par with Vietnam and we were deployed there as part of a peacekeeping force.

For my regular daily duty, I was assigned to a mobile surgical hospital—a MASH unit similar to the one featured on the television show of the same name—where I worked on the third shift as a medical specialist. My primary assignment was in a surgery ward as part of the staff that cared for preoperative and postoperative patients. Most nights I was also in charge of the medical isolation wards.

Those were my standing assignments but occasionally I was sent to work in the emergency room. One night when I was on duty we heard an explosion in the town near our base. As injured civilians arrived at the hospital we learned that someone in town had found a land mine, took it to the shack where he lived, and attempted to dismantle it in order to sell the metal parts for scrap. As he pried on the mine to open it up, it exploded, killing him and injuring dozens of his neighbors.

One of the victims, a baby not more than ten or eleven months old, arrived at the emergency room riddled with shrapnel. By the time she reached us she was in serious condition. I tore her clothes away and cleared her air passage, then assisted the doctors as they worked with her in an attempt to keep her alive. We did all that could have been done for her, but in spite of our best efforts the child died.

That was a painful moment—seeing her there, so young and tiny. An hour earlier her life and all its possibilities lay before her just waiting to be lived, and in my mind I could see a smile on her face as she laughed and played earlier in the day. In an instant, all of that was snatched away. I was heartbroken.

On another night, a Korean in his mid-twenties brought his wife to us, transporting her in a wheelbarrow. She was limp in his arms as he lifted her out of the barrow and carried her inside. I and others on the staff knew from her appearance that she was already dead, but the man's cheeks were wet with tears and he begged us to save her. So we placed her on a gurney and did everything possible to revive her, all the while knowing our efforts were futile.

Finally, when we'd done all that could be done, one of the doctors pronounced her dead. I wasn't sure what would happen next—the husband had been quite emotional when he arrived—but instead of showing more anguish, he lifted her body to his shoulder in a matter-of-fact manner and carried her back to the wheelbarrow. We watched from the doorway as he pushed her up the road and disappeared into the night.

We later discovered that she had become a prostitute—something many Korean women did in order to survive the postwar economic chaos. It was a desperate attempt to keep her family intact—and perhaps an act of heroism as well—but it was counter to Korean culture and beliefs and brought with it a profound sense of shame. To cope with the emotional trauma, she'd turned to drugs. She arrived at the hospital that night after she had overdosed.

Not all in Korea was a matter of life or death. One summer the temperature was particularly hot and the weather was dry. Water on the base came from a deep well and we had a huge tank that held thousands of gallons in reserve. Despite all of that, we constantly ran out of water, usually at the time everyone was taking a shower. This continued for several weeks and grew from a mere nuisance to an actual threat to our mission. As the situation became serious, the base commander assigned engineers and experts to investigate the matter and resolve the problem. They worked for several days trying to uncover the source of the trouble but seemed unable to resolve the issue.

The base was located atop a mountain the Koreans called Wong Tong Nee. In my free time I often went out to a quiet spot where I could pray, study, and mediate on Scripture. For fourteen months I spent my time in South Korea fulfilling my obligation to the US Army and learning to pray on what is now called "Prayer Mountain." Years later I discovered that after I returned home, Dr. Paul Cho purchased the mountain and made it a place of prayer. He said to me, "You are the first Christian to pray atop the mountain." He called me "Holy Ghost Kimchi Man, Seed of Abraham." I know now that God wanted me to learn to pray, learn to listen to Him, and learn how to seek His will and plan for my life. I knew a plan had been established for me;

I just needed to know how to allow God to unlock His purpose in my life.

One day, in the midst of our water crisis, I sat on a rock and gazed out over the landscape. It was a beautiful view and I could see for miles. That day, I noticed that all the rice fields had turned brown because of the hot summer and lack of rainfall—all of the fields except for one. It was lush, green, and well watered.

As I looked at it, a smile spread across my face. I was certain I'd found the source of our water problem.

When I returned to the hospital I reported my observation—and my suspicions—to my commanding officer. He passed the information up the chain of command. A few days later, we learned that the owner of the lush, green, well-watered rice field had tunneled under the compound fence and was drawing water for his field from our water tank.

CHAPTER
13

When I first arrived in South Korea, army life required most of my daily energy. Just getting through my shift seemed like a big task. But as the weeks passed and I became more comfortable with the rhythm of the day, I settled into a routine and—as I had during boot camp and advanced training—found I had plenty of free time to do as I pleased.

Most mornings I spent time alone on the mountain near our base walking, thinking, studying, and praying. Those mornings began more as a few minutes away from everyone else to decompress after a busy shift than anything else. Gradually, however, the time became much more than time by myself and grew into an extensive period of devotions. Not really an intense personal encounter with God, as I'd had with Him when I was a boy, but a time of study and contemplation nonetheless. In retrospect, I think it was a time when God went deeper into my life than I realized.

Early one morning, after spending a few minutes reading the Scriptures, I wandered around the mountain alone, praying and thinking about what I'd just read. As I made my way among the rocks and the sparse vegetation, I remembered again the night Jesus visited me at home in my bedroom back in Springfield. Remembering that moment made me aware of how much I longed to live every day from the vitality and power of His presence. I'd never stopped living for Him—in middle school and those first few years of high school, through boot camp and advanced training, I remained committed to God—but not every day was like that night in my bedroom. That morning on the mountain I realized how much I wanted my daily life to always be that way. To know His presence with me—really with me—like that night when I'd seen His hands stretched out before me and felt the touch of His palm on the top of my head.

As I walked along the mountain that morning I whispered, "Will you ever talk to me again? I need to hear your voice."

In an instant, the presence of God came over me and joy filled my soul—the same joy I'd experienced that night in the bedroom. The moment was overwhelming but demanded a response so, like Samuel, the Old Testament prophet, I whispered, "Speak, Lord, for Your servant is listening."[10]

With my spirit fully attuned to the moment, I sensed in my mind that I should read from the book of Daniel. So I opened the Bible I carried with me, took a seat on the ground, and read:

Yet I heard the sound of his words; and while I heard the sound of his words I was in a deep sleep on my face, with my face to the ground. Suddenly, a hand touched me, which made me tremble on my knees and on the palms of my hands. And he said to me, "O Daniel, man greatly beloved, understand the words that I speak to you, and stand upright, for I have now been sent to you."[11]

The words from that passage were spoken to Daniel by an angel who'd been sent to answer his prayers. Daniel prayed; God heard and sent an angel in response. But the angel had been delayed in arriving with the answer because of an attack that had come against him.

As I read those sentences from the Bible, it was as if the angel was speaking to *me*, telling me that God had heard my prayer and had sent a response. But what was that response? I was hoping to hear something specific—go here, say this, do that—so I remained at that spot awhile longer, listening and waiting to hear from the Lord.

After a while, when nothing further came to me, I decided it was time to return to base. Before leaving, I gathered twelve stones and stacked them up to form an altar. For me it was a monument of remembrance to the presence of God and a symbol that the place was devoted to the pursuit of the answers I needed from Him.

In the days that followed, I returned again and again to that spot to pray and seek God—during the monsoon season when the rains came, in the blistering heat of summer, or the bitter cold of winter. Not always at the same time each day but as nearly as I could manage, every day I returned to kneel beside those rocks and pray. And then it happened.

One morning, as I sat praying by my makeshift altar, studying the Scriptures, God spoke to me in a powerful way and I heard Him repeat the words He'd said to me that night in my bedroom. "Son, I love you. And I have a plan for your life."

Those were the words I needed to be reminded of. Not to remember them in my own mind—I could do that on my own—but to be reminded of them by Him, in His voice. His Spirit speaking to my spirit, bearing witness that I not only was His son but that He had a plan for me—things for me to do, a mission to accomplish.[12]

✦ ✦ ✦

In 1966, my tour of duty in South Korea came to an end and I was reassigned to the United States. I was glad to be returning home but sad to leave the mountain that had become a comfortable place for me and a place where I'd found God in a powerful way. Before leaving, I purchased a complete wardrobe of custom-made business suits, along with a cashmere overcoat and bespoke, or custom-made, shoes. Korean tailors did exquisite work at inexpensive prices and I knew I'd need suits after my service in the army was completed. God had things for me to do and though I didn't know what that might be, good business suits seemed important. So I took advantage of the moment and bought several.

When I arrived back in the United States, I was assigned to work at a recruitment office on Broad Street in downtown Philadelphia. At the time I enlisted, I owned a 1957 Chevrolet. While I was away, my sister asked if she could have it. I assumed she would keep it until I returned and then I could get it back. Instead, she sold it and bought something else. As a result, I arrived in Philadelphia without a car.

A friend from the army had a car for sale, so after I arrived from Korea one of my first stops was to view the car. It was well worn but still serviceable. I purchased it from him and loaded it with my clothes, along with everything else I owned.[13]

The assignment at the recruiting office offered even more freedom than the duty in Korea, but it also meant I needed to find my own place to stay. I intended to rent a room at the YMCA while I located an apartment and, with my belongings packed in the car, made my way in that direction.

A parking garage was located across the street from the YMCA so I parked the car there and paid the attendant ten dollars extra to watch it. For the sake of security—so I thought—I locked my wallet in the glove compartment.

The receptionist at the YMCA checked their records and told me a room was available. I asked him to hold it for me and ran back to the car to retrieve my wallet. When I arrived at the garage, the parking attendant was gone. A check of my parking space showed that my car was gone, too, along with everything and every dime I owned—except for twenty-six cents in change that I had in my pocket.

Alone and penniless, my only option was to stay at the Salvation Army. I was angry with myself for leaving my wallet in the car and for being duped by the parking attendant. And mad at the attendant for taking everything I owned. And I felt sorry for myself for having to spend a few nights with *those* people. Then I realized—I was homeless, too.

Sleeping at the Salvation Army building was an eye-opening experience. Every night, I was surrounded by rows and rows of drug addicts and alcoholics who came in for a warm bed and a safe place to sleep. Our cots were in close proximity to each other, so I struck up a conversation with those around me. As I talked with them, I learned that many were former soldiers who, like my father and other servicemen I'd known who served during World War II, suffered from Post-traumatic Stress Disorder. Unlike my father, though, these men could no longer fit at all into the society they'd given their sanity to defend.

After a few nights at the Salvation Army, I received my army pay and was able to rent a room at the YMCA. I had arrived back in the States with a car and a carload of possessions, but when I moved to the YMCA I had only my uniforms, a Bible, and a few books.

✦ ✦ ✦

Although my best friend, Jim, had been sent to Vietnam, he and I had written each other regularly. Because we'd enlisted together, he was due to return to the United States not long after I arrived. We made plans to meet at his parents' home in Springfield and go on a vacation together.

As I drove my car up there to meet him, I switched on a Springfield radio station to catch up with the local news. That's when I learned that Jim had been killed in Vietnam—shot in the head by a sniper just days before his tour of duty was scheduled to end. I was devastated. Rather than continuing on to Springfield, I turned around and went back to Philadelphia.

A few weeks later, when Jim's body arrived, I telephoned his family and learned of the funeral arrangements. The loss of their son was still quite raw and they asked me to come up before the service so we could talk. I agreed to the visit, but going up there meant staying with my parents—and that made me more than a little apprehensive.

When I arrived at the house on Pasco Road my father was home. As I entered the front room he greeted me with a gruff, "Boy, I should kick your %ss."

"No, sir," I replied. "Those days are over."

While in Korea I had enrolled in martial arts classes and advanced to a second-degree black belt in Tae Kwon Do. I also held a brown belt in Judo. I was determined that no one was ever going to take advantage of me the way he did.

As we stood there, just inside the door, he insisted that he could take me. He wore a cap atop his head, so I said, "I'll tell you what, Dad. I'm going to knock that cap off your head, and I'm going to tell you when I'm going to do it. And you can't stop me."

"Okay," he glowered. "Give it a try if you can."

I squared up to him, looked him in the eye, and said, "Now!"

Before he could react, I swiped the cap from his head with a kick of my foot. He snatched the cap from the floor and growled, "Do it again." I did a second and third time. Frustrated, he said, "Well, I can still beat you in arm wrestling." We sat at the kitchen table, locked hands, and I promptly took him down. When he lost, he jumped up from the table and went off to the basement to pout. It was the last time he ever challenged me physically.

A few days later, I was honored to serve as a pallbearer at Jim's funeral. As we lowered his body into the ground, I realized I was almost to my twentieth birthday—the year I was convinced as a young boy would be my last. Now surviving was no longer a question, but that twentieth year was the year I had promised God that I would completely surrender to His call upon my life and tell people what He'd done for me. I also realized I had not shared what had happened to me with Jim, nor had I told him the message of salvation.

Jim was turned off by religion, partly because of his experience with my father. He'd come by our house one day for a visit and as he entered through the front doorway, Dad said, "Here comes that son of a Comanche." Jim's parents were Native American. Dad's comment hurt Jim's feelings and he ran from the house in tears.

Knowing how Dad lived—booze and carousing on Fridays, beating us on Saturdays, and attending church services on Sunday—the hypocrisy of it was not lost on Jim. He understood the glaring contradiction between the way Dad talked about God and the way he lived. That, more than anything else, turned him against the gospel.

But as we buried him that day, I regretted not telling him the gospel from my perspective. He might not have accepted it, but he would have listened to me telling him about what had happened and how I'd been transformed. He would have listened to me, and the realization that I hadn't even attempted to tell him made his demise all the more painful.

✦ ✦ ✦

That year, the recruitment office was closed Thanksgiving weekend. I combined the holiday break with a few extra days off and spent the week alone in my sparsely furnished room. Shut off from the world, I used the time to pray and search the Scriptures, much as I had done while on the mountain in Korea. For added discipline, I committed myself to fasting and subsisted those seven days on nothing but water. All of my time was devoted to praying and studying. I needed to know what to do next—after my enlistment ended—and I needed to hear that direction from God, not from my own mind. I determined to fast, pray, and read through the New Testament until I had heard from God.

After two or three days, when nothing seemed to happen, I pointed to a battered chair in the corner and said aloud, "Jesus, this is Your chair. If You want to come and talk with me like You did when I was eleven, I am ready to listen and obey. I want to hear Your voice again."

When there was only silence in response, I picked up the Bible and turned to the Psalms. I intended to read the entire book but in the first one found a place in my spirit so I read it over and over, letting the words sink deep into my mind and my soul.

> Blessed is the one
>
> who does not walk in step with the wicked
>
> or stand in the way that sinners take
>
> or sit in the company of mockers,
>
> but whose delight is in the law of the LORD,
>
> and who meditates on his law day and night.
>
> That person is like a tree planted by streams of water,
>
> which yields its fruit in season
>
> and whose leaf does not wither—
>
> whatever they do prospers.[14]

As I read those verses, the Lord promised me that I would be a blessed man if I meditated on His Word, did not walk in the counsel of the ungodly, did not stand in the way of sinners, or sit in the seat of the scornful. He promised I would be like a tree planted by the rivers of water, bringing forth my fruit in good season. My leaves would not wither and whatever I did would prosper. I committed the entire chapter to memory.

My spirit was encouraged but I still had time to spend alone with God and I did not feel released to do anything else. So I picked up a copy of *The Cross and the Switchblade*, a book by David Wilkerson that told about how he ministered to drug addicts on the streets of New York. Moved by what I read, I came to the conclusion that perhaps God was leading me to do something similar in Philadelphia.

Beginning the following week, I worked full time recruiting young men to serve in the army, then spent the afternoons and evenings wandering the streets of the city, passing out gospel tracts and sharing the gospel with the people I met along the way. While I worked with people on the street, I continued to seek God's broader will for my life.

One afternoon as I worked the street, I came across a group from the Philadelphia Teen Challenge. They were doing the same thing— handing out tracts and talking about Jesus to anyone who would stop and listen. The significance of the moment was not lost on me. David Wilkerson, whose book I had read during that week alone, had founded Teen Challenge as a permanent organization through which to continue and expand the ministry he'd begun with drug addicts and alcoholics in New York.

Over the next several weeks, I continued to meet the Teen Challenge group on the street and eventually they invited me to visit their facility. After working together, the director, Bob Bartlett, invited me to come on staff. I accepted and moved into the Teen Challenge center, where I worked when I wasn't on duty at the army recruitment office.

As might be expected from the work I was already doing, my sense of the broader purpose for my life slowly moved toward a desire to minister in a more formal way—beyond working on the street and beyond the scope of the ministry at Teen Challenge. But the realization that my desire was, in fact, what God wanted for me, too, did not come on a mountaintop, or at a church worship service, or even in my room at Teen Challenge. It came, instead, at a small, run-down restaurant.

Christmas Day, I attended a worship service at a church not far from where I was living. While there, a man asked me if I could give him twenty dollars. Having been recently homeless, I understood his need and gave him the money. Doing that left me with only three dollars and fifty cents.

We'd had a blinding snowstorm earlier that morning and after the service I trudged through the snow toward my room at the Y. People who'd been at the Christmas service passed me by and as they did, the occupants waved and shouted, "Merry Christmas!" I would have much preferred a ride but I took their greeting as a blessing and waved in return.

A little before noon I arrived at a diner and went inside to eat. Having only three dollars in my pocket, I couldn't afford lunch so I ordered breakfast instead—bacon, eggs, and coffee. While I waited for my food, I leafed through the pages of my Bible and my eyes fell on a verse in 1 Corinthians. "'What no eye has seen, what no ear has heard, and what no human mind has conceived'—the things God has prepared for those who love him—these are the things God has revealed to us by his Spirit."[15]

That was encouraging but my time in the army was almost complete. I didn't want to reenlist for a second tour. I needed to know specifically, in a practical way, what to do.

As I thought about what I'd read I sensed the Lord stirring my spirit, encouraging me to ask Him one more time what direction my life should take. So I asked, "Lord, where should I go from here?"

While seated in a booth in the corner with my Bible open before me, I felt the presence of God envelop me. As I sat there, not saying a word, only enjoying His persistence, I began to think again about ministering full time. That wasn't the first time I'd thought of that topic but right then, with the Lord's presence close, I sensed the Holy Spirit bearing witness with my spirit that this was the direction I should go with my life.

At first I was excited about the idea. I'd seen Billy Graham on television—more than just that one time when my mother shouted at me for watching him. I knew the kind of crowds that gathered to hear him preach and the response his preaching produced.

But as the notion took hold in my spirit, doubts sprang up. Incidents from my past invaded my thoughts and played over and over in my mind. My father calling me moron. The kids in class laughing at me as I stuttered through a response to the teacher. My own fear at being forced to stand before an audience and speak.

After struggling for a while, I finally bowed my head and prayed. "Lord, I don't know what I'm supposed to do, but I know You are calling me. I might be the garbage others say I am, but if you can use garbage, my life is yours."

By then, my food was ready and as I ate my thoughts turned to more practical issues—the best way to go about accomplishing that goal.

In order to serve God effectively, I needed two things—training and credentials as a minister. I knew that if God called me He could, and would, empower me to accomplish His will. But in order to find my place in the existing church structure, I knew I needed to be ordained. And all of it began with training, which meant returning to school. Not just any school but a school that would prepare me to serve and work as a minister of the gospel—a preacher.

I'd already talked to Bob Bartlett about ministry and ordination. He told me, "In my opinion, there are two good schools in our denomination—Northwestern in Minnesota, and Southwestern in Texas."

Through the window next to my table in the diner I could see outside to the sidewalks covered in snow. Plows had cleared the street and the snow was piled on either side. It was bitterly cold, too, but in that moment I thought of Texas. As I did, images from my time at Fort Sam Houston played through my mind. No doubt, the weather down there was quite different from what we experienced in the Northeast. My heart quickened at the thought of returning to Texas and a smile spread across face.

Is it that easy? I wondered as I stared out the window. *Is that what You're saying to me? Do you want me to go to Texas?* The idea of doing that seemed right to my spirit and I asked the Lord, "Is that what you want me to do? Go to Texas and attend Bible school?" Right there, as I was seated in that booth, eating breakfast for my Christmas lunch, I sensed Him saying, "Go."

A few weeks after Christmas, I located the address for Southwestern Assemblies of God College in Waxahachie, Texas, and wrote for a course catalog and application. When it arrived in the mail, I flipped through the catalog pages and knew immediately that school was the place for me. I applied and was accepted for the fall term.

When I arrived on the campus, my first question was, "Where do I get my robe?" My second was, "Do you persecute Jews here?" I thought most ministers wore robes, and that at seminary we would all be given robes.

CHAPTER
14

Today Waxahachie, Texas, is a town of some thirty thousand people, lying just beyond the southern edge of Dallas' suburban sprawl. When I first arrived there in the 1960s it was a small village, and Dallas, not yet the city it is today, seemed a long way away. It was quite the change from Philadelphia, Springfield, and the crowded areas of the Northeast to which I had been accustomed as a child and young adult. Nevertheless, it was the place to which God had directed me and I intended to learn all that He had to teach me in that place, rural or not.

Although I had not completed high school, I did have the GED and was certain Bible school was what God intended me to pursue. I was older than most of the students on campus, but having dropped out of high school and enrolled in the army at seventeen, the difference between our ages was not that great. What I lacked was the experience with American popular culture and the academic background that many of my fellow students enjoyed. Although our family was not devoid of exposure to the aspects of American life—popular music, motion pictures, television shows, and the latest news—we were not participants in the cultural atmosphere of Springfield, or anywhere else for that matter. However, as a school wholly owned by the Assemblies of God denomination, most of the students came from a background that was, in effect, far more conservative than my own. The church preached a message of separation from life in the world, not involvement in it. While I might not have held my own in a more liberal environment, my exposure to the world—through my experiences in Springfield, with my extended family in New York, and in the army—made me one of the more cosmopolitan students at the school. What I lacked was the emotional stability that one receives from living in a stable, supportive family. That area of my life was more tender than I realized.

God had healed me of a near-debilitating speech impediment and physical ailments, but daily I wrestled with the pain of rejection. It gnawed at my sense of self-esteem and colored every relationship with the deep grays of despondency. There were times I thought I had those feelings under subjection, only to be rocked anew when they resurfaced.

Not long after I arrived on campus I became acquainted with a young woman named Linda. After talking with her on several occasions I asked her out on a date. Back then a date consisted of going to church and out to eat with friends afterward. It wasn't that big of a deal, but with the emotional scars I still carried from my childhood, the most difficult part wasn't the date itself but finding the courage to ask her. Still, Southwestern was a Christian college and I assumed she would at least respond in a kind and gracious manner.

Much to my surprise, instead of a gracious response she struck an arrogant pose with her hands on her hips and replied, "I'll never date you. I intend to marry someone who will make something of themselves."

I wasn't asking her for a commitment, just to join me for church and dinner, but I understood why she wasn't interested. I didn't come from a background of money or privilege. The money I did have came from working as a maintenance man on campus—for a mere thirty-two cents per hour. And I didn't have nice clothes to wear—they'd been stolen when my car went missing in Philadelphia. My father wasn't a pastor, either, and I wasn't conversant with the popular vocabulary of the day. In short, I wasn't "cool."

But her unabashed rejection of me—along with the scathing assessment of my potential future—reopened my emotional wounds in a way that I hadn't expected to encounter at a Christian college. Recovering from that encounter took a while. Not because I was particularly attached to her, but because I had not expected to be skewered in the process.

Over the next several months, I backed away from the notion of *dating* and allowed my association with women on campus to evolve more naturally—apart from any hint of romance. As a consequence, I developed a number of casual friendships. One of those friendships was with Carolyn Wedel, a fellow student in my class. We studied together and she sought my advice when dating others.

Sometime during those first few months in school, a group of us signed up to conduct worship services for a congregation out in the country, a few miles outside Waxahachie. Carolyn was part of that group. It was raining when we arrived and I held an umbrella as we made our way to the door of the church.

As the year progressed, Carolyn and I spent more and more time together, even while she dated other men. Sometimes we studied together in the library. Other times we rode up to South Dallas for worship at Oak Cliff Assembly of God Church. With Carolyn in the car, the drive up to Dallas didn't seem all that far at all. In fact, it was much too short and time passed far too quickly.

After the Sunday night service, we sometimes rode over to Kip's, a restaurant not far from the church, where we had dinner or dessert. Often we went with a group, but even when it was just the two of us there was nothing consciously romantic about those times we were together. I didn't attempt to kiss her or insist that she sit beside me in the car. I just concentrated on being the best gentleman I could be and enjoyed her company. She felt the same way. We liked spending time together—which I suppose was the most romantic time a couple could have.

Carolyn continued to have other men as her boyfriends, but when those relationships broke up, I was the one who comforted her. When other boys wanted to date her, she would come to me and ask my advice. Guys who were interested in her came to me for advice, too.

One guy named Doug was particularly interested in her and asked me everything—the kind of flowers she liked, the food she preferred, and a dozen other things. I knew all of those things about her because I'd paid attention and listened when she talked. But one day, after they'd been going out for a while, Doug even asked me if I thought he should kiss her. That was the one question I couldn't answer. Deep inside I didn't want to answer it, either. Did he really have to ask someone about that? And if he did, maybe that said more about where things were with them than he realized.

"They're her lips," I said finally. "You'll have to ask her."

Carolyn and I never really had a "first date." We were together as friends many times; we just never thought of it as "dating." I don't think I wanted to think of it that way, either. Over the course of that first year, she had become the most important person in my life. I was afraid that if I tried to take things in an overtly romantic direction, she might not be interested and that would make it all but impossible for us to continue being friends. If it was friendship or nothing with her, I wanted all the friendship I could get. But inside, in the secret places that no one reveals to anyone, I was in love with her and had been since almost the first time I saw her smile.

One Sunday, she and I rode up to her home church in Fort Worth and joined her parents—Neil and Peggy—for the morning worship service. Afterward, we went over to their house for lunch. As we entered through the back door I heard music playing in the background. The aroma of a roast cooking in the oven filled the air. It was the most peaceful home I'd ever entered.

I thought, *This is what I'm looking for. This right here. This kind of family. This kind of home. I want to be like this.*

That summer, Carolyn traveled to Jamaica on a mission trip. While she was gone, I realized that I not only loved her but wanted to marry her. That was a big step for me and although I was sure she felt something similar for me, I remained guarded in showing my affections. I wrote her throughout the summer, but they were newsy missives. More like a report of what I'd done and what was happening than the longing of a lover for his beloved. Meanwhile, her roommate on the trip received romantic letters from her boyfriend. My letters were anything but that. Carolyn was not impressed and I think she began to wonder just what sort of a fellow I really was.

When she returned from Jamaica, I asked her to marry me. She wasn't very enthusiastic at first and, in fact, told me she would have to pray about it. In retrospect, I think she might have given me that response even if she'd been wildly enthusiastic. By then she knew enough about me to know that I had endured a lot of pain in my life and I'm sure she wondered how much unresolved emotional baggage I still carried with me. I didn't blame her. I wondered the same thing, too. But I had no intention of turning out like my father. And I had no intention of letting Carolyn slip away, either.

So I gave her room and allowed her time to make up her own mind. We continued to see each other, just as before, and I did my best to do everything possible to show her how much I cared for her, but I avoided the question of marriage for a while and didn't press the matter.

Eventually Carolyn accepted my proposal and we set the wedding date for November 25, 1969—the Saturday of Thanksgiving weekend. Neither of my parents attended the ceremony but my sisters, Bonnie and Sheila, did and I was glad to have them share that moment with us. Aunt Ginger didn't attend, either, but sent us a gift of two hundred dollars, which was all the money we had at that time. It seemed like a small fortune to us and we used it to set up our apartment after the wedding.

At age eleven, I had made a vow: "God, if you will take care of me and keep me alive until I turn twenty, I'll keep myself pure from sexual sin and I'll never take your name in vain." I thought His love was conditional and that I had to do something to earn His favor. It was bad theologically, but good in a practical way.

That vow had little to do with reserving myself for a future wife—I was interested in pleasing God, how a woman I might meet in the future felt about it was of little concern to me at the time—but the effect was just the same. As a young girl, Carolyn often prayed for God to give her a husband who had kept himself sexually pure. I am so thankful I was the answer to her prayers.

CHAPTER
15

When Carolyn and I married, the front of the church was draped with a huge banner that must have been thirty feet wide and at least four feet high. It read, "Not by might, nor by power, but by my Spirit says the Lord of hosts." Those words proved to be a prophetic summary of our future as husband and wife.

Carolyn was my best friend for life and I loved her more than life itself. She was the first person who ever believed in me and I trusted her with my heart—except for one little corner. Perhaps the most important corner of all—the abuse I'd suffered as a child and the unresolved fear of rejection that came from it. That part of me was sealed away—from her and everyone else. I had never shared any of it with her, never allowed her to see the wounded child or the driven little boy longing for love and acceptance.

Although my parents did not attend our wedding, I thought it was important for Carolyn to meet them and for them to meet her. With that in mind, we planned a trip to Niagara Falls and on the way stopped at my parents' house in Springfield. I'm sure I was hoping that somehow they would finally respond in a normal way to events in my life. Or maybe I hoped they would be impressed enough by *her* to change their opinion of me. More likely, I was backing into an opportunity to explain them to her, which meant telling her about my past—a way of forcing myself to address the most difficult and painful aspect of my inner life and personality.

With that in mind, we set out for Niagara Falls and stopped in Springfield. The visit didn't last very long—we didn't stay overnight and didn't even stay for a meal. Once again, Mom was Mom. And Dad was...Dad. Just as he'd always been. Carolyn tried very hard to be polite, but I could tell she was horrified by how out of control he was.

Later, as we continued on toward our destination, she told me, "You can ask me to do anything and I'll agree. Except for one thing."

"What's that?" I asked.

"I will not move anywhere near your family. That man terrifies me." *That man* was a reference to my father and I knew all too well what she meant.

"Okay," I replied. "We won't move anywhere near them."

"I'm glad I had not met them before we married," she continued. "If I had, I'm not sure I would have married you."

Carolyn had been raised in a loving Christian home. By example and by overt instruction, she'd been taught that she should marry a man who shared her faith. Someone who came from a godly household and understood life from the gospel's perspective. Obviously, my family was nothing like that.

✦ ✦ ✦

About a month after we were married, Carolyn and I received a call from Dwayne Duck, a pastor in North Little Rock, Arkansas. Dwayne had been a student with us at Southwestern and had gone on to a career as a local pastor in the Assemblies of God church. He told us about a man in Arkansas, Troy Collier, who was trying to start a Teen Challenge Center. Troy was looking for a couple to oversee the work and asked Dwayne if he knew anyone who might be capable of directing that work. Dwayne thought of us and wanted to know if we were interested in taking the position.

Having worked previously with Teen Challenge, I understood how the program operated and was intrigued by the possibility of building a center from the ground up—facility, personnel, and program. Carolyn was familiar with the ministry from her experience growing up in an Assemblies congregation—Teen Challenge is sanctioned and administered by that denomination—but she had never been exposed to the day-to-day operation. Still, she was interested in the possibilities it afforded and excited about the prospect of us entering into ministry together.

The call from Dwayne came near the end of the first semester of our second year. Taking the position meant leaving school before we'd completed coursework on our degrees. That was an issue for me because I'd come to Southwestern in response to specific leading from the Holy Spirit. But, I reasoned, perhaps I wasn't called to finish school, merely to be there long enough for this position to come my way. Or perhaps the position at Teen Challenge was a temporary thing. I could always return later and complete my degree.

In order to sort through those competing interests—finishing school versus immediate full-time ministry—Carolyn and I committed ourselves to pray and seek the Lord about what we should do. Over the next few weeks we sensed the Holy Spirit leading us to accept the Teen Challenge position, leave school, and move to Arkansas. So, at the end of the semester we packed our belongings into the car—Carolyn's Rambler, which she'd had since high school—and drove to North Little Rock.

When we arrived in Arkansas we found the ministry—an exclusively men's program—laden with debts and facing a backlog of potential clients. Prior to our involvement, Troy and the board of directors reached an agreement with the local court to defer drug defendants to the program. When arrested, those who were willing to plead guilty were offered the option of serving their time in our Teen Challenge program—as opposed to serving time in Tucker or Cummings Prisons. Needless to say, many of them chose Teen Challenge.

The ministry owned a mansion in North Little Rock that was located a few houses down from the governor's mansion. It was a prestigious location but the house had not been maintained very well. Shortly after we arrived, we put the guys in the program to work cleaning and painting it.

As a residential program, the guys lived at our facility. Carolyn and I lived there, too, which meant we were with them twenty-four hours a day. We were newlyweds with no money and only one bedroom to ourselves. But we were happy, content, and certain we were right where we belonged.[16]

Over the course of the next twelve months, we saw many young people led to faith in Christ and redeemed from a life of addictive behavior. We kept them busy sixteen hours each day with class, exercise, and work. Anything to keep their minds off their former lifestyle and give God an opportunity to transform them. As a result, we saw lives radically transformed.

But as the end of the year approached, we learned that Carolyn was pregnant. By then, the Teen Challenge center was established and operating with a staff that was capable of administering its programs, a board capable of sustaining the ministry, and a facility adequate to the task. Long-term debt, though still an issue for the ministry, had been substantially reduced. At the same time, Troy and I reached a difference of opinion about how the ministry should operate going forward.

In praying about all of that—the pending birth of our child, the work in Arkansas, and the direction our lives should take—Carolyn and I found a renewed interest in returning to Southwestern to complete our degrees. We both lacked about a year's worth of coursework to complete the requirements for graduation. Finishing the degree was important to me for many reasons, not the least of which was the leading I'd received in coming to school at Southwestern in the first place. Moving back to complete our degrees also had an added benefit—our first child would be born in Texas, a place dear to Carolyn and rapidly becoming home for me, too.

So we moved to Fort Worth, lived with Carolyn's parents, and commuted to class at Southwestern in Waxahachie. Not long after that, Michelle was born. We spent the next year completing our degrees at Southwestern and learning the art of parenthood.

✦ ✦ ✦

During the course of that second year at Southwestern, we had received an invitation to participate in a denominational ministry located in Chicago. After graduation, we packed our belongings into the same old car, tucked Michelle onto the seat between us, and headed north to Chicago.

The work in Chicago was a rewarding experience. I spent long hours talking to people on the street—something I enjoyed very much—and opened a coffee house as a gathering place for young people from the community. I also enrolled in Greek and Hebrew courses at Moody Bible Institute. As part of the institute's admissions procedure I was required to have a physical. The doctor who did the examination performed several routine tests, one of which included an X-ray image of my chest. The image showed my lungs and indicated I had tuberculosis. I had the examination on Friday and the doctor told me to return on Monday, explaining, "We're going to do a number of tests on you and take a lot more X-rays."

Active tuberculosis would not only imperil my life but the health of Carolyn and our daughter. Not only that, it would derail pretty much everything I wanted to do with my life. But somehow it just didn't feel right. I'd been saved at the age of eleven, visited by God with power and glory in my bedroom, commissioned by Him for full-time ministry—surely this was not the end of all that.

The doctor's report rocked me rather hard but instead of sulking all weekend I spent the time in prayer, asking God what I should do, asking Him to help me, crying out to Him for healing and for peace.

Over the course of those two days, the Holy Spirit spoke to me in my spirit and reminded me of how helpless I'd felt in wanting to defend my mother—who was Jewish—from my father—who was a Protestant Christian. And He reminded me of the courage I found after my transforming encounter with Him in my bedroom that night. Remembering all of that brought back the sense of shame I'd felt as a child over my inability to make my father stop beating my mother. Then the Lord said, "I am going to redeem all of that. You couldn't defend your mother, but you will become a defender of my people. Israel and her people will become the mother you wanted to defend as a child. You will defend them now."

His voice was as clear in my spirit as if He had spoken to me aloud and I knew He was calling me to something fresh and new. A task that not only resonated in my spirit but energized my heart and my mind. "Okay, Lord," I said. "I will do whatever you tell me to do. But there's one problem. The doctor says I have tuberculosis. How can I do all the things you're showing me and do it as an active tuberculosis patient?"

Monday morning, I returned to the doctor's office and spent most of the day undergoing tests and many more X-rays than the single one the previous Friday. When all of that was finished the doctor came into the examination room to talk to me. "I don't understand it," he began.

"You don't understand what?" I asked

"The X-ray we took on Friday showed you had TB. I saw it with my own eyes. When I look at the image now, I can see it. It's there as plain as anything could be. But in the X-rays we took today, your lungs are clear. There is no sign of any problem at all." He shook his head. "I don't understand how this could happen. I've never seen anything like it."

"Well, I understand it."

"You do?"

"Yes. God has things for me to do with my life and having tuberculosis isn't part of it."

The doctor wrote a report that cleared me of any physical issues and I was accepted as a student at Bible school. Over the next several months I completed the language courses, but my refusal to accept some of their doctrinal positions placed me at odds with them and their requirements for graduation. In the end, I did not complete the coursework necessary to receive a degree.

At the same time, my diligence and exuberance for ministry placed me at cross-purposes with the ministry's leadership, which preferred a more staid, traditional approach. It's difficult for some to understand how this could happen—people were coming to faith in the Lord, lives were being transformed, God was honoring His call upon my life. But we are all as human as the next person and sometimes expectations get in the way. I expected to do the kinds of things I was doing and do them as long as I had the strength, even if it meant working every day until midnight. The ministry's leadership expected me to do as they said and limit my hours to a traditional eight-hour workday. As you might expect, tensions rose between us and rather than enduring that, Carolyn and I decided to leave and return to Texas.

✦ ✦ ✦

The decision to leave Chicago was much bigger than simply that of relocating. We were certain we were called to the ministry and, following that weekend of prayer and consideration, equally certain that our work would somehow involve the people of Israel. I was not opposed to pastoral ministry, if that's the way our calling opened up for us, but I didn't think that was where we were headed and neither did Carolyn. In human terms, we were striking out on our own. In spiritual terms we were off on an adventure.

In Chicago we lived in a small apartment and didn't own much except a bed, a table and chairs, and a television set. Michelle's belongings and the things necessary to care for her comprised the majority of what we owned. We had no money and once we left the Assemblies ministry where we'd been working, we would have no regular income. To fund this new work, we decided to sell our furniture. I placed an advertisement in the newspaper and the first person to respond purchased it all, leaving us with one mattress and the things for Michelle.

Sometime in the night, after we sold the furniture, Carolyn and I both came down with stomach flu. We spent the night crawling on our hands and knees to the bathroom. The next day, weak but determined, we climbed into our dilapidated car and made our way to a church in Columbus, Indiana, for a speaking engagement. The pastor had gone on a trip to Florida, intending to return in time for the service. But while he was away, a blizzard moved through the region, making it impossible for him to return. Only a handful of people braved the terrible conditions and came to the service—not really the kind of beginning we'd imagined.

After the service, we waded through the snow and ice to find our car reduced to a smoking hulk. A short in the wiring had caused a fire. The car was totally consumed, along with everything we owned. I thought of what had happened to me in Philadelphia when the parking attendant made off with my car and all of my possessions, but I kept the thought to myself. This wasn't just me now. I had a wife and small child.

One of the people who attended the service at the church was a man named Gene Darnell. I learned later that he was a serious believer and genuine intercessor. He saw our predicament, loaded us into his car, and took us home with him for the night. The next morning, as we pondered how we were going to get to Texas, Gene handed me the keys to a brand-new Buick Electra. I was astounded and had no idea what to say.

"I was praying about your situation," he said. "God told me to give you the car."

To say that we were overjoyed would be an understatement, and right there in his house Gene became our first ministry partner. He, like Abraham of old, believed in things that were not seen as though they already existed. We left that day to continue on our way, amazed and overwhelmed at the way God provided.

CHAPTER
16

On our way back to Texas we passed through Arkansas. When we reached Little Rock we stopped at a mobile home lot. We needed a place to live and a small mobile home seemed like our best option, though neither of us knew how we would pay for it. Carolyn and I walked the lot and discussed our options for providing a home for ourselves and our daughter, Michelle.

While we walked the lot, the owner, Bill Roetzell, was in his office having morning devotions. At the time we arrived, he was on his knees in prayer. When he finished praying he stood and looked out the window. As he did, he saw us and in that moment the Holy Spirit spoke to him, "You are to give them a new mobile home," the Lord said, "but not from the lot. It must come from the factory."

A few minutes later, Bill came from his office and told us what he'd heard. We were speechless. "There's only one thing," he added.

"What's that?"

"You'll need something to tow it with."

"Like what?"

"Well, it'll take a car at least the size of a ..." He paused while he thought, then said, "At least the size of a Buick Electra."

I laughed. "That's exactly what we have."

"Then you're all set. I'll put a trailer hitch on it for you."

The home he gave us would also become our headquarters for the ministry. We set it up in the Santa Dee Trailer Court in Fort Worth and I made a corner of it my desk. When people asked, I referred to it as "Our international headquarters for ministry to the nation of Israel."

In response, people pointed to that tiny trailer and laughed until they cried. "You've got delusions of grandeur," they said.

The trailer was thirty-two feet long and eight feet wide with a ceiling that was six feet high—which made the ceiling about six inches shorter than the top of my head. As I made my way from one end to the other, I often broke light bulbs with my forehead. The shower was so small I had to kneel down as if praying in order to bathe. A sliding door separated the bedroom from the bathroom and to make the place seem larger, Carolyn attached a mirror to the door. I awoke one night and was startled to see someone staring at me from across the room. I jumped up, ready to fight, and charged in that direction, only to crash headlong into the mirror. The person I thought I'd seen was nothing more than my own reflection in the mirror. Another night, I stepped out of bed and put my foot in the toilet.

The trailer was small and there was hardly enough room for the three of us, but we made the best of it and were glad to have it. Bill Roetzell, the mobile home dealer who gave it to us, became our second ministry partner.

We lived in that tiny home for a year, but after repeatedly breaking out the lights, stepping from the bed into the toilet, and squeezing past each other just to move from one room to the next, we were ready for a house. Michelle was getting older, too, and needed more normal surroundings. Carolyn and I started praying and then set out to look for a house that we could afford. We were encouraged by our prayers that what we were doing was right, but we could afford so little, in human financial terms, that the search seemed almost a joke.

Finally, after weeks of praying and searching, we located a house in Watauga, a suburb north of Fort Worth. The house was located on Dream Lane. As houses go in the United States, that house wasn't very large, but compared to the trailer it was a mansion. The owner wanted thirty-two hundred dollars as a down payment and was willing to finance the remainder of the price himself. That meant we didn't have to qualify for a loan with a bank, which was a good thing.

I was certain this was the house for us and that God intended for us to have it, so I agreed to buy it and told the owner I'd be back the following Monday with the down payment.

As we drove away, Carolyn looked over at me and said, "We don't have thirty-two hundred dollars."

"I believe that we do," I proclaimed confidently. "In my spirit, I am certain the money will be here by Monday."

That was a Friday. On Saturday when I checked the mail at the post office, there was nothing for us. Still, I was certain the money would be available in time.

Sure enough, I checked the mail on Monday morning and found a letter from Charlie Capps, a cotton farmer in Arkansas. With it was a check for thirty-two hundred dollars.

When I returned home I called Charlie and asked him, "What is the check for?"

"How would I know?!" he exclaimed. "Don't you know what it's for?"

"Yes, I do," I said, suddenly feeling stupid for asking. I'd believed God, He sent the money, and then I had the nerve to act surprised.

We took that money to the owner of the house on Dream Lane and in a few days we were settled. It felt great to have a home of our own—a place where we could live and move without bumping into each other and where Michelle could live a more normal life.

✦ ✦ ✦

In the months that followed, we contacted pastors and former classmates from Southwestern and arranged speaking engagements at any venue that would have us. God provided opportunities and most weeks I preached in at least two locations. He also provided the results and soon we had a number of people clamoring for further training. I wasn't sure what to do next, so I began to pray.

A few weeks later, I received a phone call from Rick Shultz. He was the business manager for David Wilkerson, the Assemblies of God pastor who founded Teen Challenge. We knew Rick from our work with Teen Challenge in Little Rock. Through our work there we had become acquainted with Dave, though we did not know each other well.

"Dave has been praying about the direction of his ministry," Rick explained. "And he wants to give you a farm that he owns on Possum Kingdom Lake. You know where that is?"

"It's here in Texas. Near the town of Graham."

"Well, he wants you to have it and he's willing to let it go for a small price."

I was interested in the property but a little skeptical about the small price part of Dave's property. Over the next few days, however,

Rick and I discussed the details and the price really was small. Not only that, Dave was willing to carry the financing himself. All we had to do was make the monthly payments.

After the papers were signed and we had title to the property, Dave came over and dedicated the facility. During the worship service, he prayed, "Lord, this place needs cows. Please send Mike and Carolyn some cows to help feed all the young people who will come here for training."

A few months later, two stock trailers arrived on our property. They came in the night and I had no idea what they were doing there. But a rancher had heard a tape of David's dedication sermon and the prayer he'd prayed over our location. In response, the rancher sent us thirty head of Black Angus cattle. I was overjoyed!

The next day, after the cows were in the pasture and the trailers were gone, I called Ben Martin, vice president of my board of directors. "Ben," I shouted, "it's a miracle! God has given us twenty-nine bulls and a cow."

Ben chuckled. "Mike, twenty-nine *bulls* and one lone cow wouldn't be much of a miracle. In fact, it would be a disaster. But twenty-nine *cows* and a bull would be something great. Are you sure that's not what you have?"

"I don't know," I replied. "I grew up in the city. We didn't have cows."

"Well, go look."

"Okay. But how do I tell the difference?" I had no idea what to look for.

He laughed. "Look in the back."

I went out, looked, and then called him back. "You're right," I admitted sheepishly. "We have twenty-nine cows and a bull."

Farm life was new to me and I might not have known much about cattle or the cattle business, but I could count and I knew what bulls and cows were supposed to do. Twenty-nine cows producing calves from that lone bull meant we had a source of income for the bank account and meat for the freezer.

CHAPTER
17

In October 1972, I held a series of meetings in Texarkana, a town located on the Texas–Arkansas border. The drive over from Fort Worth was too far to go back and forth each day so I stayed at the Texarkana Holiday Inn. One afternoon as I came from the parking lot I noticed an elderly lady who was headed toward the entrance to the hotel lobby. She was carrying a suitcase, and the thought came to me that I should help her. I stepped quickly to her side and reached to open the door. "May I carry your bag for you?" I asked.

"Thank you," she replied, "but there's no need. I am but a tramp for the Lord." She spoke with a heavy European accent and when she smiled her face lit up.

That's when I realized who she was. "Corrie ten Boom," I exclaimed like a star-struck kid. "I've read your book *The Hiding Place*. I never imagined I would get to meet you. And certainly not here."

She smiled and clasped my hand. "You can carry my suitcase if you'll join me for a cup of soup."

"I would love to," I replied.

Corrie checked in at the front desk, then we walked together to the hotel restaurant. As we enjoyed our soup together, she shared with me her great love for the Jewish people.

The ten Booms lived in the Netherlands, where her father was a watchmaker. Their home was an apartment above the shop. In 1844, long before Corrie was born, her grandfather began a prayer meeting for the peace of Jerusalem and for the Jewish people. Her father continued that tradition, even after German troops invaded the Netherlands during World War II. Faced with Nazi atrocities, the ten Booms began rescuing their Jewish neighbors, secreting them away in a hiding place inside their home and in locations throughout the country. When the Nazis learned of the prayer meeting and of the ten Boom family's work in rescuing Jews, Corrie, her father, and sister were arrested and sent to Ravensbrück, a concentration camp.

When she paused to take a spoonful of soup, I asked, "Who is your favorite Bible character?"

"David," she quickly replied. "And my favorite of his psalms is the ninety-first. God gave me that psalm on my birthday, while I was in Ravensbrück."

"Really."

"It was April fifteen, and I said, 'Lord, this is my birthday. I would like a birthday present.' And He said, 'Your present is Psalm ninety-one.'" Then she quoted the first verse. "'Whoever dwells in the shelter of the Most High will rest in the shadow of the Almighty.' Living in that shelter—*that hiding place*—means living before an audience of one and seeking Christ's affirmation above that of the world."

We talked for a while longer, then I carried her suitcase up to her room and said good-bye at the door. As we parted, she reminded, "Mike, you must remember what Jesus said."

"What's that, Miss ten Boom?"

"You shall find me when you seek me with all of your heart."[17]

I didn't know it then but that chance meeting with Miss ten Boom was the start of a lifelong association with her story and her work.

✦ ✦ ✦

That fall I held more than forty church services and conventions. One day while in prayer, the Lord spoke to me and asked, "Are the churches your source of income, or am I?"

I answered, "You are!"

Challenged by Him, I cancelled the remaining scheduled services and fasted and prayed for sixty days. While reading in the Gospel of Matthew, a scripture jumped from the page:

"Assuredly, I say to you, if you have faith and do not doubt, you will not only do what was done to the fig tree, but also if you say to this mountain, 'Be removed and be cast into the sea,' it will be done."[18]

While praying, I sensed God calling me to cease our ministry in Texas and move to another state. My best estimates indicated that making that move would cost a million dollars. As I continued to pray, I asked the Lord about that. He replied, "It will be done." I circled that scripture and believed with my whole heart that God would provide. The Scriptures are not magical chants. I knew that then as well as I know it now, but I also knew that if I followed God's will for me and kept my heart pure, I could indeed ask according to the things He shared through my spirit and through His Word.

At the time, we had no money to invest and barely enough income to meet the necessities or our daily life. Michelle, our five-year-old daughter, heard us talking and said, "Daddy, I've got a million dollars." She left the room and returned with her piggy bank. "See, Daddy, I will give you the money. It's here in my piggy bank." Then she handed it to me.

With tears in my eyes, we broke open her piggy bank and counted the money. She had three dollars and twenty-six cents. I took her in my arms and wept at the kindness in her heart. And as I cried, faith rose up in my heart.

As an act of obedience to God and an example to Michelle, I took her offering to a bank in Graham and told the banker I wanted to open an account. While he prepared the paperwork for the account, I told him I would be depositing a million dollars there and wanted to know how I could structure that deposit to attain maximum coverage under the FDIC insurance limits. He explained that I could not protect the entire amount but suggested a few ways to get the most the system had to offer.

"When do you expect to make this deposit?" he asked.

"I'm not sure. I don't actually have the money yet but God has told me that I will."

"And that's your plan?" he asked, trying to suppress a laugh. "You expect to just pray and the money will arrive?"

I was more than a little put off by his response. "Yes, I intend to pray and God intends to respond."

He laughed and shook his head. "You need serious psychiatric help."

Every day, I went to the retreat center and shut myself in the prayer room with God. At first, all we had was the money Michelle gave us, but gradually checks began to arrive. Dr. Pat Robertson heard about our effort and sent us a check for $10,000. Pat Boone learned about what we were trying to do and contributed, too. With their help, people nationwide opened their wallets and bank accounts and funded the project.

Sixteen weeks after my initial meeting with the banker in Graham, our account at his bank held a million dollars. The banker shook his head in amazement and apologized for his earlier response. Michelle's offering touched the heart of God and moved His hand.

It took longer to coordinate than I'd hoped, but eventually we made the move.

CHAPTER
18

Although at times God had been very real to me and had healed me of many things, the emotional scars of my childhood ran deep and I have spent much of my adult life trying to outrun my past. There remained aspects of my life that had yet to be touched by His grace. Running from my troubles worked at first, or so I thought, and I was able to ignore or avoid the unresolved emotional detritus from my childhood. But after a while the tension between the person I knew I should be in Christ and the deeply ingrained effects of my father's violence started to affect me physically.

Out of shame, I kept the emotional pain—and increasingly physical consequences—hidden from everyone, including my wife. Having been unable to trust my father I found it impossible to trust others, and the fear that Carolyn might not accept me after hearing the full details of my childhood left me unwilling to risk telling her about it. Although I knew in my mind that Jesus described God's love for us as unconditional, I still, in my heart of hearts, could not accept that love was anything other than conditional. Love, for me, still was something I had to earn.

Nor had I described for Carolyn, or anyone else, the complete story of seeing Jesus in my bedroom when I was eleven. I was convinced she would not understand how I could have endured such torture at my father's hands and still end up a godly man. And I wasn't entirely convinced that she could hear the account of Jesus' appearance in my bedroom without thinking I was just a little bit insane—an opinion of me that one might easily rationalize from the stories of my childhood. Believing one or the other seemed plausible. Believing them both together seemed rather unlikely.

That wariness of others extended to God as well. I had not heard His voice for a while—not like I did when I was a child—and in one of those strange twists of emotional dysfunction, I had separated Jesus the Son from God the Father. The Son seemed inviting and accepting—even though I could not accept His teachings about the nature of divine love. By contrast, the Father seemed distant, judgmental, and the thought of Him always was laden with a foreboding sense of imminent retribution—as if a punishing hand were headed in my direction.

I wanted to hear His voice, but I wanted to keep Him at arm's length. The result was an emotional state that left me hypersensitive to the opinions of others and constantly checking over my shoulder—if not literally, at least figuratively.

As a result, I become a workaholic, burying my emotional pain in work. I spent most days and many evenings dashing about at a frenetic pace. Eighteen-hour days were common, seven-day work weeks were standard, and I bragged to those who would listen that I never took vacations.

Desperate for affirmation, I tried my best to please everyone and to succeed beyond all expectations. It was a technique I'd employed with my father when I was a child, though with little success. As an adult, surrounded by colleagues who were believers, I hoped for a better result. Surely, I thought, everyone associated with our work would understand and accept me. The opposite, however, seemed to be the rule. The more I succeeded at our ministry objectives, the more I felt rejected. In the pain of that rejection, I felt my father's rejection yet again. Only, as an adult it hurt a hundred times more.

From the training we received at Southwestern and from years of sitting in church listening to sermons, I knew most of the right words and phrases to preach or witness to others. Yet inside I had never fully relinquished the old battered and beaten Mike Evans to God. The broken little boy was still very much alive and very much in need of attention. Added to that was the fact I had never met a preacher with my background, or even one who admitted making the simplest of mistakes. They all seemed to lead perfect lives—everyone except for me. So I did my best to act like nothing was wrong and kept pushing ahead.

Somewhere in all of that, an article appeared in *Time* magazine detailing my ministry. Then, as now, the magazine was widely circulated and the story attracted a lot of attention. Requests for speaking engagements increased, my calendar became even more packed than it already was, and interest in the work at our ministry center picked up.

Outwardly I had all of the trappings that defined success. And my outward emotional mask—my façade of perfection—was firmly in place, or so I thought. But inside I still felt like the moron my father said I was. I wanted to be the perfect husband, perfect father, perfect Christian, and perfect leader, but on all counts I felt as though I had failed.

Trying to fulfill my plans and achieve my goals under my own power took a toll on my mind and spirit. Inwardly, I was dry as dust. The vibrancy I'd once enjoyed was gone from my spirit and the creativity that had served me well in the past evaporated. Not only that, my obsession with the fear of rejection bordered on idolatry.

Sometime that year, I purchased a pickup truck at an auction in Connecticut. As I drove home I encountered a terrible rainstorm. In the midst of it, a trailer truck approached me from behind. I had the cruise control set on sixty-five and it seemed to me the approaching truck was traveling well above the speed limit—perhaps at speeds in excess of eighty or ninety miles per hour. The truck behind me closed at a fast pace and I realized if I didn't move over, it would run me over.

A car occupied the lane beside me, so I tapped my brakes to warn the driver behind me. That move seemed only to enrage the driver, and the truck accelerated. I realized I was now a target. Frightened, I jerked the steering wheel to the right to move out of the way. I figured the driver of the car would just have to deal with it.

The road was covered by water and when I snatched the steering wheel to make the move, the pickup spun around in a three-hundred-sixty-degree circle. I managed to regain control of it, but when I glanced in the rearview mirror, there was the truck—still bearing down on me.

As we sped down the highway, a tollbooth appeared in the distance. I made for it as fast as the pickup would take me, pointing the vehicle toward an open lane. The truck behind me followed close behind but at the last moment I switched lanes. The truck zipped past and I slowed to a normal speed. That is, the pickup slowed, but my heart raced.

I stopped on the shoulder of the road as tears trickled silently down my cheeks and no matter how hard I tried to stop them, I could not hold them back. As if a hand had ripped the door away from the secret places inside me, light flooded in and the truth followed. It was as if God had filmed every moment of my life and played it back; I saw the driven little boy crying for acceptance growing into a man struggling to keep that need hidden. Feeling inferior to other preachers who boasted larger ministries, wore better clothes, were better educated and more eloquent, I shrank from closeness as a flower shrinks from the heat of the sun at midday.

I longed for perfection thinking that production and performance were more important than caring. I strove for achievement and the favor of man when I should have been sitting at the feet of Jesus. I had become like Martha, frustrated and always working, instead of Mary, peaceful and always learning.

When I preached at a church and did what I thought was a fabulous job, I was rejected by the pastor who, rather than rejoicing at the successful meeting, said I made him look bad. It seemed that no matter what I did, acceptance was never there. Most of my peers—many of whom had attended school with me—rejected me simply because I was successful and they weren't. I badly wanted affirmation but couldn't get it from man. I had heard the voice of Jesus and it had given me affirmation and transformed my life, but I wanted to hear it again.

Desperate for help, I searched my mind for the name of someone in whom I could confide. Someone I could talk to without fear of being judged. But whom could I call?

After a few minutes, a name—Jamie Buckingham—popped into my mind. Jamie was born in Florida and grew up in the Southern Baptist

Church. After graduating from Southwestern Baptist Theological Seminary in Fort Worth, he pastored Baptist churches in Texas, South Carolina, and Florida. Later, he left that denomination and founded a nondenominational congregation in Melbourne, Florida. He spent much of his ministry being a pastor to pastors. I first met him when he lived in Texas.

When his name came to mind, I reached for the telephone without hesitation. My voice cracked as I said, "Jamie, this is Mike Evans. And I'm scared."

Jamie responded with five little words that gave me renewed hope. "It's okay to be afraid," he said. I had long felt that if someone really knew me, if my fear was discovered, I would be seen as weak and ineffective, and rejection would follow, but in the conversation that followed I found quite the opposite.

When the call ended and I hung up the phone, I knew I needed to spend time with the Lord, too, speaking to Him in the same open, honest manner. I lifted my hands heavenward in a sign of surrender and began to confess my fears. Then I pleaded for the grace and favor I needed to share my long-hidden past with Carolyn.

That evening I took a deep breath, gripped her hands in mine, and began to tell her the story of the first twenty years of my life. It took hours, but hurt by hurt, I told her everything. Our tears mingled as she realized the horror in which I'd lived.

"Actually, I'm glad you didn't tell me at first," she said when I was finished. "Since then I've had time to learn that you're not like your father."

Later, I had another conversation with God. This time I asked His forgiveness for keeping Carolyn in the dark for so long and for His help in forging close relationships in the future, not just with her but with others as well. To set aside the fear that had controlled all of my relationships and replace that fear with trust.

In response, I heard God answer in my spirit. "Will you let Me set you free from the destructive ties between you and your father?"

"Yes," I replied. "I will."

Then He said, "Go and seek your father's forgiveness."

"Whoa, Lord," I exclaimed, stunned by His response. "*Me* ask *his* forgiveness? I was the one battered and beaten. I was the one physically, verbally, and emotionally abused. Shouldn't he be asking my forgiveness?"

At once a scripture from Matthew flooded my mind.

"Therefore, if you are offering your gift at the altar and there remember that your brother or sister [*or even your father*] has something against you, leave your gift there in front of the altar. First go and be reconciled to that person; then come and offer your gift."[19]

At first I thought of all I'd done for God. I'd offered Him my life and whatever gifts and talents I possessed and was making that same offer again. Wasn't that enough? But His voice was unmistakable and His insistence unrelenting. I knew that my father would never come to me. If there were to be any reconciliation between us, it would have to begin with me. So after a moment or two spent wrestling with what I knew was inevitable, I surrendered and said, "Yes, Lord, I will."

Then that still, small voice in my spirit replied, "Now you're ready to minister."

CHAPTER
19

After my communion with God, I became more serious about addressing my work habits. I was serious about visiting my father, too, but the enemy of my soul wasn't finished with me. He was determined to end my effectiveness in the ministry and as an advocate for Israel. And he very nearly did just that...

Not long thereafter, a black cloud of depression settled over me. Many days I sat for hours on the back steps trying to pray. More often than not, I gave in to the sinking feeling inside and just sat there, crying. I felt defeated and despondent but again, in spite of what I'd learned, I kept those feelings to myself, unwilling and unable to share them with anyone. If anyone asked—and they did from time to time—

I simply smiled and assured them that I was okay. All the while, though, I knew I was a phony, only pretending to be well.

Though much of what I felt and experienced was internally generated, I could no longer handle the sense of pain, rejection, humiliation, and shame that plagued me constantly. I cancelled all pending meetings and events, then called my staff together and told them to find other jobs. I gave them a year to do so but still could not tell them who I really was, what I was going through, or what I would be doing in the future.

In the months that followed, I watched as the ministry God had given me crumbled before my eyes. Night after night I sat alone and wept over what was happening, but even in the face of ruin I held on to my prideful perspective and refused to reach out to anyone for help or even to tell them what was happening inside me.

Without consulting God, I decided there was nothing left for me to do but leave the ministry, take my family home to Texas, and try to find a different career. As a step in that direction, I secretly enrolled in a real estate sales course in preparation for becoming a licensed real estate agent.

But I couldn't escape the call of God on my life. In spite of my despondency, He kept reaching out to me in love and compassion. David, the psalmist, wrote, "He heals the brokenhearted and binds up their wounds."[20] Some of that healing came inside me as God slowly turned my eyes away from the fear that gripped me and back toward

Him. And some of the healing came from others through simple acts of kindness. I remember one day a lady came to our house with flowers. I didn't know her, but I wept because one person had reached out to me in compassion.

Gradually, the cloud of depression lifted enough for me to feel a nudge from the Holy Spirit, prompting me to face up to the crucial thing I'd left undone—to make things right with my father. Or at least to attempt to do so. I didn't want to see him. And I certainly didn't want to ask his forgiveness. But Proverbs says that humility comes before honor.[21] I knew that and I fully understood what the Lord was asking me to do. But the emotional inertia of my life pushed me in the opposite direction, and finding my way to a place of humility took some time.

Finally, when I reached the end of everything—emotionally, spiritually, financially—I surrendered. Regardless of what happened to me, or the ministry, or the future direction my life might take, I had to follow through on the commitment I'd made to God. I had to go to my father and ask him to forgive me for the way I felt toward him. He still had power over me, and I would never be free of him without righting things between us. Not only that, he needed to know that Jesus was real in my life. I wanted him to see that a true encounter with God had changed me and could change him, too.

A few days later I drove up to a place in New Hampshire where I knew my father had a hunting camp. According to my mother and youngest brother, he had been spending three or four days a week there, supposedly hunting deer. I knew he was just getting away from the house, Mom, and the things that tormented him in Springfield. And I had no doubt he used the time away as an opportunity to indulge in his favorite pastimes—drinking and chasing women.

When I arrived at the hunting camp, Dad was nowhere in sight. I waited a few minutes, thinking he might show up, then made my way to the bars and cafés I knew he frequented. After two or three stops proved fruitless, I finally found him at a bar down the road a ways, working hard to entice a young woman to go home with him. She was about the age of my sister and he was holding her hand, staring intently into her eyes, and calling her Babydoll with every other word. He didn't notice me at first but when he did, he shouted to the crowd, "Hey, there's a preacher in the house!" Then he looked over at me and in derision said, "Preach, preacher, preach."

"Dad," I replied, ignoring the tone of his voice. "We need to talk."

"Then talk," he said loudly.

"No." I shook my head. "Not here. We need to go back to the camp."

"I don't want to go back there right now," he argued.

"I realize that. But we need to talk." I was firm but polite. "So come on. Let's go."

Reluctantly, he let go of the girl's hand and followed me out to the car. He wasn't happy to be pried away from the bar or the young girl he was trying to seduce, and as we drove away, he returned to his old form, repeatedly referring to me by his favorite names—moron and bastard. I let those words slip by without response and focused on the task at hand.

When we reached the camp, he opened the door and we went inside. He collapsed in a worn-out recliner and glared up at me. "Okay," he growled. "We're here. What you got to talk about that's so important?"

In submission to what I knew God had told me to do, I got on my knees and said, "Dad, God told me to get on my knees and humble myself in your presence."

Before he could respond, I began to confess my failures as a son—pride, failing to pray for him and often refusing to do so, and many other things. I didn't enumerate his wrongs against me. Nor did I relive the beatings I had received at his hand or the curses I had received from his mouth. I didn't ask him why he repeatedly called me a bastard and a moron. I simply confessed the sins I knew I'd committed. As the words tumbled from my mouth, I found myself confessing even more. Things I had done since becoming a preacher, some of it that had nothing to do with my relationship to him.

As I continued to confess to him, a horrified look came over his face. "Stop," he demanded. "I've heard enough."

But I continued. "Dad, I have lied. I have been prideful—"

"Stop it!" he cried out again. "I can't take any more. I have committed the unpardonable sin for what I have done to you. I can never be saved. My home will be eternal hell."

Undeterred by his response, I talked to Dad about Jesus and what He meant in my life, the changes He'd brought in me, and the work yet to be done. As I spoke, his hard exterior began to crack and he opened up to me in ways he'd never done before. He told me of his childhood, the abuse he'd received from his father, and how he had been made to work in the fields from the time he was five or six years old.[22] Then he leaned forward in his seat and gripped my hands so hard his knuckles turned white. "Son," he sobbed, "I should have been put in prison for what I done to you."

Tears ran down his face, and in that moment God's grace and mercy filled me with genuine compassion for the man I thought I could never forgive, much less love. I led him to Christ that afternoon, right there in the main room of his hunting camp.

That was the beginning of a healing process between us. One that lasted until the day he died. And it was a turning point for me on my own journey to wholeness. A turning point. On a journey. But not the journey's end.

✦ ✦ ✦

During my early ministry, I was invited to go with Jamie Buckingham on a trek through the Sinai. I was traveling through my own desert place and looked forward to leaving my cares behind to hike and fellowship with Jamie and his friends for eleven days. We planned to follow the footsteps of Moses from Jebel Musa to al Arish, with side trips to other places he had traveled.

Not long into the trip it became my turn to clean the dishes. In the desert there are no dishwashers, farmhouse sinks, or even soap. There's not much water, either. So there I was squatting beneath the night sky, dodging scorpions and scrubbing the pots with sand—the universal scouring pad. But rather than enjoying the opportunity to live like a Bedouin and experience things few Westerners get to experience, I complained. Just like the people of Israel who followed Moses into the wilderness.

The next day we made plans to climb Mount Sinai and visit the spot where Aaron and Hur had held Moses' hands up for victory in the battle against the Amalekites.[23] Still full of myself, I decided to ignore the others and avoid long hours on the trail, trudging up the side of the mountain. I was a jogger. I could make it to the top in much less time.

So I left my extra gear behind—including my water bottle—took off my shirt and ran straight up the mountain. When I reached the summit, instead of celebrating in victory I collapsed in a heap. By the time the rest of the team arrived, I was in the throes of heat exhaustion. My pulse raced and my head pounded. I was weak, pale, and dizzy. And I was sweating profusely.

Rather than speaking up, I sat quietly and listened while Bill Nelson, a former astronaut, delivered a devotion on being one with

Christic.[24] By the time he finished I knew I was in trouble and had no option but to ask for help. "Bill," I croaked, "I'm sick. I think I'm dehydrated and may have heatstroke." He kindly gave me his extra shirt and hat, then offered a few sips of water.

That night, as I thought back over the events of the day, the accusing voices inside me returned, telling me what a stupid idea it had been—not the idea to run up the mountain alone but to come on the trip at all. The desert wind and heat were unbearable. The scorpions and snakes were a real health hazard. It was awful out there and the wounded little kid inside me screamed, *Why me, God? Couldn't you find someone else to torment? How can I get out of this desert?*

As I complained to God about my circumstances, I reached for my Bible. The pages fell open to the book of Numbers, chapter fourteen, the chapter that records the murmuring and complaining Moses endured from his followers. And it records God's response, which was to send them wandering in the wilderness for forty years. I certainly didn't want that.

After reading that chapter, I bowed my head in prayer and confessed my complaining spirit to God. I admitted to Him that I was proud, stubborn, and rebellious, and I didn't like to submit to authority either, which was the reason I had dashed up the mountain on my own. With that confession, the headache and fever that had bothered me all evening disappeared.

The next day, we stumbled upon a Bedouin tent and stopped to visit with its inhabitants. An Arab woman came out to greet us. When she learned there was a doctor in our midst, Dr. Angus Sargent, she ran into her tent and returned carrying her six-year-old daughter in her arms. We were appalled at the child's appearance. Flies covered a wound she'd received to her head and I could see, even from a distance, that it was badly infected. As she spoke and our guide interpreted, we learned that a family member had tried to cauterize the wound with a hot knife, which only made matters worse. My mind recoiled at the thought of the pain the child must have endured.

Angus examined her but after a moment shook his head. "I'm sorry. There's nothing I can do. I can't help her. She needs surgery, but we have no way to do that here."

As he said those words, a scripture from Isaiah came to my mind. "But He *was* wounded for our transgressions, *He was* bruised for our iniquities; the chastisement for our peace *was* upon Him, and by His stripes we are healed."[25] Remembering that passage, my heart was filled to overflowing with compassion for the child and her mother. When I looked at her, I thought of my daughters back home in the United States.

Without hesitation, I laid my hand over the girl's head, and I prayed, imploring God to heal her as tears ran down my face. I prayed in Hebrew and, as it and Arabic are similar, I hoped the mother understood at least some of what I said.

That was a special moment for us. The mother seemed genuinely glad that we'd taken the time to listen and had responded as best we could. It was also a moment for me, too, as I realized that God had affirmed me once again, just as He had when I was eleven. This time by the words He'd given Isaiah long ago and by the prompting He'd placed in my spirit.

When we arose the next morning, Angus said, "I have to set up a makeshift operating room. I have to try to operate on that little girl. Otherwise she may not survive the infection." I didn't tell him what I'd sensed as we prayed for the girl the day before.

A few minutes later, Angus walked over to the mother's tent and not long after that we heard him crying. My heart sank at the thought that he was mourning the child's death, so I eased open the tent flap and stepped inside to console him. Across the way, I saw the girl lying on a pile of rugs. The ugly wound from the day before was gone and the skin of her face was smooth and clear. She was completely healed!

When we finally came from the tent I raised my hands and lifted my eyes toward heaven. When I quit complaining, when I got out of God's way, He was able to do the miraculous through me. How like us humans to try to do our own thing—to focus on ourselves and our needs rather than on God, our Strength and our Redeemer.

✦ ✦ ✦

Not all of our experiences with Bedouins turned out as well as the one with the mother and her young daughter. Later in our trip we came across another tent and another young girl, this one about eleven or twelve years old. Her hair was braided with beads, symbolic of her tribe, and she wore a beautifully embroidered dress. As she looked at us she covered her mouth with her hand. I wanted to take a picture of her and offered a candy bar if she would remove her hand from her face and give me a big smile. She shook her head to say no, so I offered a second candy bar. Two bars did the trick and she removed her hand.

As I took her picture, I heard camel hooves behind me and a loud scream. I turned in time to see her father coming at me with a sword in his hand. From the look on his face I knew he meant to sever my head from my shoulders.

Later I learned that, in the father's opinion, I had undressed his daughter when I asked her to remove her hand—an act on my part that could only be avenged by my death. Rather than attempting to apologize or explain myself, I did what most would do. I ran.

A truck was parked nearby and everyone else was already loaded and waiting for me. I ran toward them and dove in back, the father chasing after me. The driver saw what was happening and as I landed on the back of the truck, he pressed the accelerator and we drove away just in the nick of time.

CHAPTER
20

After the trip to Sinai, I felt encouraged that the Holy
Spirit was continuing to work in me. It wasn't long before the old
feeling of worthlessness—the sense that I could not successfully live
the Christian life—returned. In a matter of weeks, I was once again
on the verge of despair.

By then we'd moved back to Texas and one day, as my mood sank
lower and lower, I walked out the back door of our home and took a
seat on the top step. As I sat there, I bowed my head and prayed. "God,
my life is in Your hands. I surrender to You once again. You told me
once that You loved me and had a great plan for my life. Please, Lord,
show me that plan."

In response that day, I heard only the rustle of a Texas breeze as it blew through the treetops. No audible voice. No memory of a scripture. Nothing. Just me, the accusing voices that invaded my thoughts, and the creeping sense of doom.

The following day, I left to preach at the church of a friend. In spite of my emotional issues and physical problems, I had booked a few events just to keep going. Deep inside, I really didn't want a different career. I wanted to live with a sense of calling. But I wanted things to be right—with me, with God—and I wanted to be at peace with myself. I just couldn't see any of that ever coming to pass. Instead, things seemed to be reaching an end and I felt that maybe God was through with me, that nothing more would come of the things I'd dreamed of and wanted so much to accomplish.

As I flew off for that speaking engagement, I sat aboard the airliner and prayed once again. "Lord, I have no joy and no peace. I'm at the end. When I finish the sermon tomorrow, that's it. I don't know what else to do but give up, once and for all. I've failed you. I've failed myself. And I'm done."

After praying awhile longer, I finally turned my face to the window and stared out at the white puffy clouds as they moved past us below the wing of the airplane. Tears rolled down my cheeks and a sense of loneliness swept over me, as if I were saying good-bye to something or someone I loved very much.

In the midst of all that, a verse from Scripture came to mind.

Several verses, actually, from the book of Isaiah. I couldn't remember all of the words, just bits and pieces of what I thought the passage said, but as I thought about it, I heard Him say in my spirit, "Pray it."

At once, I was encouraged to think God might be speaking to me again. Not in the same face-to-face way He'd spoken to me when I was eleven, but through His Word, as He'd spoken to me that day outside the Bedouin tent in the Sinai Desert. Perhaps I would again see His miraculous intervention in my life, just as I'd witnessed it in that young Bedouin girl's physical body.

My Bible was tucked inside a satchel that lay beneath the seat in front of me and I reached down to take it out, then rested it on my lap. The passage that had come to mind was from Isaiah 43:18–19 and I turned quickly to it. "Do not remember the former things, nor consider the things of old. Behold, I will do a new thing, now it shall spring forth; shall you not know it? I will even make a road in the wilderness and rivers in the desert."[26]

As the Lord told me, I began to pray those words, repeating them over and over, internalizing them and objectifying them—as words of Scripture and as His words specifically directed to me. As I did, He declared those verses back to me. "This is not the end. It's not over. This is only the beginning. I'm doing a new thing in your life. You're going back to the original vision I gave you that night in your bedroom. And to the calling I've already shown you. You will be a protector of the nation of Israel and of her people."

My mouth fell open in amazement and my heart leapt with wonder. Just moments before, I'd been convinced that God had turned away from me. Certain that He and I were done. And in an instant, I again felt affirmed as His child. Expectation rose up in me, and my spirit was energized with a renewed sense of purpose. God was at work, accomplishing His will in me and for me and through me. I would become the protector of Israel and of her people—defending Israel as an adult in ways I'd never been able to protect my mother as a child.

Although God had spoken to me and my spirit was renewed, I still had no clue what to do next. Just the outline of what would happen—that He was doing something new and that I would become a defender of Israel. To find out what that meant in terms of a next step, I began to pray, even as I flew on to my destination.

For the remainder of that day, I continued to seek the Lord and slowly He impressed upon my spirit that I should travel to Israel. When I asked why, I sensed Him telling me that I should request a meeting with Menachem Begin, Israel's prime minister. Now, I'll admit that to the human mind alone, that sounds rather farfetched—go to Israel, ask for a meeting with the prime minister—but after imploring God to speak to me, and then finally hearing His voice, I wasn't about to turn my back on Him. I had come to my end—spiritually, emotionally, physically—and He had renewed me in an instant. I was committed to following through on the direction I'd received.

As planned, I preached at the Sunday morning service, then returned home to Texas. However, instead of going home to Carolyn to announce my retirement from the ministry, I met her with an announcement. "I'm going to Israel!"

She had a puzzled look. "You're doing what?"

"I'm going to Israel."

Her forehead wrinkled in a frown. "But why?"

"I'm going to meet with Prime Minister Begin."

"How do you know this?"

"God told me to go," I replied confidently. "And He told me to ask for a meeting with Begin. I've run from a lot of things in my life. I can't run from God. I need to run *to* Him. I *want* to run to Him."

We talked awhile longer, and then she realized my mind was made up. The decision had been made. I was going to do this. I intended to ask the prime minister's office for an appointment and then I was going to fly to Israel—regardless of whether I received a response from Begin's office.

The next day, I made an airline reservation for a flight to Israel, then made a hotel reservation and located a fax number for Menachem Begin's office. With those arrangements in place, I composed a letter requesting an appointment with Begin, advising him of my planned arrival date and giving him the location where I would be staying. When the letter was finished, I signed it, inserted it in the fax machine, and sent it off with a prayer that God would have His way.

Having dealt with politicians and government officials in the past, I knew that decisions like my request sent to Begin's office might take days, if not weeks, to resolve. In addition to the usual delays, Menachem Begin didn't know me and there was no compelling reason for us to meet. After all, I was an unknown Christian minister, not someone like Billy Graham or a noted official. I was just a boy from the other side of the tracks, determined to obey God and watch Him order events according to His purposes.

In spite of that, I secretly hoped for a quick response. By the end of the week, though, no response had arrived. Still, I was undeterred in my resolve to obey the Lord and so I placed my luggage in the car, and Carolyn drove me to the airport for a flight to New York City, the first leg of my trip to Israel.

Several hours later, I arrived in New York, took a room at the Plaza Hotel, and retired there to pray and read. As I sat in the hotel, reading my Bible, God reminded me of another scripture from Isaiah that He had given me, this one from a time when I was on the mountain in Korea. "But those who wait on the Lord shall renew *their* strength; they shall mount up with wings like eagles, they shall run and not be weary, they shall walk and not faint."[27] That evening, as I sat alone in the room, I sensed the voice of God assuring me that I was following His will. That things would turn out right. That my strength would be renewed—and I could feel Him doing that, right there in that hotel room.

The following day, I took off from the airport in New York. After a long and tiring flight I landed in Israel and checked into a hotel in Jerusalem. I asked at the desk about messages that might have been left for me, hopeful that the prime minister's office had called while I still was in the air, but the hotel clerk informed me there were none. I felt a twinge of discouragement but pushed it aside and went up to my room.

For the next couple of days, I prayed and fasted in my hotel room, believing God was at work and that I was in the right place at the right time. Finally, one morning early in my second week, the phone on the nightstand rang. When I answered the call a voice on the other end said, "Mike Evans? This is Yehiel Kadashai, Prime Minister Begin's personal secretary. The prime minister would like to meet with you. Are you available to meet this afternoon?"

My heart stood still. "Yes," I stammered. "What time should I come?"

Mr. Kadashai confirmed a time and I hung up the phone. Suddenly my knees turned to jelly and I sank onto the edge of the bed. God had honored His promise to me. I was going to meet the prime minister of Israel!

At the appointed time that afternoon, I took a taxi and made my way to the prime minister's office. He was a small man but had a commanding presence, and as I entered the room he reached across the desk to shake my hand.

After we exchanged greetings he directed me to a chair in front of his desk. We sat across from each other and I began with a feeble, "How are you?" He gave a polite response and then talked for thirty minutes, which was good because I knew of nothing else to say beyond "hello." I'd come all the way from Texas at the instruction of the Lord, and I knew the outline of what God had said He was going to do—that I would become a protector of Israel—but I hadn't a clue what I was supposed to talk about with the prime minister that day.

Four times during our conversation Prime Minister Begin asked, "Why did you come to see me?"

And every time he asked, I repeated his question, "Why *did* I come?"

Finally, after the fourth time, he asked, "Do you know why you came to see me?"

"No," I replied awkwardly. "I don't know."

He looked astonished. "You don't know?"

"No," I said. "I don't."

A faint smile turned up the corners of his mouth. "What *do* you know?"

"I know God sent me."

He looked confounded. "God sent you, but He didn't tell you why?"

I shook my head. "No, He didn't tell me why."

"God sent you," he chuckled as he repeated the question, "but

He didn't tell you why?" Without waiting for a reply, he called Mr. Kadashai into the room. A moment later, the door opened and Mr. Kadashai appeared.

"Eight thousand miles, Kadashai," Begin roared. "This man traveled eight thousand miles to meet with me and he says nothing except that God sent him." He gestured in my direction. "Kadashai, shake his hand. We have found an honest man! He believes God sent him, he came in response, but he doesn't know why." Then he turned to me. "When God tells you why, will you come back and tell me?" I assured him I would.

The meeting went as well as one could expect, but I came away as perplexed as Menachem Begin. I'd heard the Lord telling me to go to Israel. And I'd come all the way there. And I'd heard Him tell me that I was to meet with Menachem Begin, and I'd done exactly that. But the question remained—why? Why did I come all that way?

When I returned to the hotel, I went up to my room and spent the remainder of the day asking the Lord for an answer. The following morning, as I prepared to spend another day in solitude, He gave me the answer. I was there to build a bridge between Christians and Jews. Not a physical bridge but a bridge of love. This was the "new thing" He was going to do with my life.

At once, I reached for the phone, called Mr. Kadashai, and arranged to meet with Prime Minister Begin again.

As I entered his office later that day, Begin held out his hand and asked, "So, why did you come?"

"To build a bridge," I blurted out.

"Oh, I see," Begin said, not as impressed as I'd imagined. "A bridge?"

"Yes, a bridge."

"What kind of bridge? Like the Brooklyn Bridge in New York City?"

"No, Mr. Prime Minister, a bridge of love." As I shared those words with the prime minister that day in his office, they sounded out of place and I'm sure I appeared more than a little awkward, but I'd come that far believing that the things God had spoken to me were actually from Him. He had opened doors for me that I never could have opened on my own, and I wasn't backing down.

"A bridge of love," Begin mused. "But a bridge for whom?"

"Between Christians in America and Jews in Israel," I smiled.

"I like that," he replied with a grin. "I will help you build that bridge."

And right then I knew the answer to the question I'd asked that night in my bedroom when I was eleven. I'd cried out, "Why was I born?" And this was the answer. I was born to build a bridge of love, understanding, and friendship between Christians in the United States and Jews in Israel. At last, I had found my place.

✦ ✦ ✦

The next morning I awakened with the sense in my spirit that I should go and sit in the lobby. After breakfast, I made my way downstairs, took a seat on a bench near the hotel's front entrance, and waited to see why God had sent me there.

When several minutes passed and nothing obvious occurred, I picked up a copy of the *Jerusalem Post*. Somewhere on the first or second page I read a story about Jonathan Netanyahu.

Jonathan was the eldest son of Benzion Netanyahu, a leader of the Zionist movement that brought thousands of Jewish settlers to Palestine in the early twentieth century. During the 1967 War, Jonathan had volunteered for duty in the Israel Defense Forces. Not long after that war ended, he'd been assigned to a Special Forces unit. In 1976, when Israeli airline passengers were held hostage at the airport in Entebbe, Uganda, Jonathan led the elite commando team that rescued them. The raid was a success but Jonathan was killed during the attack.

The day that I read the *Jerusalem Post* article was July 4, the anniversary of Jonathan's death, and as I sat there in the lobby I sensed the Lord urging me to go to the Netanyahu home and offer my condolences.

As with the other things I had recently heard from Him—go to Israel, meet with Menachem Begin, tell him I sent you to build a bridge—the notion that I should visit Benzion Netanyahu was capricious. I'd never met him and knew but a few details about him. He'd been an early advocate of Zionism. And he'd been one of the founders of New Zionism—an attempt to return Zionism to that earlier emphasis—but that was about all I knew. Nevertheless, God had spoken and by then I was convinced He would open a path before me to accomplish His will through my efforts.

After I finished reading the article, I put aside the newspaper, rose from my place on the bench, and walked outside to the front of the hotel. A taxi was parked there and I leaned down to speak to the driver.

"Do you know where Benzion Netanyahu lives?" I asked quietly.

"Certainly," the driver replied. "Everyone knows where he lives."

"Good. Please take me to his house."

A few minutes later the driver brought the taxi to a stop and pointed out the window. "There it is," he said. I paid the fare, stepped from the car, and pushed the door closed behind me, never once wondering if we were at the correct location.

To my surprise, when I rang the doorbell, Benzion answered. As quickly as possible, I explained who I was and why I'd come to see him. He listened intently, then graciously invited me into his home. As we entered the living area he pointed to an overstuffed chair. "Have a seat, Mr. Evans. Would you like some tea?"

After our tea had been served, I said, "Mr. Netanyahu, I saw a picture of you standing on the tarmac when your son's body arrived home from Uganda. That must have been the worst day of your life, yet you held your head high."

"I was sad, but very proud," he replied.

"Your eyes in that photograph captivated me. They were filled with the pain of a father who had just lost his son."

Benzion's eyes brimmed with tears. "That was, indeed, the worst day of my life."

Just then a door opened behind me and a young man entered the room. Probably about thirty years old, he was dressed in a suit and carried himself with purpose. He glanced at me and shyly smiled. "I heard your American accent and wondered who was visiting us today."

Benzion glanced over at me and gestured in the young man's direction. "This is my son Benjamin." I rose from my chair and we shook hands, then Benjamin asked, "What brings you to our home?"

"I was just telling your father, I came to offer my condolences on the anniversary of Jonathan's death."

Benjamin took a seat on the arm of a nearby chair, and I sat down again. "You were intrigued by Jonathan's story?"

Benzion looked at Benjamin. "A father's loss of a son can only be understood by a father."

"I wanted you to know that you are not alone," I said. "You do not face the loss of your son alone. And Israel does not face her enemies alone. You have friends who stand with you. I think God wanted me to come here and tell you that, and so I have come."

As Benjamin looked into my eyes, his pain at the loss of his brother was palpable. In an instant I felt the anointing of the Holy Spirit rising within me. I stood slowly, put my hand on Benjamin's shoulder, and said, "You loved your brother Jonathan as Jonathan of old loved his friend David. From the ashes of your despair will come strength from God."

While I spoke, I took a small vial of oil from my pocket. I carried it with me as a matter of practice and hadn't brought it there that day for a specific purpose. But as I spoke I sensed the Holy Spirit directing me to anoint Benjamin and so I opened the vial, dabbed a drop of oil on my finger, and touched it to Benjamin's forehead.

As I continued to talk, the words rolled off my lips like water cascading over rocks. "Yet unlike Jonathan of old," I continued, "who died in battle defending his country, you will accede to the seat of power. One day you will become the prime minister of Israel."

As those last words slipped from my lips, my voice trailed off and I sank back to the chair where I'd been sitting, suddenly weak, as if delivering those words had drained all my energy. The smile vanished from Benjamin's face and his forehead wrinkled in thought. In Hebrew, he called me a moron. His father answered, "Not just a moron, a genuine moron."

"We shall see if you are a prophet," Benjamin quipped. "Lucky for you, we do not live in ancient times. You know what happened to the prophet whose words did not come true."

I nodded. "But I am not afraid to be held accountable for the words God has given me."

"Perhaps not," he said. "But I have no interest in politics. I am going into business."

We talked a few minutes more, then I pushed myself up from the chair and said my good-byes. Benjamin walked me to the door and I made my way out to the street.

The next day, I met for the third time with Prime Minister Begin and told him of my encounter with the Netanyahu family. He asked how the visit went and I said, "I met the prime minister of Israel yesterday."

"No," he chuckled. "You met me two days ago."

"That's true," I replied. "But I met the man who will one day be prime minister of Israel." Then I told him the prophecy that Benjamin would be prime minister of Israel, more than once.

"Isn't once enough?"

"You should give him a post in your government," I suggested. "He's bright, well-educated, and talented. If you don't give him a start in government, he'll go into business. Israel can't afford to lose potential leaders like him."

Begin agreed with a nod. "He is a fine young man. But he withdrew from public life after the death of his brother." He thought a moment longer, then abruptly stood. "My friend, I am glad to have this time with you." He came from behind the desk and embraced me. "I hope we can enjoy many more times like this together." When I finally left his office, Begin gave me two letters—one to Billy Graham and one to Jerry Falwell. I asked his advisor why the prime minister had given me those letters. He replied, "He is trying to provoke you. He suspects these people don't know you."

Not long after that meeting, Benjamin was offered the position of Deputy Chief of Mission at the Israeli Embassy in Washington, D.C.[28] That was, indeed, the beginning of his political career. And it was the start of my friendship with him, Menachem Begin, and a relationship with Israel that has defined the rest of my life.[29]

CHAPTER
21

As strange as it may sound, the misery Dad inflicted on us when we were children actually bound us together as a family, at least for a while. We had a sort of negative love, if such a thing is possible. An emotional connection, nonetheless, created by the pain he inflicted on us. When you're young, vulnerable, and hungry for attention, and the only attention you can get is negative attention, even that can draw you to each other.

That's what happened with us. We were together in that house, united by our desire to survive, hoping the next day would be the day when things finally changed. Hoping that the next day would be the day that Dad stopped beating us. That next day would be the day Mom or Dad said "I love you" and gave us the positive affirmation we all needed and craved. That, of course, never happened. Not then. Not later. Not ever.

As we grew older, all but one of us left that house on Pasco Road. My older sister moved out to live with a friend. I left for the army. My brothers, each in turn, ran out the back door to avoid yet one more beating and never returned. Finally, there was only my Mom, Dad, and youngest brother, Danny, living in the house.

With just the three of them at the house, Dad started spending more and more time at his hunting camp in New Hampshire. He made Danny go with him sometimes, to cut the grass or help with maintenance. Finally, though, he sold the hunting camp and moved to Alabama.

Not long after Dad left, Mom became ill. She was sick on and off through the last year of her life and though I didn't visit her as often as I should have, we spoke regularly by telephone. There wasn't much for us to say. She just kept repeating, "I want to die, Mike. I just want to die."

When she told me about Dad leaving, it seemed like a good thing— him down in Alabama and her in Massachusetts. I said, "Rejoice, Mom. He's gone and you don't have to worry about what he's going to do next."

"But I love him," she replied. Hearing her fall apart over him was distressing, but I pushed aside my personal feelings and kept talking.

As our last conversation came to an end, I asked if I could pray with her. I was astonished when she said I could. That was the final thing I did for her. As a little boy, I'd been unable to save her from Dad and now as an adult, I couldn't save her from the memory of him, either. Praying for her didn't really seem like much at the time, but as the years have gone by I am more and more grateful for that moment.

Mom died on December 14, 1982, when she drew her last breath and slipped into eternity. It was a bittersweet moment for me. She was gone and I would never see her again, but she was free of the pain Dad inflicted on her. I only wish she had come to know Christ first.

There were times as a child when I wondered why my mother didn't pack up our few belongings and take us away from Dad. Certainly, she had the opportunity. Most weeks, he was gone from Monday morning until Friday afternoon. Her sister, Ginger, would have been glad to pay for our trip out of there. She could have taken us to New York where their brothers lived. They would have seen to it that we were protected. But she never did. That was a troublesome issue for me as a child—why she didn't step in to save us from him—and no doubt contributed to the hurt that I still, at times, feel inside over my past.

As I grew older I came to recognize her dilemma. She, like me, had been beaten and abused until she had no self-esteem left. And like me, she believed that she deserved the treatment she received from Dad. No doubt also lurking in the back of her mind was the question, "What would he do when he found out we were gone?"

Later in her life, Aunt Ginger told me that she and Mom had been abused by their father. Because of that, both of them were removed from their father's home and taken to an orphanage.[30] I've never been able to confirm any of that from official records, but I know Mom had a number of nervous breakdowns. My youngest brother, Danny, cared for her through many of those episodes.

There were a few times when Mom did get in front of us when my father came toward us in a rage. Sometimes he backed off. Other times, he simply beat her into submission. He was six feet four inches tall and weighed well over two hundred pounds, most of it solid muscle. Physically, she was no match for him. Most of the time, though, she just turned away and disappeared into the kitchen.

That's how it was with Mom. She never told us she loved us. Never asked about our day. Never sat with us at the table and helped with our homework. Never attended parent meetings at school. And yet, in spite of all that, I miss her and I cherish the few good memories of moments we had together. The religious celebrations in New York. The memories of our relatives in Belarus. And my identity as a Jew. As lacking as she was as a mother, for most of our childhood she provided the only glimmer of light in our lives.

CHAPTER
22

After my first trip to Israel to meet with Menachem Begin I returned again and again, one trip leading seamlessly to the next. Soon I was flying back and forth across the Atlantic with regularity, traveling from our home in Texas to Israel multiple times each year, working to build the bridge I'd described during our first meeting: A bridge of love, understanding, and support between Christians in the United States and Jews in Israel.

As my relationship with Begin grew and developed, he introduced me to Dr. Reuven Hecht, one of the prime minister's principal advisors, and to Isser Harel, the head of Mossad, Israel's intelligence agency.

Harel was born in Vitebsk, Russia, during the final years of the Russian Empire. His father operated a vinegar factory, but the family business was confiscated by the Soviets after the Russian Revolution. Eventually, the family left the Soviet Union for Latvia, then immigrated to Palestine when Harel was sixteen. He lived through and participated in most of the major events in the founding of the modern state of Israel. As an adult, he was the founder of Shin Bet, Israel's internal security service, and became the director of Mossad the year after it was formed. By the time I met him, he had experienced fifty years of Middle Eastern history and knew at least as much about terrorism as any person alive.

While on a visit to Israel in September 1980, Harel invited me to dinner at his home. We'd enjoyed several long conversations together already and I was looking forward to another opportunity to talk with him at length. Reuven Hecht joined us, and the three of us sat around the dining table, eating and talking about a wide range of topics. Before long, however, our conversation moved to the topic of terrorism and I asked Harel, "Do you think terrorism will ever come to America?"

Harel leaned away from the table in a thoughtful pose. "America is developing a tolerance for terrorism," he said after a moment.

"Oh? How so?"

"You've already experienced terrorism. The assassination of President Kennedy. And of his brother. Those were terrorist attacks. Americans just haven't seen them that way and view those events as criminal acts, rather than as terrorist acts. That approach has rather unwittingly raised the American tolerance for politically motivated violence."

"I never thought of it that way."

"Nor have many other Americans. The United States has the power to fight terrorism, but not the will. The terrorists—the kind we experience here every day—have the will but not the power. But to answer your question—yes, I fear terrorism will come to the United States in time."

"So, where will it come? What's the most likely target?"

"New York," he replied. "New York City. It's the symbol of your freedom and of capitalism. That's the most likely place they would strike and I think it would be the location of their first big, organized attack. Probably your tallest building."

"For the effect?"

"That and, being the tallest, Islamic terrorists would see it is a symbol of your strength and power." Harel paused before continuing. "As I said, America has the power to fight terrorism but not the will. The terrorists have the will but not the power. But all of that could change in time. Oil buys more than merely tents, so to speak. Much more, I'm afraid."

"And they have a long memory," Reuven added.

"Yes," Harel responded. "You in the West kill a fly and rejoice. In the Middle East, we kill one and one hundred flies come to the funeral.

And they all remember."

"The long game."

"Yes, they play the very long game. And I fear it will come to your own shores in time."

In 1993, when Pakistani Ramzi Yousef led the first terrorist attack on the World Trade Center, Harel's comments and insights took on a sense of the prophetic.[31] In the months that followed, I became convinced that an even greater attack would occur. That conviction led me to write *The Jerusalem Scroll*, a novel about a second attempt to blow up the Twin Towers. Most people who read that book believed it was nothing more than fiction—that an attack of the magnitude necessary to destroy those buildings would never happen in the United States. The events of September 11, 2001, proved otherwise.

Using hijacked airliners like missiles, terrorists struck not only the World Trade Center in New York City but also the Pentagon in Washington, D.C. Though ultimately unsuccessful in destroying the nation, they nevertheless dealt powerful blows to our government and financial system. Carefully coordinated and well planned, the events of that day brought us the worst terrorist attack ever on American soil and made the truth of Harel's warnings all the more evident.

✦ ✦ ✦

In 1984, the threat of attack took on a more personal meaning for me and our family. In June of that year I received a phone call from an agent with the Bureau of Alcohol, Tobacco, Firearms, and Explosives (ATF). The agent phoned to tell me about recent activity involving Richard Wayne Snell, a member of a white supremacist group called The Covenant, the Sword, and the Arm of the Lord (CSA).

More than merely another quirky religious cult, CSA was a toxic blend of racism, warped pseudo-Christian belief, and radical activism. Many of those beliefs were decidedly anti-Semitic.

One of CSA's primary teachings was that the United States government had come under the domination of a select group of Jews who used the government to suit its purposes. CSA members were convinced that Jewish influence had corrupted the government to the point that it would soon collapse, resulting in chaos that would quickly turn violent. To prepare for what they believed lay ahead, CSA trained its members in survival techniques and devoted itself to hastening the day of collapse and chaos, in the mistaken belief that doing so would usher in the return of Christ. The FBI designated them as the second most dangerous group in the United States.

Although Snell was not widely known to the general public, I knew about him and the CSA from my work with Jewish organizations. He knew about me through a television special we produced and aired for my first book, *Israel: America's Key to Survival*. That telecast identified me as Jewish and as an advocate for Christian support of Israel.

Snell was a dangerous person, but I wasn't concerned about him posing a threat to me or my family until the agent who phoned me said, "Mr. Evans, I need to tell you—Snell's most recent activity involved plans to kill you."

"Just plans?" I asked.

"No, sir," the agent replied. "When we arrested him, Snell was on his way to make good on those plans. He was driving to your house to kill you."

That part of the conversation got my attention. Snell was a domestic terrorist—a homegrown, American terrorist. The kind of person security experts spent long and sleepless nights worrying about. And this one had been arrested—on the way to my house to kill me. Not someone else. Me! And most likely, anyone else who was at home with me when he arrived. I'd never experienced anything like that before and the thought that my work with Israel—fulfilling a sense of calling from God to protect and defend the nation of Israel and her people—might put my family in harm's way cast the issue of terrorism in an entirely new light.

Snell's involvement with CSA apparently began a year earlier when he met the group's founder, Jim Ellison, at a CSA conference. The two men reportedly struck up a friendship as they discussed how they might blow up the Alfred P. Murrah Federal Building in Oklahoma City. Apparently Snell intended to do that job himself but his plans were sidetracked by another more overwhelming desire—his desire to kill Jews and Blacks.[32]

On November 3, 1983, Snell gunned down the owner of a pawn-shop in Texarkana, Arkansas, apparently under the belief that the man was Jewish. He wasn't, and the case confounded investigators for more than eight months. Then, on June 30, 1984—which was my birthday—Snell was stopped by Louis Bryant, an Arkansas State Trooper, on a lonely stretch of highway in western Arkansas. As Bryant, who was African American, approached Snell's vehicle, Snell opened fire with a modified Colt .45, fatally wounding the trooper.

A truck driver who saw the shooting followed Snell across the Oklahoma border and contacted the police. Not long after that, Snell ran into a police roadblock. Rather than surrendering peacefully, he fought back and a gun battle ensued. Eventually, Snell was wounded and taken into custody.

In the trunk of Snell's car, police found a pistol with a silencer, a submachine gun, and grenades. When they searched the interior of the vehicle, they found a single piece of paper lying on the front seat. Written on the paper were my name, address, and unlisted telephone number.

As agents pieced together Snell's activities leading up to Trooper Bryant's murder, they soon learned he was committed not only to killing African Americans and Jews, but to killing as many high-profile Christian Zionists as possible. My name was at the top of his list.[33]

CHAPTER
23

As the implications of Snell's plot sank deeper into my soul, and as I realized anew each day that not only was my life at risk but that of my wife and children as well, a spirit of fear rose up inside me. Fear so strong it all but overwhelmed me. Little things took on an increased significance. When the garbage truck slammed its hopper closed outside our house, I jumped. When the phone rang, I felt my heart leap inside me. I was edgy, irritable, and jittery all the time. In short, I was terrified of being killed.

Having studied Scripture and listened to the Holy Spirit most of my life, I knew that peace—true peace—was not the absence of fear but the strength and courage to face the conflict in one's life and make the right choices. I also knew that the way to peace lay in getting my attention off my predicament and onto God and His promises. *Knowing* that was one thing, *doing* it was quite another. And the more I tried, the more I resembled a caged animal prowling around the house day after day, constantly in fear and, at the same time, aching to break free.

One morning as I prayed and studied Scripture, I came to Psalm 20 and I read:

"May the Lord answer you in the day of trouble; May the name of the God of Jacob defend you; May He send you help from the sanctuary, and strengthen you out of Zion; May He remember all your offerings, and accept your burnt sacrifice. Selah. May He grant you according to your heart's desire, and fulfill all your purpose. We will rejoice in your salvation, and in the name of our God we will set up our banners! May the Lord fulfill all your petitions. Now I know that the Lord saves His anointed; He will answer him from His holy heaven with the saving strength of His right hand."

As I thought about those words, I sensed the Lord telling me that psalm wasn't merely a prayer of David but a prayer for me as well. That I could pray the same prayer David prayed and do so in the same faith, power, and authority.

In thinking about it further, I also knew that I couldn't overcome my fear by avoiding it. I had to confront it. Confronting Richard Wayne Snell was impossible. He was incarcerated in an Arkansas prison and awaiting execution. So I decided to confront my fear another way.

As I traveled to and from Israel, met with Israeli leaders, and kept abreast of the latest developments in the Middle East, I had become increasingly aware of conditions in Israel's neighboring countries. Beginning in 1975, Lebanon had been torn by a civil war that pitted Christian forces against armed units from the Palestine Liberation Organization (PLO) and various radical Muslim groups. In 1976, as conditions deteriorated further, the president of Lebanon asked for help from Syria. Later that year, an Arab League force comprised mostly of Syrian troops occupied the country and attempted to instill order.

With a measure of peace restored in Lebanon, the PLO turned its attention to Israel and began firing rocket and mortar rounds across the border into Galilee. Israel responded by invading Lebanon, and the international community intervened with a multilateral peacekeeping force, including elements of the US military.

Angered by the presence of foreign troops in Lebanon, and enraged by the presence of Israeli troops inside its southern border, Muslim clerics organized a paramilitary group known as Hezbollah. The group, comprised of followers of the Ayatollah Khomeini, was trained and financed by Iran.

All of that served only to stoke the anger of the Lebanese—anger against Israel, the United States, and nations of the West who supplied peacekeeping troops. Each one shooting at the other. While civil war raged, hundreds of thousands of soldiers, terrorists, and civilians were killed, wounded, or displaced in the prolonged fighting.

As I thought about their situation and my own, I felt impressed to travel to Lebanon and bring them aid. I was under no delusion that I could end all of the suffering the Lebanese experienced, but I knew I could do something for them. And I hoped that in going there, I could confront my fears in a real and tangible way. A way that might bring a sense of relief from the fear that had such a tight grip on me. For me, Lebanon was the most dangerous place on earth. If God could send me there, and deliver me back to safety, I knew I could put aside the fear that tormented me.

As I wrestled with being obedient to the leading I'd received and the fear that I felt, the Lord gave me another scripture. This one was from Deuteronomy 31:8. "And the Lord, He is the One who goes before you. He will be with you, He will not leave you nor forsake you; do not fear nor be dismayed." After reading that, I resolved to believe the scriptures I had been directed to. To believe them, to pray into them, to mediate on them, and I pressed ahead with plans for the trip.

In preparation for the trip, I arranged for several containers of food and medical supplies to be sent ahead of us to Jerusalem. I also contacted two friends—L. W. Dollar and Charlie West—about joining me for the trip. I wanted L. W. to see firsthand the importance of our work and thought Charlie should come along as our videographer, to document and preserve a record of our effort. They were apprehensive about venturing into the unrest that had occupied much of the recent news cycles but eventually agreed to accompany me.

When we arrived in Jerusalem, I rented a car, loaded it with supplies, then the three of us started north toward the Lebanese border.[34] I had previously informed the prime minister's office of our intentions, and he had insisted we allow him to arrange for our safety. At the border, we were supposed to encounter an IDF colonel who was to direct us to a place where we would switch from our rental car to a taxi owned by Mossad. The driver and another person, both of whom were Mossad agents, were to accompany us across the border into Lebanon.

When we arrived at the border crossing near Metula, the IDF colonel stopped us, but I misunderstood what he said. Thinking he was telling us to hurry on our way, I pressed the accelerator and we sped away from the checkpoint into Lebanese territory.

Our plan had been to head for Sidon, then drive up the coast to Beirut. We had been warned by Israeli officials not to go there, and one of my companions had been told specifically that an attack on Sidon was imminent, but I was determined to follow through with the goal of our trip and confront my fears.

The information about Sidon proved to be valid, however, as we found the city had been targeted just minutes before our arrival. Many of the buildings had been badly damaged and bodies still lay in the street. We parked the car and got out, then spent a few hours distributing our supplies, comforting the wounded, and sharing God's love with the suffering who'd been caught in the crossfire—Muslims and Christians alike.

From Sidon, we continued north to Beirut. Our objective there was to meet with and minister to the US Marines who were part of a peacekeeping force stationed near the airport. The trunk of my car contained not only medical supplies but Bibles as well, which we intended to distribute to the troops.

We found the troops without much difficulty at a beachhead where they'd landed earlier and through which they conducted resupply for the soldiers manning positions around the perimeter of the airport. As I shared the gospel with them, I handed each Marine a Bible. In the course of doing that, I realized they would not be home to celebrate Christmas with their families, so I asked our cameraman to record Christmas greetings from them that we could deliver to their families.

Later that evening most of the troops returned to their barracks, a four-story building approximately five hundred yards from the beach. Our team unrolled our sleeping bags and made our beds on the sand with the few Marines who remained there.

A little after six the following morning, I was standing near the water's edge talking to a contingent of marines who had just taken up their posts on the beach. Suddenly a terrific explosion shook the ground and in the distance a dark cloud of smoke billowed into the sky.

Not long after that, we learned that a truck loaded with the explosive equivalent of more than ten tons of TNT crashed through the gate outside the marine barracks. Once beyond the gate, the driver—an Iranian national—crashed the truck into the lower floor of the barracks and detonated the charge. In seconds, the building was reduced to a pile of rubble.

Two-hundred forty-one US servicemen lost their lives that day. Two-hundred twenty marines, eighteen navy personnel, and three soldiers from the army. Many of the dead were not killed by the blast itself but by the crush of debris that buried them.

Two minutes after the blast at the Marine Corps barracks, terrorists attacked French troops stationed at the Drakkar building not far away. As a result, the First Parachute Chasseur Regiment lost fifty-eight paratroopers. Another fifteen were wounded.

For the United States, the attack marked the single deadliest loss of Marine Corps lives since the battle of Iwo Jima during World War II. For the French, it was the most deadly loss since the Algerian War (1954–1962). And for me, it was an introduction to how vile and deadly terror attacks could be.

With the area near the airport and beachhead suddenly transformed into an active war zone, my friends and I hurriedly gathered our belongings and started down the coast for Nahariya, the nearest crossing on the Israeli border. To get there, we followed the sea from Beirut, keeping it always to our right.

That worked for a while, but as darkness approached I made several wrong turns that took us into the center of Tyre, where we found ourselves in the midst of a funeral procession for a Hezbollah operative. Our vehicle was an Avis rental car from Jerusalem with a distinctive Israeli license plate—not a good thing to have when surrounded by raging, grieving Muslim terrorists. Somehow, though, God blinded their eyes and we made it through the city without incident.

Once we reached the outskirts, however, I made another wrong turn. Instead of going to Nahariya, to the south, we were headed northeast, toward Damascus. Before long our vehicle was spotted, apparently for its obvious license plate, and tracer bullets raced overhead. Not long after that, 135-millimeter shells began to explode around us.

As if that weren't bad enough, our car sputtered and died. We had left Beirut so quickly I had forgotten to check the fuel in the tank. Now we were lost on a desert road, amid hostile fighters, and out of fuel. With shells continuing to drop around us, slowly moving closer to our location, I was certain we had but minutes before our vehicle would be blown to shreds. Still I was not ready to give up.

One of the men traveling with me shouted, "We're dead!"

"No," I replied. "You're not dead. You're still talking. If you're talking, you're alive. We have to pray."

As I began to pray, I was startled by a knock on the car window beside me. Despite my bravado, I jumped at the sound of it and thought,

This is it! We're going to meet our Maker on the backside of nowhere. God help us!

But when I looked to the left I saw a young Arab man standing beside the car. His head was covered by a *kaffiyeh*—the traditional Muslim head covering—in the color and design worn by members of Hezbollah. Only, he wasn't carrying a gun but a fuel can. He pointed to the can, then made his way to the rear of the car, unscrewed the cap to the fuel tank, and poured in the contents from the can. When the can was empty, he came around to the passenger door and pointed to the lock. I hesitated only briefly before pulling it up, then watched as he opened the door and climbed inside.

"Drive," he ordered and pointed out the windshield.

I had no idea where he was taking us and no workable alternative, either. So I started the car, steered it back onto the road, and drove in the direction that he'd pointed. As we picked up speed, I glanced in the rearview mirror at my passengers, who simply shrugged in response.

For thirty-two kilometers the young man did not speak another word. When we reached a junction, he simply pointed in the direction he wanted us to go and I guided the car as he directed. After what seemed like hours, he barked, "Stop." I brought the car to a halt, and the young man opened the door and climbed from the car. He slammed the door, stuck his head back inside, and said, "Safe."

Before responding, I turned to look over my shoulder at my friends huddled together in the back seat, as if to make certain of what the young man meant. Once more, they only shrugged in response but when I turned back, the young man was gone. We were stopped out in the open. There was no place for him to disappear. And yet, he was gone.

"Did you see where he went?" I asked.

"No," L. W. replied. "It's like he vanished."

We talked about it a moment longer, but none of us wanted to sit out there like that for long. So, reluctantly, I pressed the accelerator and we started forward in the direction we'd been traveling, still with no idea where we were or where we were headed. Only the young man's assurance that we were safe.

Half an hour later, we topped a hill and suddenly the Israeli border checkpoint appeared before us. A shout went up from all of us as that sight came into view. As we passed through to the Israeli side, one of the guys in the back seat caught my eye in the mirror. "Can you explain what just happened?"

"Not really," I said. "Other than to know that God answered our prayers for safety."

Scripture says, "Do not forget to entertain strangers, for by so *doing* some have unwittingly entertained angels."[35] No doubt—God sent an angel to help us that night. An angel dressed as an Arab terrorist. I can think of no other way he would have known where we were, that we were out of fuel, or that we wanted to get to the Israeli border.

CHAPTER

24

Had I attempted to orchestrate the events of my life I never would have thought to include some of the things that happened. I don't think I would have included the call from an ATF agent telling me that a domestic terrorist intended to kill me. And I doubt I would have included the trip we took into Lebanon with the mysterious young man who helped us reach our destination. I'm equally certain that involvement in the Iran Contra Affair, however minor, would not have been on my list, either. And yet, that's what happened.

One day in March 1989, while I was at home in Dallas, I received a rather cryptic phone call from Carolyn Sundseth, a friend who had served as religious liaison in Ronald Reagan's administration.

Carolyn and her husband had been on their way to the mission field when President Reagan asked her to help coordinate religious support for his administration. Realizing what a great opportunity that position offered, Carolyn and her husband redirected their foreign missionary plans and decided, instead, to become missionaries to Washington, D.C. She and I became acquainted as the president put together his administration and as she worked on several initiatives involving Israel.

She called one day and asked, "Mike, would you fly to Washington tomorrow? I have a man here who needs prayer. Don't ask his name, his position, or why he needs prayer. Just come up here and pray with him."

Although puzzled as to why she called *me*—many Bible-believing men lived much closer—I readily agreed to her request. That night, as I made plans to leave on the trip, I opened my Bible and read before going to bed. A few verses into the night's reading, I came to a passage in Isaiah. "Then you shall delight yourself in the Lord; and I will cause you to ride on the high hills of the earth, and feed you with the heritage of Jacob your father. The mouth of the Lord has spoken."[36] I wasn't completely sure how that applied to me or my situation, but I knew in my spirit that the encounter I would have the following day would be important, that God had something to say to whomever I was to meet with, and that I should be attentive to His voice.

Mrs. Sundseth was waiting for me when I arrived at the White House and led me through the building. As we walked down a hallway lined with windows, she pointed ahead to a solitary young man staring pensively at the landscape outside. "That's him," she whispered. "Just give him whatever word you feel God has given you."

The man wore a Marine Corps dress blue uniform and on his shoulders I saw the insignia of colonel. I'd never met him before and had no idea who he was, even when he turned to face me as I approached.

Suddenly, my mind was flooded with a portion of Scripture—another passage from Isaiah—verses that I knew by heart. Instinctively, I rested my hand on the young man's shoulder and said, "Sir, you don't know me, but I have a message for you. God wants you to hear His Word. 'But now, thus says the Lord, who created you, O Jacob, and He who formed you, O Israel: "Fear not, for I have redeemed you; I have called *you* by your name; You are Mine. When you pass through the waters, I *will be* with you; and through the rivers, they shall not overflow you. When you walk through the fire, you shall not be burned, nor shall the flame scorch you.'"[37]

The barest hint of smile flickered across his face and he acknowledged me with a nod, then without another word between us, he turned and walked away. As he started up the hall, I retraced my steps to Carolyn's office and told her good-bye.

From Washington, D.C., I flew the next day to meet with Juan Martinez Varela, the El Salvadorian minister of the interior. We were planning an area-wide meeting at a stadium in San Salvador, that nation's capital, and needed the Salvadorian government's cooperation to make it happen.

When I arrived, I took a room at the Sheraton Hotel in San Salvador and the next morning had breakfast with Minister Varela. While we ate, a waiter handed me a copy of the morning newspaper. I laid it aside but took it with me when I left the table after the meeting. In the elevator on the way to my room, I opened it and was stunned to see a picture of the young man I had prayed for at the White House the day before. In the caption I discovered that he was Oliver North, the marine colonel embroiled in the Iran–Contra Affair.

As a result of the government's Iran–Contra investigation, North had been convicted on multiple charges. At the time when I saw him in Washington, he was awaiting sentencing. Eventually, after a lengthy appeals process, the charges against him were dropped and his conviction dismissed, but that day when I prayed with him, he was staring into the depths of a very dark abyss.

Years later, I was at the White House covering a meeting between President Bill Clinton and Benjamin Netanyahu. During a break in events, my cell phone rang. The caller was Oliver North. He'd heard I was in town and wanted to talk.

"The words you gave me that day were from God," he said. "After you spoke, I knew He would deliver me."

"Those weren't my words," I replied. "They were from the Lord. I only shared with you what He gave me."

"I appreciate that. Thank you so much for coming when Carolyn called. I didn't know she was going to do that, but I'll never forget the scripture you shared with me. It was a dark time in my life. You brought light into the darkness with God's Word. It literally transformed my life and after that I knew the Lord would deliver me. I quoted the scripture you gave me several times daily during that crisis. Nothing meant more or comforted and strengthened me more during that entire crisis than that scripture."

Light into the darkness—that's what God did for me all those years ago. He brought His light into the darkness of my battered young life. Now He was giving me the opportunity to share His light with others. I never dreamed that His plan would take me from my childhood house in Springfield to the White House—or to the offices of presidents, prime ministers, and kings around the world. But that's exactly what He did. None of it has been my own doing. All of it has been from Him.

Equally important, I've been allowed to share the good news of Jesus Christ with people in tents and tenements, on city streets, and on the backside of the desert. God in His grace has enabled me to speak of "things I did not understand, things too wonderful for me to know."[38] As an example, I'll share one more thing that happened on that trip to El Salvador.

As was my practice, before Minister Varela and I ate breakfast that morning in the Sheraton Hotel, I prayed a blessing over our meal. While I was praying, I heard the Lord say, "At this time, you will meet with the president." When I finished praying, I glanced over my shoulder and saw El Salvador's newly elected president, Alfredo Cristiani, coming through the restaurant. Emboldened by what I'd heard from the Lord, I walked over to him, introduced myself, and asked if we could meet. He agreed and we scheduled an appointment for the following day.

At the time, El Salvador was embroiled in a violent civil war. When I prayed about what I should say at my meeting with President Christiani, the Holy Spirit told me I should talk to him about how to end the civil war and that I should give him a verse from 2 Chronicles. "If my people, who are called by my name, will humble themselves and pray and seek my face and turn from their wicked ways, then I will hear from heaven, and I will forgive their sin and will heal their land."[39]

When I met with President Christiani the next day, his secretary of state joined us, along with two generals from the Salvadorian army. I told Christiani what I had heard from the Lord and gave him the verse from 2 Chronicles. "Mr. President," I said, "if you will lead the nation in a day of humility and repentance, God will heal the land."

As I quoted the scripture, the general hurriedly wrote it in the palm of his hand.

The words I shared with them that day found a place in their hearts, and Christiani agreed to call for a national day of prayer and fasting. Christians in the nation already had been praying and God graciously answered their prayers, as revival erupted.

✦ ✦ ✦

Not long after my meeting with President Christiani, I was invited to speak on a Salvadorian television program. I had the entire morning to preach the gospel. One of the program hosts asked me to pray for him and afterward he was healed by the power of God. News of his healing spread and not long after that, the vice president's wife called and asked me to pray for her at the vice president's palace.

On the way to the palace, we rode with a military escort down a heavily congested street. As we inched along in traffic I noticed a crippled man who was seated on the sidewalk, begging. The Holy Spirit nudged me to stop and pray for him.

"Yes, Lord," I replied. "I'll pray for him after I pray for the vice president's wife."

A few minutes later we arrived at the palace. I came from the car and started up the steps toward the entrance. As I did, the Holy Spirit said, "If you go in now, you're going in alone. Go back now and pray for the man you saw on the street."

Sheepishly, I excused myself, returned to the car, and rode back through traffic toward where we had seen the man seated on the sidewalk, begging. As we made our way in that direction, I sensed the presence of the Lord with me in a powerful way. Even while I still was seated in the car, I knew that I knew that Christ was with me.

In a few minutes, we found the man seated right where we'd seen him before. I got out of the car and walked over to him. As I approached, the man looked up at me with a startled expression—our motorcade created quite a commotion when it arrived. Undaunted, I glanced down at him and saw a patch above the pocket of his shirt. Written on it was his name: Jesus. It's a common name for men in Spanish-speaking countries but, given the context, it struck me as humorous. Rather than laughing, though, I said, "Silver and gold have I none, but such as I have I give to you. In the name of Jesus, be healed."[40]

At once, the man threw his canes over his head and ran away down the street, screaming and shouting at the top of his voice. An interpreter was with me and I asked, "What is he saying?"

"He's saying, 'I am healed! I am healed!'"

On the street around us, car horns blared and drivers shouted, "Creo en Jesús! Creo en Dios!" I knew those phrases. They were saying, "I believe in Jesus. I believe in God!"

We celebrated with them a moment longer, then continued on our way back to the vice president's palace. As we drove in that direction,

I knew again that God was with us and that something great was going to happen there, too. When we arrived, we talked with the vice president, then I prayed for his wife. As I did, the Lord's presence fell on us.

✦ ✦ ✦

Not all the things I've seen and participated in were easy or obvious. Like Oliver North, I've stood at the crossroads, not knowing which way to turn or what path to take. And as God did for him, He also has delivered me.

Although I've seen many times when the Holy Spirit spoke to me, and I stepped out in obedience, that obedience didn't come without a long list of failures, many of which I've already shared with you in this book. But the successes I've seen have multiplied with each moment of obedience. Enough so that I'm convinced the reason we don't see more miraculous moments isn't because God is unwilling or because believers don't hear from Him. More often than not, I think it's because we who hear don't step out, speak up, and take the supposed risk of doing what He says. I say "supposed risk" because the real risk is in not acting.

The end of the Marine colonel's story was one of victory and deliverance. The beggar on the streets of El Salvador found healing. God is always above our circumstances and is infinitely able to deliver us in times of storm, to provide the things we need, to heal our brokenness—physical as well as emotional. And He continues to show me that the same Jesus who appeared to me at the age of eleven still speaks to me today through His Word and through His Spirit.

CHAPTER
25

One night in November 1988, as I read through Scripture, I came to a passage in Isaiah.

"So do not fear, for I am with you; do not be dismayed, for I am your God. I will strengthen you and help you; I will uphold you with my righteous right hand. All who rage against you will surely be ashamed and disgraced; those who oppose you will be as nothing and perish. Though you search for your enemies, you will not find them. Those who wage war against you will be as nothing at all."[41]

That was a familiar passage, one I first circled in my Bible when I was thirteen, but as I read it that night I felt my spirit quicken within me. As if the Holy Spirit was nudging me that something important had happened, or was about to happen. I didn't know what that might be but I knew something was in the offing and that these verses from Isaiah were important for whatever my involvement in the as-yet-unspecified moment might be.

This is something that I've described earlier and that has happened to me many times since—a moment I think of as the Word being activated. Others talk about it in the sense that God gave them a scripture or verse. Still others talk about it as a word from the Word—more than merely flipping through Scripture, finding something we like, and believing we can see it happen simply by believing it. It's that, to some extent, but it's more than that. And it's more because the One calling our attention to this or that verse is God and He's calling our attention to a particular verse for a particular reason. I think of it as activation.

What we call it or how we label it isn't nearly as important as listening and being committed to acting in obedience to the thing we hear next from Him. A few days later, the next thing came to me...

For most of that year—1988—Yasser Arafat, the leader of the PLO, had been lobbying international leaders for their support in finally recognizing the West Bank and Gaza Strip as an independent Palestinian state, with or without Israel's agreement. In conjunction with that effort, Arafat was scheduled to address a November session of the United Nations General Assembly in New York City.

In the months leading up to that session, Arafat had been pushing hard to achieve his goal of Palestinian independence and on several occasions had come close to declaring it on his own. Each time, however, he pulled up short of an outright announcement. Many expected that after giving this speech in New York, he would finally make that move.

All of that depended on one thing: As a precursor to Arafat's address, the Reagan Administration required that Arafat and the PLO acknowledge Israel's right to exist. By late November, with that acknowledgment not forthcoming and the date for Arafat's arrival looming ever closer, the US State Department reached a decision. Arafat would be denied permission to enter the United States on the basis of his known involvement in, and support of, terrorist activities. That decision was announced on November 26.

The decision to deny Arafat entry into the United States played well with supporters of Israel, but many in the international community still favored Palestinian statehood. Tension between those perspectives created a diplomatic impasse among UN member delegations. Many wanted to give Arafat an opportunity to plead his case before the world. Others acknowledged the United States' right to determine who entered its borders.

To maneuver around that impasse, a proposal was offered that would move the session to a temporary site outside the United States and beyond its control. That proposal quickly gained support and on

December 2 delegates voted to adjourn the General Assembly meeting in New York and reconvene in Geneva, Switzerland. Arafat was invited to deliver his address there.

When I heard news of the UN decision, I knew I was supposed to be at that meeting in Geneva. I wasn't a diplomat—not by official government standards—and I didn't know exactly what I would do at the meeting, but I knew I was supposed to go. Suddenly, those verses from Isaiah took on added significance. "Do not fear, for I am with you; do not be dismayed, for I am your God. I will strengthen you and help you ..." As I made plans for the trip, I repeated them over and over in my mind and let them sink deep into my spirit. More than simply inspiration, they were my source of protection.

The following week I flew from Texas and arrived in Geneva that Friday. I checked into the Hilton Hotel, believing that somehow God would cause me to ride upon the high places of the earth—that, because I took delight in Him, He would open doors with leaders of nations.

To my amazement, I was allowed into the facility where the General Assembly meetings were being held, though at first only in the upstairs section. During breaks in the meeting, I shared the gospel with dozens of ambassadors and foreign ministers.

Advance copies of Arafat's speech contained language deemed sufficient by the State Department to indicate acceptance of UN resolutions 242 and 338, explicit recognition of Israel's right to exist, and renunciation of terrorism—major elements in gaining US agreement to discuss the Palestinian question in direct talks with the PLO. During his deliver, however, Arafat departed from key portions of that language.

Afterwards, US officials reiterated their earlier position that he had not done enough to win their participation in talks. As a result, Arafat was forced to hold a press conference to straighten things out. The moment I heard the news, I got up from my seat and began walking the halls of the building, praying with every step, searching for the room where the meeting would be held.

Not far down the hall, I sensed the Holy Spirit directing me to a room identified as simply number 401. Inside I found an auditorium with a platform down front. On that platform was a long table and behind it was a single chair. I paused a moment to scan the room, then made my way toward the front of the room.

Rows of seats lined the room and as I neared the platform I sensed that I should stop at the second row from the front. I carried a briefcase and as I stood there at the end of the row I heard the Lord tell me to place my briefcase on the chair at the center of the row, directly opposite the platform, and leave the room. I did as He directed.

By the time the location of Arafat's news conference became public, the room was filled with members of the PLO executive council and others who were fully sympathetic to the Palestinian cause. Security for the event, most of which was provided by agents loyal to the PLO, turned everyone else away. Even some accredited members of the press corps were denied entry.

Just before the conference began, I approached one of the security guards. "Excuse me, sir," I said. "I need to go to my seat."

"What seat?" he snapped as he moved to block my entry. "You have no seat here. You cannot enter."

"But I've already been inside," I replied.

"You have no seat."

"Go to the front of the room. Look on the middle seat of the second row. My briefcase is on that seat. Open it. I'll give you the combination. Inside you will see my passport. It has my name and my picture. You'll see. It's really me."

Reluctantly, the guard turned away and stalked up the aisle. A moment later, he returned and escorted me to the chair that held my briefcase.

Minutes later, Arafat entered the room to find I was seated directly in front of him. Camera crews that were permitted to attend had been assigned to the third row—just behind me. Not even the executive council had been permitted to sit on rows one and two.

When Arafat was settled in place at the table, he read a prepared statement designed to satisfy the Reagan administration and open the way for direct talks between the US government and PLO representatives. His remarks were carried live in many places and reported on newscasts around the world.

When he finished Arafat said, "I shall allow three of you to speak. You may choose among yourselves."

I knew no one would choose me, so I took my Bible from the briefcase, secure in the scripture that God had activated in my life: "So do not fear, for I am with you; do not be dismayed, for I am your God. I will strengthen you and help you; I will uphold you with my righteous right hand ..."

In my other hand I held a copy of the PLO covenant, which called for the destruction of the state of Israel, and I rose to my feet. "Mr. Arafat, if you denounce terrorism, then also denounce this covenant that calls for the destruction of Israel." I gestured with the PLO covenant as I spoke.

Before he could answer, I began to recount the biblical position of the Jewish people—a position in stark contrast to that outlined in the PLO document. As I spoke, I gestured with the Bible.

Arafat screamed, "Shut up! Shut up! What must I do to make you shut up—striptease for you? It would be absurd."

When I'd made my point—that nothing about him had changed, that he had no intention of taking a serious stand against terrorism or in favor of Israel's right to exist—I collected my briefcase and turned to leave. As I did, I was met by an audience whose eyes were filled with unspeakable hatred.

Lord, I prayed silently, *You divided the sea for Moses. I only need six inches to get out of this room.*

Suddenly a path opened before me and I walked quickly through the midst of the gathering into the hallway outside the room. As I made my way through the building, the voice of the Enemy taunted me. *You'll never make it out of here alive. They will stab you in the back before you get outside.*

I focused on the voice in my spirit and sensed the Holy Spirit guiding me this way, then that. At first there was only the hallway, then another, then at last an exit appeared. I quickened my pace as I headed for it.

When I was a few feet away, the Spirit said, "A cab will be waiting with the door open. Get in and go to your hotel. The phone will be ringing when you arrive. No man will harm you."

As the door opened and I stepped outside I saw a taxi waiting at the curb. The door was open, but no passenger was inside, so I climbed into the back and told the driver to take me to the hotel.

When I reached my room the phone indeed was ringing. The caller was my friend Reuven Hecht, the senior advisor to the prime minister of Israel.

"Mike, we are hearing you in Israel," he said. I didn't know it at the time but Arafat's remarks had been broadcast live on Israeli television. Reuven was worried for my safety and had phoned the room to check on me. "Do you know where you are? How many bodyguards do you have? Arafat and his people are terrorists."

"Oh, I have many guards—I am surrounded by angels."

"Good ones?" Reuven asked, not realizing I meant heavenly angels.

"Yes," I assured him. "Very good ones."

"In that case, will you speak for Israel tomorrow on *Nightline*? They want to interview someone."

"I would be honored," I told him.

As we talked, the phone beeped with another call and I excused myself to take it. That call was from a producer with ABC's *Nightline* program, asking me if I would consent to be interviewed on the show. Instantly the Holy Spirit said, "Don't do the interview."

I told the producer, "No. Not me. Interview Benjamin Netanyahu."

Back then, Benjamin wasn't well known and I had to explain to the caller who he was and why they really wanted him. When I finished with the producer, I returned to my call with Reuven.

"Where is Bibi? Tell him to go to Capital Studios. They want him to do a simulcast." Reuven had no idea what a simulcast was but Bibi did and readily agreed. The interview was the first of many for him on network television.

✦ ✦ ✦

The evening before I left Geneva I was seated in the hotel restaurant, sipping coffee. As I relaxed, I overheard a conversation taking place in the booth behind me. Stunned by what I heard, I took my pen from the pocket of my jacket and scribbled the details on a napkin.

One of the men, an American with close ties to former president Jimmy Carter, was meeting with someone who, when I later saw his face, appeared to be a Saudi prince. As they talked, the American said to the prince, "George has everything under control in Washington. Harry is working on the project with the Japanese. There's a special meeting set up at the Tokyo Club. I've just heard from Rome—we have the support of our partners throughout Europe."

That was intriguing enough but the next statement horrified me. "We should have Jerusalem in your hands by '96—at the very latest by 2000," the American said. "We're certain we can get you a good piece of Israel by then, too."

Jerusalem in your hands—a good piece of Israel, too. I felt as though I'd been kicked in the stomach...or suddenly thrust into a scene from a very bad James Bond movie.

Since the late nineteenth century, when the first Jews returned to Palestine, the question of control over Jerusalem has been a deeply divisive issue. The earliest UN proposals to partition regions, giving part for an Arab state and part for the new state of Israel, had been unable to satisfactorily resolve the matter. Arabs and Jews held deep-seated and irreconcilably opposite views of the same city, the same sites, the same mountaintops. So divisive was the issue of Jerusalem that the UN had finally suggested the city remain an international territory, governed by neither party. Whatever tenuous peace that proposal might have offered was forsaken by the Arabs when they rejected the UN offer in its entirety and chose instead to wage war against the state of Israel, in the vain hope of winning control over the entire region. They lost and in the process lost control of Jerusalem.

Now the Arabs wanted the city for themselves. Many in the international community wanted to give it to them and, based on the conversation I'd just heard, members of our own government wanted them to have it, too. I was incensed but there was little I could do about the situation but listen, take notes, and pray.

The next day as I boarded the flight from Geneva, I saw the same American seated in the row in front me. I stepped out of the aisle and stood at my seat, then leaned forward and touched his shoulder. He looked back in my direction and I repeated the conversation I had heard the day before. As the color drained from his face, he said, "You're scaring me. Who are you?"

I looked him directly in the eye and said, "Don't fear me. Fear God! 'He who watches over Israel will neither slumber nor sleep.'"[42]

The man from the restaurant didn't reply and we didn't speak again for the remainder of that flight. But when the plane landed in Zurich, he left his seat and deplaned. From the look on his face, he appeared still unsettled by my remarks. And well he should have been.

The following day, the Reagan administration announced, through Secretary of State George Shultz, that Arafat's statement during the special UN session and the follow-up press conference had satisfactorily met his obligation to acknowledge Israel's right to exist and that the United States would immediately begin discussions with the PLO on the topic of a two-state solution in Palestine. I couldn't help but think the conversation I'd heard in the hotel was part of that effort. I only hoped my comment to the man on the plane had some influence on his participation in the matter.

CHAPTER
26

As I mentioned at the outset, my mother's family came to the United States from Belarus. At the time they immigrated, Belarus was part of the Russian Empire, where their life was marked by cyclical periods of anti-Semitic persecution.

After the fall of the empire and the rise of Communism, that religious intolerance deepened and spread to include systematic attacks on the church, religious educational institutions, and individual Christians.

Following the death of Soviet Premier Nikita Khrushchev a period of tolerance emerged, but by the end of the 1970s, government leaders became aware of a growing apathy among young people toward the government's official anti-religious position. It wasn't that more young people were turning to Christianity, or to any religion at all. Rather, they simply didn't care for the issue one way or the other.

At the same time, the government learned to its horror that, in spite of its prolonged effort to the contrary, many Russian Christians had continued to worship. Some in private, others in apartments and houses. Previous campaigns to wipe them out, the government realized, had served only to remove the external trappings of religion but had done nothing to change the hearts and minds of believers.

The same was true for Jews. Although many Russian synagogues no longer existed, Jewish beliefs ran deep. Like Christians, they simply went underground, meeting in homes and other locations without public fanfare.

In response, the government renewed its anti-religious campaign and once again turned to the task of rooting out religion in all its forms. This time, the focus was on the underground church and on Jewish congregations. Unlike before, however, life in the Soviet Union was far more accessible to the West and it wasn't long before news of the government's treatment of Jews and Christians began to trickle out. Many in the West felt led to respond, and before long a steady stream made the trip from the United States to bring fellow believers their support. Some of that support was in the form of money, food, and material items like blankets and clothes. Some of it was in the form of the printed Word, either Christian Bibles or the Tanakh—canonical Hebrew scripture.

At the time we began smuggling Bibles, bringing even a single copy of the Bible into the Soviet Union was a criminal offense. Foreigners who were caught doing that, particularly those from the United States, often managed to avoid lengthy prison terms, but Soviet citizens who were caught possessing a Bible were sent to Siberia. So those of us who engaged in smuggling the Scriptures learned to be careful.

On each trip, the routine was much the same. After the airplane landed, usually in Moscow, we gathered our luggage and made our way down to the customs inspection point. A soldier or law enforcement officer inspected our luggage and we proceeded on our way.

One day I was met at the airport by a young soldier who dutifully checked my luggage. In the first suitcase he found the usual clothes on top, but underneath were rows and rows of neatly wrapped packages, all of a uniform size and shape. He gave me a questioning look, to which I replied, "Soap."

He nodded, opened my second suitcase, and found the same contents. Clothes on top, rows of neatly wrapped packages underneath. The ones in the second suitcase were smaller than those in the first. "Small soap?" the soldier asked.

I nodded. "Small soap."

He glanced at the first suitcase, then back to the second. "Big bars.

Small bars." There was a twinkle in his eye and I knew he knew what the packages really contained, but I played along. "Yes," I nodded enthusiastically. "Big bars and little bars."

For that trip I carried five suitcases and he looked at them all. When he was finished he pointed to them and said, "You may close your luggage." I wasn't sure what would happen next—arrest, detention, deportation—then the soldier leaned toward me and whispered, "Slava Bogu." In Russian the phrase means, "Praise the Lord." I walked out of there with a skip in my step, a shout on my lips, and tears of joy trickling down my face.

During that trip I noticed several of the pastors to whom I was bringing the Bibles were not there to meet me. Members of their congregations met me instead and took me to a secret rendezvous in the forest, where I ministered to them. They told me their pastors were back in Bible school. I later discovered that the expression was a euphemism in the underground church for prison. The pastors were missing because they'd been arrested.

✦ ✦ ✦

Psalm 122 contains the simple admonition, "Pray for the peace of Jerusalem," and for most of my adult life I've done just that—I've prayed for the peace and safety of that magnificent city, for its leadership, and for all who live there. That God would lavish His favor upon them, restrain the forces of evil that threaten to overwhelm them, and cause them to thrive even as they live in the midst of unprecedented challenges.

As I've grown in my understanding of what it means to be both Jewish and Christian, I've expanded my prayers to include that same supplication for Jews everywhere. It's been a fascinating effort, praying in a way that is informed by a knowledge of events affecting us all around the world.

Among the churches where I speak and minister I've taught leaders about the importance of praying for Jerusalem, too. I've emphasized the necessity for us to come alongside the people of Israel, and Jerusalem in particular, to pray for their safety and well-being and I've done my best to show pastors how to educate their congregations on this topic—to move beyond the typical questions of doctrine and polity to confront the actual, real-world issues that Jews in many nations face. I do that in every church, every conference, and every event both in the United States and abroad.

As my work with the underground church in the Soviet Union expanded through the 1970s and into the 1980s, I came to know an ever-widening circle of Christian leaders there. I also became acquainted with rabbis who lived in the areas where I visited. On each trip, I equipped the pastors with Bibles, gave them instruction, and helped educate their congregations. I also worked to put copies of the Tanakh—canonical Hebrew scripture—in the hands of Jewish leaders, many of whom were as much without their scripture as the church members. To make that effort even more successful, I recruited leaders and members from the underground church to distribute copies of the Tanakh to their Jewish neighbors. No agenda. No strings. Just one oppressed group trying to help another.

As part of that effort, I invited Christian leaders and church members from all over the Soviet Union to attend a gathering at the Olympic Convention Center in Moscow. They were a little concerned about meeting in public. Most of the time they gathered in apartments, arriving in ones and twos, each of them coming at different times so as to arouse as little suspicion as possible. But I had prayed about it and the Lord assured me that this event would be held without causing anyone a problem. So we notified the country's Christian leaders about the gathering, rented the hall, and located hotel rooms for everyone to stay. We paid their travel costs and food expenses, too. And they came from everywhere.

During that event we prayed for many things, but one morning I led them in prayer for the Jews of Russia, many of whom came from families who had been oppressed for multiple generations. As I prayed, a verse from Isaiah exploded in my spirit. "I will say to the north, 'Give them up!'"[43] Instantly I knew that God was on the move and as I prayed I heard Him say that He was going to release the Russian Jews in a modern-day fulfillment of that prophecy.

Later, I met privately with bishops and pastors from the underground church. I told them what I'd seen and heard while I prayed and asked them to enlist their pastors and congregations in an effort to take literature to the Jews living near them, literature that would instruct them to prepare for an exodus—a mass immigration of Jews from Russia to Israel. The bishops and pastors agreed and before long we began an amazing prophetic journey based on that single scripture that had been activated in my spirit. One that saw tens of thousands of Jews released from the grasp of the Soviet Union and freed to make the journey to safety.

✦ ✦ ✦

While we moved forward with the literature distribution effort in the Soviet Union, the Holy Spirit said to me, "You must go to the home of Corrie ten Boom and pray. As you pray, I will open up Russia in a mighty way for you."

Corrie ten Boom's family home was located in Haarlem, Holland. It seemed rather strange that the way to Russia led through Holland, but Corrie and the entire ten Boom family had been at the heart of the Jewish rescue effort during World War II. Not only that, her grandfather began a prayer meeting in his clock shop that continued with a ten Boom leading it until well into the twentieth century. The focus of that prayer meeting was to offer prayers for the peace of Jerusalem.

In obedience to the Holy Spirit, I flew to Holland and visited the ten Boom home. By then, Corrie had gone on to her heavenly reward and we'd formed the Corrie ten Boom Fellowship, which purchased and restored the house. It has since operated as a museum and I've spent many hours there familiarizing myself with the house and meeting people who still remembered her.

During that particular trip, I spent a lot of time in prayer, trying to listen to what God had to say about the things we were doing in Russia and hoping not to miss the reason He'd sent me to Holland.

As I sat in the clock shop in prayer, there was a knock on the door. A woman named Erica van Eeghen entered and asked if she could see the Hiding Place—the room where Corrie and her family hid Jews while they worked to get them out of the city. I was glad to show her around and gave her a tour of the property. As she was leaving she handed me her card and invited me to join her and her husband for dinner that evening at their home.

Because she was a stranger, I would not normally have accepted her offer, but I found the Holy Spirit urging me, "This is the key to the Soviet Union." I accepted her invitation and later that evening a car arrived to take me to their house.

As I ate dinner that evening in their beautiful home outside Amsterdam, I learned that the woman who'd invited me was married to Ernst van Eeghen, a Dutch businessman who owned one hundred fourteen corporations in Holland and the Soviet Union. He held several Dutch consular titles and was a born-again Christian.

As I learned about this, I was all but overwhelmed. I had accepted the invitation to dine with them knowing nothing about their wealth or social status, or of their involvement in Russia. I'd come only out of obedience to the Lord, and the realization that He was using that moment to make possible the fulfillment of the Word He'd declared to me as I was praying that day in Moscow left me several times on the verge of tears.

Ernst noticed the look on my face. "Is there something wrong with the food?"

"No. It's just that, while we were sitting here talking, the Holy Spirit revealed to me that you are going to be a major key to revival in Russia."

He looked over at his wife. "You told him?"

"No," she assured him. "I told him nothing."

As our conversation continued I learned that Van Eeghen had used his business influence in the Soviet Union to host several human rights conferences. Those gatherings, which came to be known as Berkenrode Consultations—a name derived from the title of the estate where the Van Eeghens lived—addressed a number of key issues affecting Soviet relations with the West. Along the way, Van Eeghen had become one of the most influential Westerners in the Soviet Union.

What Van Eeghen thought his wife had told me was almost exactly what I had said to him. "God told me," he explained, "that my ministry is to open up the Soviet Union for the gospel."

As we talked, he told me about a time when the head of the KGB had come to his house in great distress. "He said to me, 'I can't get the blood off my hands. I've scrubbed and scrubbed, but I can't get the blood of the innocent off my hands.'"

Ernst explained that only the blood of Jesus could cleanse his hands and then led the leader of the KGB to Christ. He showed me a letter he had received from the man filled with questions about the meaning of Scripture. The born-again KGB leader was used mightily as an instrument of God to help a number of ministries obtain permits to enter the Soviet Union.

Through our conversation that night, Ernst van Eeghen became involved in our effort to bring as many Jews as possible from Russia to Israel. The underground church distributed literature telling Soviet Jews about the opportunities that awaited them in Israel and instructing them how to apply for travel documents. And with the help of Van Eeghen's contacts at the Dutch Embassy, their visas and passports were approved without a glitch. Together, we helped thousands find freedom and safety and watched while God fulfilled His word.

✦ ✦ ✦

Striving to help Russian Jews return to Israel was a highlight of our work in the Soviet Union, but it wasn't the end. In 1985, I felt prompted by God to produce a television special based on my book *Let My People Go.* One of the people highlighted in that production was the Russian dissident Natan Sharansky.

Sharansky was born to a Jewish family in Donetsk, a city in Ukraine. He was a child chess prodigy and graduated from Moscow Institute of Physics and Technology with a degree in Applied Mathematics. After graduation, he applied for an exit visa to travel to Israel but was denied permission to leave the country. Authorities supported their decision by asserting that he had been exposed to information that was vital to Soviet security and thus could not be permitted to travel outside the country.

After his exit visa was denied, Sharansky became involved in the protest movement, becoming a founding member of the Moscow Helsinki Group—one of the Refuseniks, a group of young Soviets who'd been denied travel permission. In 1978, he was convicted of spying for the United States and sentenced to thirteen years in prison. He served time in several penal facilities.

Sharansky's wife, Avital, had been permitted to leave the Soviet Union and while he was incarcerated she traveled throughout the West working to keep Sharansky's story and the plight of Soviet Jews always before the public. She lobbied leaders at every level of government to help gain his release and even published her own book giving an account of their life and work among dissident Russian Jews. I was well aware of their situation and wanted to help.

My goal for the television project was to use it to acquire one million signatures on a petition calling for Sharansky's release. I intended to present that petition to President Reagan in an effort to enlist his help in freeing Sharansky. He and Soviet leader Mikhail Gorbachev enjoyed a sometimes tense but quite personable relationship. I thought that if Reagan pressed for Sharansky's release, Gorbachev might just let him go.

We created a script and sent crews all over the world to obtain footage for the show, then purchased television time to air it in every major market around the United States. Viewers responded enthusiastically and we accomplished our goal. I presented the petition with well over a million signatures to President Reagan and asked him to help. He agreed and, after an intense effort, Sharansky was released.

When he arrived at the Ben Gurion Airport near Tel Aviv, Sharansky phoned President Reagan to thank him for his help. I was glad to have helped, though I wasn't the only one and perhaps not the most important. Still, I know God had determined in His heart to set Sharansky free, and my participation was part of that.

✦ ✦ ✦

After Soviet authorities began issuing exit visas for Jews to return to Israel, and after Sharansky had been released, I sensed the Holy Spirit telling me that I would preach in the Kremlin Palace. I was astounded by what I heard but certain the voice I heard in my spirit was indeed the voice of the Lord.

The Moscow Kremlin is a vast complex that includes five palaces, four cathedrals, and many other buildings. It sits atop Borovitsky Hill, a strategic location that has been occupied since the eleventh century and has been the seat of power, more or less, since that time. Today, the Grand Kremlin Palace, the largest building in the complex, is the official residence of the Russian Federation president. However, it is little used as a residence and its five reception halls are rented out for special events. I intended to hold an event in one of those halls.

In addition to having many historic buildings, the Kremlin has come to be the home of the Russian government. During the Soviet era, it was the site where Communist leaders cursed God and vowed to bury America. It is the site from which various leaders issued edicts and decrees that resulted in the persecution of the Jews, the church, and imposed limitations on personal freedom suffered by many, including Natan Sharansky and the Refuseniks.

In obedience to what I'd heard from the Holy Spirit, I flew to Moscow and applied for permission to hold a meeting in one of the Kremlin Palace's reception halls. I was turned down seventeen times, but on the eighteenth time, they said yes.

We advertised the event as an Easter musical, hired an orchestra, and located a ballet company that was interested in performing. As a way of saying thank you to the underground church, I invited them to attend and made sure a place was available for those who came.

On the night of the event, every seat in the palace hall was filled. The orchestra played magnificently. The dancers performed beautifully. And then I preached—it was Easter, God said I would preach, so I preached. As I spoke that evening I said, "Stalin is dead. Lenin is dead. But Jesus Christ is alive."

You can imagine, those words did not sit well with the palace guards. When I continued, they attempted to remove me from the stage. They quickly saw that would produce a major incident so they cut the electrical power to the microphone and turned out the lights in the room where we met.

Inspired by the Holy Spirit, I shouted, "Those who have shut off the lights and microphone do not respect your president! I was about to pray for him." Seconds later, power was restored to the microphone and lights in the room came back on.

It was a marvelous evening—as Easter should be. Not only did God permit me to proclaim the gospel in the Grand Kremlin Palace, He also arranged to have it aired on Moscow's Channel One, at that time the largest network in Russia. Its viewership included more than 125,000,000 people in eleven time zones, which made it also one of the largest networks in the world. We aired the event live during prime time that evening, and then rebroadcast it a few days later. That was the first time anyone had ever proclaimed the gospel in the Grand Kremlin Palace, held an altar call, and had it aired live over Russian television. God certainly does the impossible!

CHAPTER
27

One year, we had invited my father to Texas for Thanksgiving, but I knew we couldn't have him at the house. As it turned out, circumstances were such that we had to postpone his trip.

I phoned Dad to tell him and, as I expected, he didn't take it well. Just like when I was a child, he screamed and ranted, calling me a liar and a phony. "You moron," he chided. "Now what am I supposed to do? You screwed up my Thanksgiving!" I let him say whatever he wanted but held firm on my resolve that he couldn't come to the house, and the call ended as badly as it had begun.

For a week after that, I endured the "slings and arrows of outrageous fortune"[44] flung at me by the consummate liar, Satan himself.

And then I got mad. That's when I began to pray. God's answer was not at all what I expected.

I thought God would comfort me while I complained. Instead, He said very plainly, "So, the Enemy is doing exactly what he is supposed to do. Why don't you do something about it? Don't get mad—get even. Take control of the situation."

As I thought about His answer, I prayed, and God reminded me of a scripture He'd given me years before. As with many others, this one was from Isaiah, too.

"Arise, shine; for your light has come! And the glory of the Lord is risen upon you. For behold, the darkness shall cover the earth, and deep darkness the people; but the Lord will arise over you, and His glory will be seen upon you. The Gentiles shall come to your light, and kings to the brightness of your rising. Lift up your eyes all around, and see: They all gather together, they come to you; your sons shall come from afar, and your daughters shall be nursed at your side."[45]

Having reminded me again of that passage, I knew God would honor it in my life, but like many other scriptures He'd given me, this one was quite general in its application. It could apply to a broad context. I needed to know what He meant on a practical level, and so I asked. The response He gave was even more astounding and incisive than His admonition to take control of the situation.

As clearly as I've ever heard Him, the Holy Spirit said, "Go to Saudi Arabia, defend Israel, and preach My Word."

Go to Saudi Arabia? I'm Jewish. Saudis are Arabs. And not just Arabs but Muslims. And not merely Muslim but Wahhabi, one of the strictest, most orthodox of all Sunni Muslim groups.

"I can't go to Saudi Arabia," I argued. "Billy Graham hasn't even been there. And I'm Jewish. They cut off the heads of Jews in Saudi Arabia."

The Lord replied, "Billy never applied for a visa. Apply."

I drove down to a visa processing service and applied for a visa to Saudi Arabia—never for a moment thinking my request would be approved. One week later the visa arrived at our house.

After all that had happened in my life, one might expect that I would have realized God was at work. And, having come to that realization, that I would repent of my attitude, align my actions with God's actions, and rejoice. Instead, I continued to argue.

"Okay," I said. "I have a visa. But I have no invitation to speak. No meetings scheduled. And no other reason to go." I didn't even know a single person who lived there.

In response to all of that, God was surprisingly silent and in that silence all I heard was the memory of His voice when He told me to go. And that's when I knew beyond question that I had no choice but to obey Him.

With visa in hand, I quickly made flight arrangements and, just two weeks later, I climbed aboard a British Airways flight for Saudi

Arabia. Twenty hours later, I landed in Dhahran, a Saudi Arabian city on the Persian Gulf. I was exhausted.

After clearing customs I took a taxi to the Gulf Meridian Hotel in Al Khobar, checked in to a room, and collapsed on the bed. "Father," I prayed. "Here I am. Now what?"

When I looked up, I saw a Saudi telephone book sitting on the nightstand beside the bed. I opened it and randomly flipped through the pages. I can't read a word of Arabic, but the book fell open to a page with an advertisement for the *Dhahran Hotel*. The advertisement was written in English. And once more God said, "Go."

Suddenly energized, I ran into the bathroom, splashed some water on my face, and combed my hair. Then I re-tucked my shirt, straightened my jacket, and raced downstairs to the concierge. Minutes later, I was seated in a taxi for the ride to the Dhahran Hotel.

As we arrived at the lobby entrance, I saw a banner draped across the front of the hotel that read Joint Operation Command. I grinned from ear to ear. The hotel was headquarters for US forces being assembled to liberate Kuwait from Saddam Hussein and his Republican Guard. The army's effort was still part of Desert Shield. The Gulf War—code named Desert Storm—was still months away.

In addition to housing the Army Command, the hotel also was headquarters for television networks that were covering the war. Americans were everywhere.

Without a moment's hesitation, I climbed from the taxi, tucked my Bible under my arm, and started through the hotel lobby entrance. I stopped the first official-looking person I met, stuck out my hand, and said, "How are you?"

The man—an American—looked at me in horror. "Who are you? And what on earth are you doing with that Bible?"

"I'm Mike Evans," I replied. "I'm from the United States."

"You can't be," he muttered in a tone of disbelief.

"But I am."

"Then you're going to jail."

I frowned. "Why? I just got here."

"Christian ministers are not allowed into the country. How did you get here?"

"British Airlines," I smiled. "They have flights in here three times a week."

His tone changed and his demeanor became all business. "Go back to your hotel," he directed. "Pack your belongings. And be out of here within forty-eight hours. If you aren't gone by then, you will go to jail."

He seemed so certain, I began to think maybe he was right—maybe I would go to jail. Perhaps God's will for me was to preach in prison like Paul. Or maybe I was mistaken in what I thought I was supposed to do. Maybe I wasn't supposed to be there at all. Or maybe just not at that hotel.

Perplexed by what the man said, and with no other plan to follow, I made my way back to the hotel lobby door and stepped outside. A few minutes later, a taxi arrived and I climbed into the back seat. I gave the taxi driver directions back to my hotel and began to pray.

En route, we passed in front of a gate at the headquarters compound for the Eighty-Second Airborne—the army unit my friend Jim and I had wanted to join when we enlisted as teenagers almost thirty years earlier. I ordered the driver to stop and got out, then paid for the ride and walked over to the gate. A guard stepped out to meet me.

"I need to speak to the chaplain," I told the guard.

"Who are you?"

"I'm Mike Evans from Dallas."

The guard looked as puzzled as the man at the hotel. "How did you get here?"

"British Airways," I again replied. If they could ask silly questions, I could give silly answers.

"You, sir, will go to jail."

"I've already been told that. Now, may I please speak to the chaplain?"

A flurry of phone calls followed, but eventually the guard let me enter and directed me to the chaplain's office. The chaplain, however, gave me the same response as everyone else. "I don't know how in the world you got here. What do you want?"

Later I learned that chaplains assigned to the US military in Muslim countries were not allowed to wear crosses on their uniforms. Nor did they walk around with a Bible tucked under their arm. In fact, they weren't even called chaplains. Instead, they went by titles like Recreational and Motivational Coordinator. I didn't know that when I first arrived. I just knew God told me to go to Saudi Arabia. So in response to the chaplain's question I said, "I want to speak to the troops."

He shook his head in wonder. "Well, I'll call them together for you and then I'm leaving."

From that day until the day I flew back to Texas, I was privileged to preach to our troops stationed in Saudi Arabia. It was both humbling and encouraging to know that God was using me to minister to men and women serving so far from home and in such precarious circumstances.

✦ ✦ ✦

One day, while riding through the streets of Dhahran, I noticed a group of soldiers gathered on a street corner. I stopped the cab, paid the fare, and climbed out. Though I'd been warned many times about openly sharing the gospel, I walked over to the group, turned to a passage of Scripture, and began to preach.

From behind me I heard a beautiful baritone voice singing "His Eye Is On the Sparrow." I turned to see an army sergeant from the

United States and stopped what I was doing to listen. Tears streamed down my face as he sang and soon the other men joined him.

At the conclusion of the song, they began to share testimonies of God's grace and protection. It was a magnificent display of God's presence and several of the men that day gave their lives to Christ.

As we talked and prayed, a military policeman appeared. He pushed his way into the center of our gathering and glanced warily in my direction. "What are you doing? It's against the law to preach in public. We can take you to jail."

"That's fine," I said. "Do whatever you have to do. Everyone tells me I'm going there anyway." The officer wasn't amused but he didn't arrest me, either.

✦ ✦ ✦

When I returned to my hotel that evening, I wanted nothing more than a shower to wash away the dust and grime of the sand-covered streets. I was hot and tired, and my bed with cool, clean sheets was calling my name.

As I walked through the lobby though, I saw members of the Kuwaiti royal family gathered in one of the lounges. They'd been forced out of Kuwait when the Iraqi army invaded. Most of them had taken up residence in Saudi Arabia. Their presence in the lounge surprised me but I was further stunned when one of the young men from their gathering left the others and hurried in my direction.

"I know you." He grinned as he reached me. "You're a friend of Yasser Arafat. I saw you with him in Geneva."

The irony of the situation was not lost on me. True, I had been with Arafat in Geneva, but he and I were not at all on friendly terms. I was about to laugh at the young man's remark when the Holy Spirit nudged me. Rather than refuting his assertion, I found myself saying, "You will soon be going home. This war will be short and with little bloodshed. You will regain your country and when you do, you must give the glory to Jesus."

"Are you a prophet?"

"No, I am not. But this is a word to you from God."

The young man leaned away and looked at me intently. "If this prophecy comes to pass, you shall be a guest of the royal family in Kuwait." I smiled, shook his hand, and continued on my way toward the elevator.

That night as I lay in bed, thinking about the events of the day and about the young man I'd seen in the lobby, the Enemy once again attacked me. *"You are going to jail. You are doomed. They will hide you away in there and you'll never get out. You had better just pack up and go home now."*

As I prayed and rebuked Satan, the Holy Spirit spoke to me. "Return to the Dhahran Hotel. Speak to the first person you see and ask if you can go with him."

The next morning I took a taxi to the Dhahran Hotel and entered the lobby. As I entered, a man was coming toward me. He was an Arab, about six feet tall, with short black hair and dressed in a Saudi Arabian military uniform. From the insignia I could see he was a four-star general.

As the Lord had instructed me, I stuck out my hand and said, "Can I go with you?"

The man shook my hand and stared at me with a puzzled expression. When he didn't respond, I repeated my question. "May I go with you?"

"What is your name?"

"Mike Evans."

"And you are from where?"

"The United States of America."

His demeanor changed. "Be here tomorrow at 0600 and you shall go with me."

The next morning I stood outside the hotel at 0545. At precisely 0600 a dozen vehicles drove up and in the fourth jeep was a four-star general, Prince Khalid, the man whose hand I had shaken the day before. I was waved inside and sat down beside General Khalid.

As the jeep started forward, General Khalid glanced down at my lap. A Bible rested there and he looked up at me. "Are you a Christian?"

"Yes," I replied. "I am a minister."

"We behead ministers every Thursday. Would you like to go there with me, too?"

"I'm busy Thursday," I answered.

A grin broke over General Khalid's face. "I like you."

That morning, General Khalid took me by helicopter up to the Kuwait border where we met the Syrian High Command and the leaders of the Egyptian Third Army. I listened while they briefed Khalid on their invasion operations.

When the briefing concluded, Khalid asked me to accompany him as he inspected the troops. I had no idea what I was supposed to do and turned to one of the men in the entourage. "What do I do?"

Because I was an American, the man thought I was from the Defense Department and assigned to General Khalid in an official capacity. He also thought I was aware of his own assignment and therefore kept no secrets from me. From him I learned details about Operation Bright Star, a joint US–Egyptian exercise that took on added significance with the approaching 1991 Gulf War.

Later that day we joined the military leaders for lunch. Surprisingly when Prince Khalid introduced me, he became my interpreter, as I was able to share a short presentation of the gospel with him and the soldiers.

After lunch, Prince Khalid asked me what was next on my agenda and I replied that I wanted to speak to the troops in the field. He called in a French Foreign Legion helicopter to take me to minister to the men and women who had dug in on the front line.

Several years after that trip to the Persian Gulf and my meeting with Prince Khalid, I preached a crusade in the Philippines. A trio of Filipino pastors greeted me warmly after the meeting and one even began to cry. I hadn't preached well enough to bring tears to anyone's eyes, so I asked why he was crying. Shocked that I didn't know, one of the other men told me they had been in jail in Dhahran—condemned to be beheaded for preaching the gospel. One day, their cell doors opened and they were told they could leave. It seems one Prince Khalid had arranged for their freedom. The Filipino pastor was weeping because he knew what I'd never known—that my witness to Prince Khalid had saved their lives.

✦ ✦ ✦

Shortly before I left Saudi Arabia to return to Texas, God spoke to me that I should go to Iraq to comfort the suffering. He said, "Take food and medicine to the Kurdish people who have been targeted by Saddam Hussein."

I assembled a group and we made the trip, passing out supplies while doctors treated the sick. In the middle of a field, I preached to the refugees day and night for a week. Finally my strength was gone and I was almost too hoarse to speak.

Gathering all the strength I had left, I tried to think of a topic for my last sermon before our departure. Then I heard that still, small voice of the Lord instructing me to preach on Jonah and Nineveh.

I did the best I could, telling how Jonah rebelled against God but finally went to Nineveh. And I told of the king's repentance and the revival that broke out because of Jonah's obedience. When I asked if anyone wanted to come to Christ, only one person responded—an old man in a dusty robe. I was as disappointed by the lack of response as Jonah had been. My interpreter noticed my reaction and asked with concern, "Why aren't you rejoicing?"

"I'm happy for one soul, but I was hoping for more."

"My dear brother," the interpreter said, "the one who just found Jesus is the king of Nineveh.[46] He is the Kurdish sheik of sixteen provinces and the capital is the site of ancient Nineveh. He has accepted Jesus and has invited you to go to Nineveh, because he believes if you will preach, they will repent."

Truly, "to obey is better than sacrifice."[47]

CHAPTER
28

As I noted earlier, troop buildup for the US-led effort to liberate Kuwait from Iraqi occupation was known as Operation Desert Shield. It began in August 1990. The actual invasion of Kuwait—Operation Desert Storm—did not begin until January 1991. And although Saddam Hussein had threatened a long and bloody war, fighting was over and the Iraqi army defeated by the end of February that same year, barely a month and a half after fighting commenced.

At the end of the war, the United States enjoyed substantial goodwill in the Middle East, particularly among Arab nations located around the Persian Gulf. President George H. W. Bush, who by then had succeeded Ronald Reagan in the White House, saw the moment as an opportunity to accomplish something no one else had been able to achieve—a lasting peace between Arabs and Israelis in Palestine.

In an effort to further that desire, Bush announced the peace process—an on-again, off-again effort conducted by US presidents at least since the Carter administration—would begin yet again, this time at a conference in Madrid, Spain. The conference was scheduled for October 30 through November 1, 1991.

Though with perhaps the best of intentions, the Bush plan for peace was little more than a warmed-over version of every other plan put forward by the West to solve the problems in Palestine—plans that shifted the burden of peace to Israel, calling for her to give up large portions of her territory. The arrogance of the West telling Israel how to solve its problems made me angry. None of the other major powers of the world would allow another country to dictate the terms of their policies. Yet they saw no problem with telling Israel the great price it must pay for a peace pleasing to nations that had not the slightest care for Israel's future.

Not only that, much of the territory controlled by Israel was won as the result of a war initiated by the Arabs—a war that ended badly for the Palestinians. Now they wanted the lost territory back and they wanted the nations of the world to force Israel to return it. I've often wondered if things had gone the other way—if Israel had lost ground allotted to it by the UN—would the nations of the world require the Arabs to return it to Israel? I doubt it.

When I learned of the gathering in Madrid, I remembered that conversation I'd heard at the restaurant in Geneva. *"We should have Jerusalem in your hands by '96—at the very latest by 2000. We're certain we can get you a good piece of Israel by then, too."* That plan, it seemed, was going forward and I knew Israel needed someone to stand in her defense.

As I mulled over what I should do, God again gave me a word from Scripture. Like many others, this one, too, was from Isaiah.

For Zion's sake I will not hold My peace, and for Jerusalem's sake I will not rest, until her righteousness goes forth as brightness, and her salvation as a lamp that burns. The Gentiles shall see your righteousness, and all kings your glory. You shall be called by a new name, which the mouth of the Lord will name. You shall also be a crown of glory in the hand of the Lord, and a royal diadem in the hand of your God.[48]

Acting in faith on that Word, I made plans to attend the conference. As with the UN session in Geneva, I had no invitation, no recognized international credentials, and no official status as a diplomat or adviser. Still, I was convinced I should be there and equally certain that God would make a way.

One of our ministry partners, Dr. Bob Skinner, joined me for the trip. Together we boarded a plane in Dallas and flew to Spain. As we went, we prayed that God would open the doors He wished for us to enter. The specifics of what we were to do at the conference were still unclear, but somewhere over the Atlantic, God infused us with the gift of faith to accomplish the task—whatever that task might be and however it might unfold.

In preparation for the trip, my assistant had discovered the name of the hotel where many of the conference delegates were staying. When Bob and I landed in Madrid, we went directly to that hotel and managed to secure a room. Already, it seemed, God had done the seemingly impossible. We had a room at a hotel that was central to the conference and were rubbing elbows in the lobby with ambassadors, secretaries of state, and other diplomatic officials. With an afternoon free, I used the time to witness to them about the Lord.

A few hours after we arrived, I learned that Mikhail Gorbachev, president of the Soviet Union, and Yitzhak Shamir, prime minister of Israel, were going to meet at the Soviet Embassy. This would be the first time the leader of the Soviet Union would meet with the leader of Israel. If it happened, it would be an historic moment and I knew I needed to be there. So I hired a taxi and rode over there from the hotel.

The complex included a tall white building surrounded by a fence twelve feet high and made of wrought iron. A gate blocked access to the driveway, so the taxi stopped at the street. I paid the driver and climbed from the back seat.

A light rain was falling as I stepped out, which made the temperature feel even cooler. I ignored the weather, walked over to the gate, and called out in a loud voice, "Who is in charge here?"

A guard approached. "I am in charge," he answered with a thick Russian accent. His eyes focused on me with an intense look, and the muscles along his jaw flexed with tension, but I wasn't backing down. "Please open this gate and let me inside."

The guard glanced at me, apparently looking for the usual visible identification, then said, "You have no credentials." He was right, of course. I had no official credentials as a delegate to the conference or as a member of the permanent press corps. There was no lanyard around my neck with a picture ID hanging from it and nothing pinned to my lapel. I held no office as a minister of any nation represented in that meeting. I was not an ambassador nor did I have an official invitation.

My only authority had come from God's directive. I knew God had sent me, so I instinctively held up my Bible—as a standard practice I carried it with me everywhere I went. "Here are my credentials."

The guard looked disdainfully at my Bible, stuck his nose in the air, and turned to walk away. "Come back here," I ordered in an authoritative tone.

When he turned toward me I pointed through the fence and said sternly, "In the name of Jesus, whom I serve and who has sent me, open this gate and let me inside!"

In robotic fashion, the Russian walked over to a control panel near the gate and pressed a button. Seconds later, the gate swung open.

God had acted and I didn't hesitate. When the gate was open wide enough for me to squeeze past, I hurried onto the embassy grounds and started toward the main building.

A few minutes later, I was ushered into the very room where Gorbachev and Shamir were to meet. I remained there throughout their discussion, praying for God to pour out His wisdom and courage on Shamir, and His grace and mercy on Gorbachev.

✦ ✦ ✦

Official sessions of the conference were held at the royal palace, located in downtown Madrid. It was a beautiful location from an aesthetic perspective, but I couldn't help seeing the glamour as little more than a disguise for the actual purpose of the gathering, which was to wrest more land in Palestine from the Jews and give it to the Arabs. Land for peace, they called it. The only problem was, the Arabs didn't want peace. They wanted Israel and the Jews gone, and the so-called land for peace initiative was simply an attempt to nibble away at Israel's territory.

As the meetings progressed, I spent most of the time praying. During one of the sessions, I gazed up at a fresco on the ceiling above the grand Hall of Columns. Painted in a magnificent hand, it portrayed an array of false gods. Apollo, Aurora, Zephyrus, Ceres, Bacchus, Diana, Pan, and Galatea. From their lofty perch, they looked down on the proceedings—false gods watching over a gathering that searched for a false peace. The symmetry of the moment seemed somehow altogether fitting. False gods, false peace, and the smugness of those gathered to pursue it. Like the apostle Paul at Mars Hill, I found myself praying to the one true God while under this canopy of idolatry.

As I prayed, the irony of the moment became even more apparent. Israel had been forced to attend the meeting, strong-armed by the United States to endure yet one more international peace conference. And this one was in Spain, of all places, where one-third of the Jewish population had been massacred during the Inquisition.

Day after day, I watched as representatives from nation after nation mounted the podium to insult Israel. Accusing her of innumerable atrocities, all of that as false as the gods on the ceiling, and to demand that her leaders give up the majority of her land. I can still hear their voices as they reverberated through the marble halls. "We will accept your land in exchange for peace."

What they really were saying was, "This is a stick-up. Give us all your land and you won't get hurt—much." One tends to think of a mugging as something that happens on the streets of a major city. Yet the Madrid Peace Conference, by any measure, was an international mugging of Israel. And the West was the silent witness, too timid to intervene and too intimidated to report it for what it was. Like most of the nations represented there, even the United States pretended not to see the gun pointed menacingly at Israel's head.

On the second day, I found myself in the midst of Israel's first press conference and I was astonished to see Deputy Foreign Minister Benjamin Netanyahu presiding. The young man I had anointed all those years before was now a polished speaker and an effective representative of his homeland.

Only sixty observers were allowed inside the room where he spoke, and I was seated in a chair on the front row. When Netanyahu finished his prepared remarks, he asked for questions from the press corps. I offered several that pointed to the critical issue of Jerusalem, perhaps the most intractable problem of the two-state peace plan. My initial question led to a statement and as I continued to speak, Netanyahu handed me the microphone. My statements affirming God's plan and purpose for Jerusalem—as documented in the Bible—were covered by the world press.

✦ ✦ ✦

During a break from one of the sessions, the Syrian foreign minister showed me a photograph of Yitzhak Shamir. The picture had been taken when Shamir was part of Irgun, an Israeli paramilitary organization active in the years long before statehood was achieved. The Syrians intended to use the picture the next day to accuse the prime minister of being a terrorist. When our conversation ended, I borrowed a cell phone and called Netanyahu to tell him what I had learned.

The next day was Friday, the final day of the conference. All of the heads of state were present, including President Bush and President Gorbachev. As they watched, Shamir stood and announced to the gathering, "I have to leave now. I am an Orthodox Jew and must return to Israel before sundown to observe the Sabbath. However, I leave these proceedings in the hands of my able delegation that will carry on without me."

Thirty minutes after he departed, the Syrian foreign minister stood to speak, intending to confront the Israeli prime minister face-to-face. Instead, he faced only an empty chair where Shamir had sat. With Shamir no longer in attendance, and the photograph obviously fifty years old, the Syrian's remarks came off as petty and mean-spirited—which is precisely the way reporters wrote about it. The incident that had been designed as the final and determinative accusation against Israel instead became a final word against the Arab argument. I was glad to have been there and thrilled to have participated in thwarting the Syrian minister's plans.

✦ ✦ ✦

Throughout the conference, the favor of God rested on me as I found myself in every session, admitted to rooms where others were excluded, privileged to speak to heads of state and diplomatic officials without credential or invitation. To my knowledge I was the only minister of the gospel present for those meetings and I did not shy away from using the access I had been granted. Nor did I retreat from asserting my position as a spokesman for the Kingdom of God.

At the conclusion of one session, the Egyptian foreign minister and the Syrian secretary of state met me in the hall and asked if I was a minister. "Yes," I replied. "I am." I knew what they meant, but after all I'd seen God do for me and through me, I wasn't going to let them maneuver me around with clever questions.

The Egyptian asked, "From what country?"

"The Kingdom," I responded.

He had a puzzled look. "Are you Semitic?"

"Yes."

"From what kingdom?"

"The Kingdom of God."

The Syrian minister chuckled. "It must be a very small country."

"No," I said. "It is much larger than yours. In fact," I added, gesturing to them, "it would swallow up both of your countries."

They laughed but I was serious, and while they were laughing I looked the Egyptian foreign minister in the eye and said, "Will you obey the words of your most distinguished prime minister and secretary of state?"

His laughter faded and the puzzled look returned. "Egypt has never had a person who was both prime minister and secretary of state. If we had such a man, I would certainly obey his words."

Then I told him the story of Joseph from the Old Testament, especially the part about how he forgave his brothers for selling him into slavery and how he later rose to the most influential positions in the Egyptian government. "Joseph was both prime minister and secretary of state of Egypt," I explained. "And yet he forgave and embraced his brothers. Will you do the same?"

Both men abruptly walked away.

✦ ✦ ✦

Perhaps the most important press conference I attended was held by US Secretary of State James Baker. Although the room was filled with press representatives from around the globe, the Lord granted me favor and I was able to ask the first question.

"Why does America continue to refuse to recognize Jerusalem as Israel's capital? Wouldn't such recognition be a gesture toward peace?"

Baker lost no time in replying, "That is a matter that we think should be determined by negotiations. That has long been the policy position of the United States and I'm not going to engage in a debate with you or anybody else about specific policy issues or specific US positions. That is not really the issue here. The issue is whether Arabs and Israelis can begin to talk in a way that can resolve these very, very difficult and fundamental differences."

My second question was about offering military assistance to Israel, in light of the price Israel paid in lives and property during the

Gulf War. During that war, the Iraqi army launched numerous Scud missiles into Israeli territory. At the urging of the Bush administration, Israel had heroically refrained from retaliating; a move the United States feared would fracture the coalition of allies fighting against Iraq and rephrase the war as Arab versus Israeli. As you might expect, Baker conveniently ignored my question.

✦ ✦ ✦

Throughout the conference, scriptures rolled through my mind and into my spirit. I was reminded that in the last days, the Bible tells us Israel will become the center of world attention, though her problems would defy human resolution. I thought of Zechariah's prophecy about Jerusalem, under siege by all the nations of the world, yet described by him as an immovable rock. Surely I was seeing the precursor of those events, and yet Jerusalem remained.

That week I had many opportunities to ask questions at press conferences and to address world leaders. They kept saying over and over, "Israel is not the Promised Land, and the Bible has nothing to do with this issue." To which I repeatedly responded, "You are wrong. God will have the final word."

On the flight home, I couldn't help but think about how an abused little boy from the wrong side of the tracks had found himself in the presence of presidents and kings in a palace in Madrid, Spain. And I was amazed at how God's great plan for my life continued to unfold.

CHAPTER

29

God's plan for my life has included sharing His Word in places few would dare even go, much less preach the gospel. Places like the Soviet Union during the 1970s persecution of the underground church. War-torn Lebanon of the 1980s. Somalia in the 1990s during the week of the Somalia Civil War that saw an attack on a US 101st Airborne's Blackhawk helicopter. Cuba long before normalization. And the Democratic Republic of the Congo during the massacre in neighboring Rwanda. As with the apostle Paul, I heard the Macedonian call[49] and could not refuse to answer.

When God directed me to a worldwide ministry, the same old doubts and fears I'd wrestled with other times in my life assailed me once again. In response, I opened my Bible and began to read. As I read, I spoke the Word out loud, repeating verses like, "Greater is he that is in you, than he that is in the world."[50]

None of us fully comprehend what God will do to change the world. This became apparent one day as I prayed and God told me that He wanted me to preach in Third World countries—undeveloped nations whose lifestyle falls far below that of the West and who lack meaningful participation in the current globalized economic system. Since money isn't plentiful in those countries, I reminded God that I would need a way to cover travel and crusade expenses.

"How much do you need?" He asked.

"About a hundred thousand dollars," I replied.

"Is that all?"

I felt a bit like Abraham bargaining for Sodom and Gomorrah.[51] How much would be enough, but not seem too much? "I'd have to put pencil to paper to get an exact figure," I replied. "So make it two hundred fifty thousand. That should be enough."

"Is that really all you will need?"

"Well," I shrugged. "Half a million, then."

"Is that all?"

"Okay, let's round it off and make it a million."

Years before, when we still were living in the thirty-two-foot trailer, I circled the verse from Philippians, "And my God will meet all your needs according to the riches of his glory in Christ Jesus."[52]

Our income that year had been four thousand dollars. As I prayed about ministry in developing countries, I remembered that verse and felt a surge of faith, as if God had activated that scripture in my spirit.

"So be it. But don't reveal this to anyone. Don't ask for it and don't tell anyone the need."

I was flabbergasted. "Don't tell anybody?"

"That is the condition for getting the million dollars. Don't tell anyone and don't ask anyone."

Not long after that, I was seated at my desk when my secretary came to the door of my office and said, "There's a woman on the phone who wants you to pray for her."

As a matter of general practice, it's impossible for me to personally pray with everyone who calls our ministry. The call volume is simply too high. But rather than simply fielding prayer requests and praying for them en masse, we have a team of intercessors who actually pray with callers. That day, however, the Holy Spirit impressed on me that I should pray with this particular person, and so I agreed to take the call. The woman's name was Madeline Chaffin.

The following week Mrs. Chaffin phoned again. This time, she asked if Carolyn and I would have dinner with her. The Holy Spirit whispered, "Say yes," so I did, although I still had no idea who she was or why she wanted to meet with us.

On the appointed day, Carolyn and I met Mrs. Chaffin at a restaurant in one of Dallas's distinguished hotels. As we were seated at our table, she smiled and said, "I know you must wonder why I asked you here for dinner—especially since we've never met."

"Yes," I admitted. "I've been rather curious about that."

"My husband is a very wealthy man, and he's placed me in charge of our charitable giving. As I was praying about what to do, the Holy Spirit told me to call several ministries—I had a list of the ones I was interested in working with. When I called, I was to ask the head of each of those ministries two questions. The first was, 'Will you pray with me?' and the second was, 'Will you share a meal with me?'

"So I picked up the phone and called the first one on my list. It was a very large ministry, but I couldn't get through to the leader. Then I called another and I couldn't get the leader of that one on the phone, either. Finally, I called your office and you prayed for me. When I called back later and asked, 'Will you have a meal with me?' you said you would. So I'm going to give you a million dollars."

As I sat there in stunned silence, I heard God whisper, "It pays to listen to the voice of the Spirit. Now you have the funds for the overseas crusades." And that isn't the only lesson I have learned about God's miraculous provision...

✦ ✦ ✦

Sometime after that, the door opened to minister in Cuba before the ban was placed on travel to that country. I was delighted to have the opportunity to further expand our reach into developing nations.

We gathered a ministry team, made arrangements for travel and lodging, and flew from Dallas to Miami, then on to Havana.

One night as I walked to the field to preach at a crusade, I failed to see a concrete arch across the walkway. It was dark and the arch was only about six feet high. I am six inches taller than that and hit it with my forehead. Blood ran down my face and seeped from my ear. I mopped at it with my handkerchief and continued on my way, but my head pounded with pain.

When I reached the platform where I was to speak, the service was just beginning. I took a seat and sat with my eyes closed against the harsh glare of the lights. Later, as I rose to preach and looked out over the crowd, my first thought was, *What a massive crowd.* Then I realized I was seeing double. I don't remember much about the sermon but when I finished the crowd surged forward in response to the invitation to receive Jesus as Lord.

When the meetings in Havana ended, we flew back to Miami and from there to Amsterdam to witness in the city's infamous Red Light District. My head was still pounding, only now it was with a migraine headache. We landed and went to De Wallen, the city's largest Red Light District. There, I asked the team to pray for me—the pain from the migraine was blinding and I was too exhausted to minister.

As we gathered in a circle, holding hands and praying, prostitutes, drug addicts, and homosexuals walked up to see who was in the center of the circle. More and more came until a large crowd of people surrounded us. I don't know how many were saved that night, but it was a miracle.

✦ ✦ ✦

At this point in my life I was no longer taken aback by God's whispered commands. "Go. Preach. Witness. Pray. Bless. Minister." The next different from the last, but each equally important in God's eyes—a wounded soldier, a starving child, a victim of terrorism, a prostitute, a gay man with AIDS—Christ died for all. His love is all-encompassing. And so I was not surprised when the call came during prayer one evening. "Go to the Killing Fields of Cambodia."

This time, instead of wrestling with why or how or should, I simply responded in obedience. We put together a crusade team and prepared to follow God's directive.

As the plane carrying our team descended through the clouds to the airport in Phnom Penh, I was reminded of yet another scripture from Isaiah.

Have you not known? Have you not heard? The everlasting God, the Lord, the Creator of the ends of the earth, neither faints nor is weary. His understanding is unsearchable. He gives power to the weak, and to those who have no might He increases strength. Even the youths shall faint and be weary, and the young men shall utterly fall, but those who wait on the Lord shall renew their strength; they shall mount up with wings like eagles, they shall run and not be weary, they shall walk and not faint.[53]

In the history of Cambodia, no one had ever preached a nationwide crusade. More than two million people had been slaughtered by Pol Pot and his Khmer Rouge followers between 1975 and 1979. It was exceeded in executions only by the Holocaust during World War II.

Before our first night's events, I took a pastor to the stadium at the National Sports Complex and asked, "Do you see this stadium full?"

"No," he said, "there are only eighteen hundred Christians in the whole nation. This stadium may have the capacity to hold forty to sixty thousand. But I see it empty."

"Close your eyes again and pray." We prayed for more than thirty minutes. Then he saw a thousand people in the stadium. We prayed again and as he wept, he said he saw five thousand people. We continued to pray until he could see the stadium packed full. At that moment I said, "Now it's time to have this crusade. Now that you've seen what Jesus sees, the Holy Spirit will empower you and you can do what Jesus did."

Thousands of Buddhists and Khmer Rouge murderers gathered as we proclaimed the message of the gospel. Many of them responded to the message by surrendering to Christ. It was the largest harvest of souls in the history of that nation.

The crusade was so successful, with so many people attending and responding, that the prime minister, a former member of the Khmer

Rouge, and his staff were determined to destroy our efforts. One night he ordered a squad of soldiers to our hotel to keep me from reaching the crusade venue. Then he sent a second group to the meeting to tell those gathered that I was in the hotel sipping tea and eating cookies and that I didn't really care about them. They were told that even though they had sacrificed much to attend, I wasn't interested in them. Some of the people rioted, set all the billboards afire, and came to our hotel armed with AK-47s to try to kill me. There even were threats to dynamite the stadium where we were meeting.

Things got so bad, a US security team stationed in Bangkok, Thailand, was dispatched to get us out. They entered the country dressed as Khmer Rouge soldiers and traveled in older vehicles so as to avoid drawing attention to themselves. When they reached our hotel they escorted us out and drove us to the airport.

In the airport waiting area, we were ordered to sit on the floor, hidden behind a concrete barrier until the planes were ready. Then we made a dash across the tarmac to the planes and they flew us out.

More than ten thousand souls came to know Christ in Cuba, Amsterdam, and Cambodia. Many more were added as we went on to minister in other countries, too. And as we ministered to large crowds, we also trained pastors to follow up with those who responded to our message, to make certain they continued to walk in faith as a member of a congregation.

CHAPTER
30

Although I was committed to follow God wherever He led and however strange that leading might seem to my natural mind, I still didn't understand how that all worked or how I understood what I was supposed to do—how I knew that God was giving me a scripture, as opposed to me giving one to myself. Or how I knew that God was sending me to a particular place or event, even though none of the outward signs indicated I could gain access to those locations or events. Many times when I felt led to go somewhere, I didn't know all that I was supposed to do once I arrived, but even then I knew God would meet me there when I arrived—and He always did.

How that all fit together remained a mystery to me until a conversation with Oral Roberts.[54]

"You operate in the gift of faith," he told me. "You've preached to larger crowds than I. You've spoken to more world leaders than I. You go places and say things about what will happen and actually believe they will happen before you go."

"Yes," I admitted. "I actually do."

"That's the gift of faith, Mike."

That's when I realized the direction God had been giving me actually came from His voice—the same voice I heard that night in my bedroom when I was eleven, only now He communicated with me through my spirit and through scripture. I received those scriptures as an impression on my spirit, a sense that this one applied and not that one. The power, though, came from His voice. He was the One who empowered me, not my manipulating Him. And when He spoke and I responded, His presence was made real and powerful in my life through the gift of faith.

Not long after that conversation with Oral Roberts, I had a dream about a man in Africa. The dream seemed more than merely a dream and I began to pray about a ministry in Africa. After praying about it, we started to work on a preliminary effort to organize a preaching effort there. We worked hard to do that but didn't have much success.

As we continued to pray, I sensed the Holy Spirit directing me to travel to Mexico City, where I was to pray. With nothing more than that simple instruction, I boarded a flight from Dallas, flew down to Mexico, and took a room at a hotel. For the next several days, I prayed.

One morning the Holy Spirit spoke to me, "Go downstairs to the sidewalk outside the hotel. Stand there and wait. Someone will speak to you and that person will have the key to your ministry in Africa."

In obedience to that direction, I left my room, took the elevator to the lobby, and stepped outside to the sidewalk in front of the hotel. A few minutes later, I was surprised to see Maureen Reagan Revell and her husband, Dennis, coming toward me. Maureen was the daughter of President Reagan. They seemed as surprised to see me as I was to see them.

"Mike Evans!" Maureen exclaimed. "What are *you* doing down here?"

"I was wondering if we could talk about Africa."

They seemed taken aback. "How did you know about that?"

"About what?"

As we talked, I learned they had just returned from a fact-finding mission to Africa and were in Mexico City for a few days of rest and relaxation before returning to Washington, D.C. I didn't know that when I boarded the plane in Dallas or when I came down from my room to stand on the sidewalk. I didn't know it, but the Holy Spirit did.

Maureen and Dennis agreed to join me for a meal and we went inside the hotel. As we ate, I related the dream I had about the man in Africa and our interest in developing a ministry there. Based on the description from my dream, Maureen identified the man I'd seen as President Yoweri Museveni of Uganda. Just knowing that much—the name of the person I'd seen and the country—was enough to give focus to our ministry. But that wasn't all. They knew Museveni and had spent time with him just a few days before.

Emboldened by their response and empowered by the Holy Spirit, I asked Dennis and Maureen if they would issue an invitation to Museveni, inviting him to bring his cabinet to meet with me in Washington, D.C. They readily agreed and we made tentative plans for a date and time when the meeting could take place.

With the promise of an invitation for Museveni, I telephoned Ben Armstrong, executive director of the National Religious Broadcasters (NRB).[55] He was both a colleague and a friend and I was certain I could count on his help. I asked Ben if I could invite Museveni to speak to the NRB at one of its regular gatherings. He was eager to help and agreed to my request on the spot.

Six weeks after my conversation with Maureen and Dennis, President Museveni and his cabinet were seated in a hotel suite, with Carolyn and me, and several other leaders. During that meeting, God opened an opportunity for our ministry in the Republic of Uganda.

In preparation for our ministry in Uganda, God's remnant of believers in that country organized prayer teams that prayed earnestly for our meetings. That effort went on for weeks prior to our arrival as they asked God to pour out His spirit in revival on their nation.

We joined them from our offices in Dallas and bathed the ministry in prayers of expectation.

✦ ✦ ✦

The crusade services in Uganda were held at a large soccer field. We set up a platform on one end with seating for special guests and a sound system strong enough to reach the surrounding neighborhood. Prior to our first service I went to the field and surveyed the site. *This is great,* I thought. *God is going to show up and people are going to flock to the meetings.*

The next day, thirty minutes before the gates were to open for our first worship service, the sky darkened and a deluge began. It was one of the worst rainstorms I had ever seen. I ran for cover along with everyone else on our team.

When the rain ended, I walked back to the stage, expecting a crowd to be there. Instead, I saw only about fifty people. All of them were soaked from the rain and they were standing ankle deep in mud. At first I thought they were a hardy group to have braved the weather, then I realized the only reason they had stayed was because they were handicapped in some way and couldn't leave on their own.

This was not what I expected. I looked out at the small group gathered before me, then glanced up at the heavens and whispered, "God, this isn't Your will. You want more people than these few here tonight. What if we cancel the event and try again tomorrow night?"

God's reply was terse and to the point. "It's My will, son. Preach!" And so, I preached.

The second night the crowd was larger and the third night the soccer field was packed with thousands of people. When called to the microphone to preach, I simply held up my Bible and said, "The Word of God is the power of God unto salvation."

Suddenly the people began to shake as if they had been plugged into an electrical charge. As I continued to hold God's Word aloft, they ripped demonic fetishes from around their waists and wrists and threw them into piles all around the field, all while denouncing the powers of darkness. As the piles grew larger, someone touched them with torches, setting them ablaze.

As I stood there, watching the crowd react, I heard the whistle of a train on track outside the field. *That's it,* I thought in relief. *It's the train that's causing the people to shake.* It sounds silly now, but that's what I thought.

From my place on the stage I could see the train and watched as it slowed to a stop, then the conductor jumped from one of the train cars and ran toward the soccer field. When he reached the crowd, he started shaking, too.

Something happened in the spirit realm that brought about this incredible breakthrough. The anointing of Christ was on His Word and His spirit moved among the crowd, convicting and convincing of sin, bringing them to repentance. It was an astonishing thing to see.

So much so that I was afraid to move—even to lay my Bible on the podium—or to say a word. With our own eyes we saw what Isaiah said long ago. "I send it out [His Word], and it always produces fruit. It will accomplish all I want it to, and it will prosper everywhere I send it."[56]

From the meager crowd of those first meetings, revival grew and spread across the country, becoming one of the greatest gospel crusades in Ugandan history. Before our ministry concluded, I had the joy of leading President Museveni to Christ. After his conversion, Museveni publicly challenged Uganda's religious leaders to enter into a born-again experience with Christ and urged them to lead their parishioners into a relationship with Him, too. He implored them to preach against the witch doctors that held many in bondage and to instruct their members to cast off the fetishes they used in an attempt to ward off evil.

✦ ✦ ✦

After we returned from Uganda, the Lord placed on my heart a desire to minister in India, a country that is eighty percent Hindu. I knew it would be a challenge to preach there. Powerful spiritual forces were arrayed against us and the logistics of conducting a week-long preaching crusade in a far-off place posed a daunting task. But when the Lord prompted me to go there, He also gave me a scripture. This one was from Jeremiah. "Call to Me, and I will answer you, and show you great and mighty things, which you do not know."[57]

As I meditated on that verse, the Holy Spirit told me to believe for a total crowd of one million people. "You will see the greatest harvest of souls ever." The response in Uganda had been tremendous and I wondered how we could top it. Not only that, I had never been to India.

As the weeks went by, my flesh seized on those two things—the seeming impossibility of surpassing the response we'd seen in Uganda, and the fact that the people of India did not know me. A voice inside my head said, *They don't know you. They've never even heard your name. No one will show up.*

When I prayed about those concerns and told the Lord about what I heard, He said, "Be grateful they don't know you. It's a blessing. This way, the only Name they will know is Mine."

The night before our first service, I was praying in our hotel room when I saw a vision. Before me was the throne of God. He was seated there with Jesus at His right hand. On the floor before them were hundreds of idols; as I looked at them, Jesus asked, "Whose idols are these?"

I was about to reply, "They're the idols of India," but I stopped short when I saw the names on them. The idols belonged to me! One of them was labeled "pride," another "selfishness." I realized they were things that hindered my relationship with God and my usefulness to Him in ministry.

When the vision ended, I fell forward on my hands and knees and crawled across the floor into the next room. Our daughter Shira was with us, and when she saw me crawling into the room she began to weep. Soon our entire crusade team joined us and we spent the night interceding in prayer, humbling ourselves before Him, praying diligently, and seeking God in repentance.

When I arose from prayer early the next morning, I felt like the most unqualified man in the world to preach, but once again God was faithful. That night I stood before a sea of people and preached about seeing Jesus. The Holy Spirit moved among the crowd and many were saved. The next night, six blind Hindu girls were gloriously healed. More than 250,000 Muslims and Hindus came to Christ that week. People flew in from all over the nation to attend the services.

In the daytime, crowds gathered in front of the hotel where we were staying, all of them wanting us to pray for them. Even a government official came with his aide to ask for prayer.

It seemed as though once we knew that we had exhausted our own efforts, the Holy Spirit released the ministry of Christ through us. He ministered that week in a way that reminded me of the description in the Gospel of Mark. "And they were astonished beyond measure, saying, 'He has done all things well. He makes both the deaf to hear and the mute to speak.'"[58]

CHAPTER
31

After the terrorist attacks of September 11, 2001, the United States went to war against a group of terrorists in Afghanistan known as Al-Qaeda and its sponsor, a quasi-Islamic government known as the Taliban. Two years later, the United States invaded Iraq as part of a global war against terror. As US troops advanced across Iraq, the Holy Spirit prompted me to write a book on the war and what would happen once it ended.

As is often my practice when presented with a challenge from God, I opened my Bible and began to read. The scripture that leapt from the pages was from Psalm 1:1–3 (NIV).

Blessed is the one who does not walk in step with the wicked or stand in the way that sinners take or sit in the company of mockers, but whose delight is in the law of the LORD, and who meditates on his law day and night.

That person is like a tree planted by streams of water, which yields its fruit in season and whose leaf does not wither—whatever they do prospers.

This was the same scripture God had given me years before, after I had returned from Korea and lived at the YMCA in Philadelphia. He reminded me of it again in 1979, when He prompted me to write my first book, *Israel: America's Key to Survival.* The manuscript for that book turned out well and I thought it would make a great documentary, but no traditional publisher would publish it, and no producer would make a movie about it. So, after eighteen publishing houses rejected it, I published the book myself. I also produced my own documentary, trusting God that whatever I did, He would prosper. That book sold more than fifty thousand copies the first week it was released.[59]

This time, the book I was to write was to be entitled *Beyond Iraq: The Next Move—Ancient Prophecy and Modern Day Conspiracy Collide.* I was certain it might become a *New York Times* bestseller. I went to work on it the moment I thought of it, hiding in my study for nineteen hours a day. A few days later, the first draft of the book was completed.

When the book was released, I received another scripture from the Lord. This one from Joshua. "No man shall *be able to* stand before you all the days of your life; as I was with Moses, so I will be with you. I will not leave you nor forsake you."[60]

Energized by that verse, my staff and I placed phone calls to all the major networks in New York City, looking for an opportunity for me to appear on camera and discuss the book. After hours of hard work, we secured one commitment from a single program airing on a Christian network. It was only one show, but I was overjoyed to have that opening—then the show's producer called to cancel my appearance.

News of the cancellation was disappointing but rather than wallow in it I left my study, went to our prayer room, and fell on my knees before God. I reminded Him that I wrote the book at His prompting. It was His idea and I had done my best to be obedient in producing it. Now I needed Him to intervene once more and help us publicize the book.

As I lay on the floor before God, the Word from those verses in the Psalms flooded my mind and I heard the Lord say, "Whatever you do will prosper." With those words resounding in my spirit, I knew what to do. I would travel to New York City and call on every news personality at every major network.

That was a big job, so I left the prayer room, called my daughter Rachel, and asked if she would accompany me. She readily agreed to help, and the next morning we boarded a flight from Dallas.

When we reached our hotel room in New York I told Rachel, "If Jesus doesn't make this publicity effort a success, we will have failed completely. But I'd rather fail knowing I had faith in the Lord than in the flesh."

The next morning, we each took a stack of books and made the rounds of the television studios, handing out copies and asking for interviews. After we'd visited all the studios, we returned to our room and waited for the phone to ring. But nothing happened.

On Sunday, Rachel and I attended Times Square Church, which was pastored by my old friend David Wilkerson. After the service, he agreed to pray with me about the launch of the book. I appreciated his prayer, but as we left the church I was unsure whether to stay in New York or return to Texas. Rachel and I talked about it on the way back to our room and by the time we arrived I decided we should stay one more night.

The next morning, as we prepared to leave, my cell phone rang. The caller was a producer for Neil Cavuto from the Fox News Network, asking if I would appear for an interview on Neil's program. We were delighted for the opportunity, but that was only the beginning. Over the next several months, I scheduled appearances to promote the book on sixty-one television and radio programs. By June of that year, *Beyond Iraq* had sold 53,000 copies. In July, it hit the *New York Times* bestseller list, reaching as high as the top ten.

That book marked the beginning of a long list of books for me.

In 2003 alone, I released three titles—*God Wrestling*; *The Unanswered Prayers of Jesus*; and *The Prayer of David*. A steady stream of books followed as God blessed me with favor in an unusual way.

✦ ✦ ✦

By 2006, the war that had started well in Iraq seemed to have no end in sight as what appeared to be a quick operation bogged down in the face of local resistance. As the pace slowed, casualties mounted with more and more American soldiers being killed or maimed on the streets of Iraqi cities.

One day as I watched the latest reports on the evening newscasts, I realized that this was the first war of the twenty-first century. But it was not merely a war against terror, as some supposed. Instead, it was part of a much larger battle—the battle for the soul of America. I let that idea roll around in my mind a moment and slowly felt the Lord nudge me to write a book entitled *The Final Move Beyond Iraq: The Final Solution While the World Sleeps*.

As I gathered information for the book, the Lord brought to mind a list of people I needed to interview. Men such as the prime minister of Israel Benjamin Netanyahu, former CIA director James Woolsey, Israel Defense Forces Chief of Staff Lt. Gen. Moshe Ya'alon, Harvard College of Law Professor Alan Dershowitz, and Mort Zuckerman, Editor in Chief of *U.S. News & World Report* and owner of the *New*

York Daily News, among others. As the list grew, I started phoning each of them to schedule interviews.

In the midst of juggling the interview schedule, God directed me to go to Iraq—specifically to Iraqi Kurdistan, where I had visited years before. I was certain God was speaking to me, but the idea of going there gave me pause to consider the risk. At the time, there was a war going on in Iraq. From reports on the news channels, improvised explosive devices seemed to be planted along every roadway. Suicide bombers struck daily.

"And you want me to go to Kurdistan, God?"

God replied with a resounding definiteness. "I want you to go." So I went to work figuring out how to get to Kurdistan.

Using contacts developed in 1990 when I flew into the Kurdistan Region with Prince Khalid, and from my personal relationship that developed with the man who had been described to me as the king of Nineveh, I secured an invitation from the Kurdish regional government. My son, Michael, and a businessman from Texas agreed to accompany me.

Commercial travel was arranged that would take us as far as eastern Turkey. From there we would be in the hands of the Kurds.

A few days later, we flew from Dallas to New York and then to Turkey. From there we flew to Erbil, the capital of Iraqi Kurdistan. When we landed in Erbil we were greeted by a group of Kurdish dignitaries and then provided with a military escort to the vice president's guesthouse, where we stayed for the duration of our visit. While there, we were provided the finest food and accommodations the Kurdish government had to offer. During the day, we met with President Barzani and his cabinet, whom we interviewed for the book.

While we planned the trip, and even after we left the United States, we took steps to keep the details of our journey away from reporters and media outlets. The Kurdish region was part of Iraq, which still was embroiled in war, and my connections with leaders in Israel were well-known. I didn't want to reach Iraq to find Arab terrorists waiting at our door.

In spite of that effort, we arrived for our first meeting with President Barzani to find representatives from twenty-one media organizations waiting in his office. We'd kept things quiet on our side, but the invitation we'd received came from the State, which was a public matter. Coverage of our visit was broadcast during prime time and appeared on every television channel in Iraq.

Our visit with the Kurds lasted four days, during which we were allowed access to President Barzani and other leaders in the region, including Prime Minister Nechervan Barzani, Interior Minister Karim Sinjari, Minister of Peshmerga Affairs General Sheikh Ja'afar, Vice President Kosrat Rasul Ali, and others whose names even now I cannot divulge.

The trip went off without a serious problem but shortly after we returned home a truck bomb was detonated in front of Karim Sinjari's office, the interior minister whom we had interviewed just a few days earlier. He was unharmed, but others in and around the building were unable to escape the blast. Nineteen people were killed and seventy wounded, many of them women and children.

✦ ✦ ✦

In 2009, I went to work on a book entitled *Jimmy Carter: The Liberal Left and World Chaos*. As I gathered information for that book, I learned that Valery Giscard d'Estaing had been president of France when Mohammad Reza Pahlavi—the shah of Iran—had been deposed. For much of his life, Pahlavi had been a devotee of all things French, copying French architecture in some of Iran's buildings and going to great lengths to develop relationships with French leaders. The sentiment ran in both directions, and when d'Estaing served as the French president, he asked Pahlavi for a loan on behalf of the French government, a request Pahlavi granted.

As I thought about all of that, it occurred to me that I should interview d'Estaing. He had been in office when Pahlavi was deposed, an event that took place during the Carter administration. Not only that, both the Ayatollah Khomeini, who led the Islamic uprising in Iran that eventually toppled Pahlavi's government, and members of Pahlavi's family lived in Paris. I thought a discussion with d'Estaing might cast an interesting light on those events and circumstances.

While working on that book I took a trip to Jerusalem. One morning, as I spent time in my hotel reading and praying, I felt impressed to open my Bible to the book of Joshua. A verse I had underlined long before caught my eye. "Every place that the sole of your foot will tread upon I have given you, as I said to Moses."[61] I thought about that and about my desire to interview d'Estaing and wondered how the two might be related—what ground I might tread upon that would take me to an interview with him.

Later that morning I was seated in a restaurant downstairs. As I continued to think about the verse from Joshua, the Lord said, "There's a woman seated at the last table in back. Go over to her and tell her that she is special." I glanced in that direction and saw a beautiful woman seated on the far side of the dining room.

"That woman?"

"Yes. Tell her she's special."

The suggestion made me uncomfortable. *Lord, I don't want to go over to her. If I go over there, she'll think I'm flirting with her. I've been faithful to my wife and I've been careful to avoid even the appearance of evil.*

But the more I argued, the more persistent the impression became. "Tell her she is special."

When the Lord told me the third time, I rose from my chair, made my way across the dining room, and came to her table. "Excuse me,"

I said nervously. "I promise I'm not flirting with you, but I wanted to tell you. You are special."

As you might expect, she gave me a startled look. "I...don't even know you," she stammered.

I smiled. "No, you don't. And I don't know you, either."

At that, she seemed to relax. "My father always told me I was special. That's the most important word in my vocabulary." She gestured to a chair across from her, inviting me to sit. "You're not special," she said. "I don't know you, but I know you are no one special. What do you want?"

I had no idea who she was, but because this had all come about while I was praying and thinking about my interest in interviewing d'Estaing I thought perhaps it was an opening in that direction. So I said, "I want you to arrange a meeting for me next week with the former French president Valery Giscard d'Estaing."

A frown wrinkled her forehead. "Are you out of your mind? Just because I am his personal assistant doesn't mean I will do that for you. I most certainly will not."

I was floored. Like I said, I had no idea who she was, and certainly not the slightest inkling she had a connection to d'Estaing, but right then I also knew in my heart that my desire for an interview with him was about to be fulfilled.

"Monsieur," she continued, "the only way I would do that for you is if I really believed you were special." She tilted her head at an angle in an indignant gesture. "And obviously, you are not."

Without thinking, I took my cell phone from the pocket of my jacket and dialed the private number for Benjamin Netanyahu. He answered immediately. "Bibi," I began, "I'm sorry to bother you, but I need a big favor. Would you please tell this lady that I am special?" He chuckled, said that he would, and I handed her the phone.

A shocked expression came over her when she heard Netanyahu's voice. She listened a moment, then I heard her say, "Yes, Mr. Prime Minister, of course I will. Have a good day."

When the call ended, she handed the phone to me with a look of awe. "That was the prime minister. Benjamin Netanyahu."

I tucked the phone back into my pocket. "Yes, it certainly was."

"Well," she smiled. "I guess you're special after all." She leaned back in her chair and smiled. "Then I will set up a meeting for you with Mr. d'Estaing. In Paris. That will work for you?"

"Paris will work great for me."

"Good. He will see you within the week."

Two days later, the meeting was arranged and I left Jerusalem for Paris. When I arrived at d'Estaing's office, his assistant was waiting and ushered me in to meet him.

CHAPTER
32

As I mentioned earlier, later in his life my father left Massachusetts and moved back to Alabama. He settled into a house that was located in Dothan, a town not far from the area where he grew up and where some of his siblings lived. I visited him there with as much frequency as my schedule allowed and did my best to continue the reconciliation process with him.

Even then, after all those years, it wasn't easy to be around him and I think it wasn't easy for him to be with me, either. Often, when things didn't go his way, he resorted to the language he'd used against me when I was a child. In spite of the healing I'd received, hearing those words brought back a flood of memories, none of which were good.

For his part, my presence seemed to remind him of how badly he had treated me and my brothers and sisters when we were children. More than once in those later years he said, "I should have been locked up for the things I did to you kids." I had forgiven him and urged him to think on that—as well as on the Lord's forgiveness for him—rather than on the things that had happened in the past, but I'm not sure it had much effect on his thoughts and attitude.

Alabama suited Dad far better than Massachusetts. He liked the people, the warm climate, and enjoyed living alone. As he grew older, however, his condition deteriorated and his inability to care for himself became painfully obvious. I insisted that he find a different living arrangement but he resisted until finally, after more than a few arguments, we succeeded in moving him to a nursing home. In his typical fashion, he complained about it at first but soon adapted to the routine and before long seemed to enjoy life there, though he would never admit it to anyone. He spent the last year of his life there and died in 2010. Carolyn and I drove over for the funeral. I preached at his service and told the congregation about how he had been a decorated war hero, a construction contractor, and had come to know the Lord. There was no point in telling them the rest of the story. Those who knew him best already knew that part anyway.

Wrapping up Dad's affairs took an extra day or two, but as we returned home from the service, the Lord reminded me of a scripture from Revelation. Like many of the verses I've mentioned before, this was one I had circled years ago. "See, I have set before you an open door, and no one can shut it."[62]

The verse resonated with my spirit and I knew immediately that God was speaking to me about something specific He wanted me to do. When I prayed into that sense of leading, I heard the Holy Spirit tell me, "You are to go to New York City now. To the hotel of Mahmoud Ahmadinejad, the president of Iran. And meet with him." The tone of the Lord's command implied a sense of urgency. I had no idea why.

Ahmadinejad was elected president of Iran in 2005. Since taking office, he had made numerous speeches decrying Jews, Zionists, and Israelis, stating emphatically his desire to wipe them from the face of the earth. I was both a Jew and a Zionist, albeit a Christian Zionist, and a friend of many of Israel's most prominent leaders.

In addition, I had written four books that spoke directly against Ahmadinejad and the role he had staked out for Iran—*The Final Move Beyond Iraq*; *Jimmy Carter: The Liberal Left and World Chaos*; *Showdown with Nuclear Iran*; and *Atomic Iran*.[63] Just the year before, I had given a copy of one of those books to Ahmadinejad's chief of staff and asked him to pass it on to the president. Then, in the course of promoting those books and in response to various world events, I had given numerous interviews, many of them on the Fox News Network, decrying his terrorist activities.

All of that was well-known, and in my natural mind I was certain that no one in Ahmadinejad's administration or security detail would allow me anywhere near him. But I was equally certain that I had heard the voice of God—the same voice I had heard at eleven and the same voice that had directed me to do the things I've described in the previous pages of this book, all of which the Lord had successfully brought to pass. So in obedience to Him I set aside the thoughts of my natural mind, packed my bag, and prepared to travel.

The next day I flew from Dallas to New York and arrived fully prepared to meet with the president of Iran. He was in New York that week to attend a meeting of the United Nations General Assembly. That much I knew. What I did not know was the name of the hotel where he was staying.

The United Nations is located in the borough of Manhattan, an area of New York City that has hundreds of hotels. However, only a few of them are capable of attending to the needs of high-level officials and dignitaries, especially those who travel with large entourages that require special security measures. One of those hotels is the Waldorf Astoria.

With that in mind, I took a taxi from the airport to the Waldorf, checked in to a room, and began calling around to people I knew who might know where Ahmadinejad was staying. It didn't take long to learn that he wasn't staying at the Waldorf. When a few more calls failed to yield news of his location, a foreboding sense of gloom settled over me—as if I had been given an assignment from God and might actually fail to accomplish it. I knew that was a lie and that as long as I acted in obedience nothing could stand against me, but the voices that had assailed me before now tried to return. This time, though, rather than dwell on the negative, I decided to take the elevator downstairs to the lobby, get a soft drink, and see what I could learn down there.

When the elevator reached the first floor, the doors opened to a lobby crowded with people; some obviously with a sense of purpose, some apparently with time to spend. In the midst of that, a group of three gentlemen caught my eye. They were seated in an area to one side and by their appearance I thought they might be from Africa. The hotel was filled with people who had come for the UN meetings, most of them international guests.

The three men seemed friendly and I felt drawn in their direction, so I walked over to them and said, "How do you do? My name is Mike Evans."

All three jumped to their feet with a startled look. "You're not *the* Mike Evans, are you?" the first one asked.

His question caught me off guard but I quickly recovered and said, "Well, I *am* Mike Evans."

The man beside him spoke up. "Are you the Mike Evans that President Museveni and his wife talk about? The man who hosted his first event at the National Religious Broadcasters Conference and who prayed with them?"

"Yes," I answered, realizing they were talking about Yoweri Museveni—the president of Uganda, whom I had met through Maureen

Reagan Revell and her husband, Dennis, and who had opened the door for our ministry in his country. "Yes," I replied to the three men that day. "I am *that* Mike Evans."

Their faces brightened. "Praise the Lord," they all said with a smile. "The president is about to make his entrance."

Through the windows I saw a motorcade parked in front of the hotel and I started across the lobby in that direction. As I reached the entrance, the doors opened and President Museveni appeared. I was grinning from ear to ear as I shook his hand and said, "Welcome to New York, Mr. President."

Museveni was as surprised to see me as I was to see him, and equally as happy. When he asked why I was there, I told him I was looking for the hotel where Ahmadinejad was staying. He shook his head, "I don't think he's staying here." Then he turned to one of the men traveling with him and said something I didn't understand. A moment later, Museveni smiled back at me, leaned close, and said in a low voice, "He is staying at the Tudor Hotel."

When I arrived in the city, I didn't know that much about the details of how to accomplish the task God had given me. I didn't know where Ahmadinejad was staying and had not even thought about Museveni, much less consider that he, too, might be staying at the Waldorf and that our paths might cross. But God already knew all of that. I thought I was in the wrong hotel, but He had other plans and one of the things He'd planned was that I would not fail in the mission He had given me.

President Museveni and I visited a few minutes longer and then I returned to my room, put on my best suit, and headed for the Tudor. It was just one block from the United Nations.

Security at the Tudor was tight. Fire trucks blocked the cross streets, and policemen swarmed the sidewalks, along with Secret Service agents and many other law enforcement personnel. As I started toward the hotel entrance, a policeman stopped me. "Where are you going?"

"I'm going to my room in this hotel."

"No," he replied. "You don't have a room here."

"Yes I do, and I'll show it to you if you like."

After a few more questions, the policeman allowed me to continue through the entrance doors, but just inside the lobby a Secret Service agent stopped me. He had a list and only people on his list were allowed inside. "Where are you going?" he asked.

"I need to get to my room."

The agent glanced at his list and said, "You don't have a room here. You're not on the list. Please leave."

"But I do have a room," I insisted. "Come up to the desk with me and I'll show you my key."

In the natural realm, I didn't have a room in the hotel, but the scripture I had received from God had assured me, "See, I have set before you an open door, and no one can shut it." Every room has a door and if God had given me a door, then surely it led to a room. And if He sent me to an open door at a hotel, then I must have a room there. This was, after all, the hotel where Ahmadinejad was staying and to which I had been directed by Him.

The Secret Service agent accompanied me from the hotel entrance to the front desk, though I was convinced he was only humoring me, ready to remove me from the premises at once or, more likely, to place me under arrest. When we reached the desk I said to the clerk, "Could you give me my key, please? I'm in a hurry."

She frowned at me. "You have no room here."

"Surely I do. May I speak to your supervisor?"

A moment later, the supervisor came to the front desk. After an amicable exchange, he handed me a room key. The agent was surprised. I was relieved.

During the next two days, I sat in the lobby of the Tudor Hotel and approached anyone who seemed interested in talking. In the course of doing that, I had the opportunity to talk and pray with twenty-one Iranian cabinet ministers. Several times they shouted at me, "Zionist! We know who you are." But I didn't let that stop me.

On the third day, I talked to Ahmadinejad's chief of staff and asked if I could have a meeting with the president. To my great surprise, he agreed—without an argument or fuss.

The news left me so excited that I immediately phoned one of the key producers at Fox News and asked if one of their program hosts would like to interview the president of Iran. He was interested but told me in no uncertain terms that it would take an enormous amount of work on their part to make it happen. If I was wrong, he assured me, my name would be "mud" with the network.

The interview was tentatively scheduled for the same day Ahmadinejad was scheduled to deliver an address to the UN General Assembly. That address turned into a belligerent, acrimonious rant, the reaction to which was so adverse that my meeting with him was cancelled. I called Fox with the message and won't repeat what the producer said. He didn't believe there had ever been the possibility of a meeting in the first place and wasted no time in telling me so. I felt totally humiliated.

To add to my troubles, one of my brothers phoned me, cursing and screaming because he'd found out that when our father died, he left everything to me. What my brother didn't know was that before I left Alabama to return to Texas, I had disclaimed my right to inherit from him and signed over all of Dad's estate to my siblings.

After the phone calls with the Fox producer and with my brother, I went down to the lobby and spent the night pacing back and forth, praying and reciting the scripture God had given me and claiming His word to me as a promise. "See, I have set before you an open door, and no one can shut it."

Early the next morning, as hotel guests congregated in the lobby,

I saw a rather distinguished-looking man making his way through the crowd. I didn't know who he was but sensed in my spirit that I should approach him about seeing Ahmadinejad. In obedience to what I sensed, I walked over to the man, touched him on the arm, and said, "Sir, I only want to thank you for setting up the meeting with the president of Iran today."

He looked at me with the most vacant gaze. "Who are you?"

As briefly as possible, I told him who I was and why I was in New York. He listened intently but had very little to say, then continued on toward the front of the lobby and stepped out to the street.

Two hours later, when it seemed as if everyone was packing to leave the hotel, an Iranian came to me and said, "Go to the Barclay Hotel. The president will meet you there at ten."

In spite of the way things had turned out when I was promised a meeting with Ahmadinejad before, I called the Fox News producer that I spoke to earlier and told him I'd received a new invitation. I don't know if he believed me or not but the possibility of interviewing the president of Iran was too great an opportunity to miss. He arranged for a camera crew to meet me at the Barclay.

When I reached the hotel I was escorted to a room where the Fox News crew was already setting up. A few minutes later, Ahmadinejad entered and we went on the air with an interview. What had seemed impossible just a few days earlier now unfolded before my eyes and before the eyes of millions of television viewers.

It brought to mind a quote I remembered from President Obama, who was in office at the time. "**We can absorb a terrorist attack. A potential game changer would be a nuclear weapon in the hands of terrorists, blowing up a major American city.**" That day, with the interview proceeding, I felt as though I had played a part in seeing that such an attack never happened and that perhaps that was the reason I was sent to New York to meet with Ahmadinejad.

To be honest, when I heard the Lord speaking to me as I returned from my father's funeral, it seemed like an interruption. The month was planned well ahead of time, some of it from the year before. My father's death had disrupted that schedule and then when the Lord spoke to me, the month's timetable was turned on its head. But that was only how it felt. A disruption from God isn't a disruption at all but a blessing. A holy rearrangement. And always for a much larger purpose than our original plans. He was continuing to speak to me, a thing for which I had fervently prayed, and I was glad to hear His voice.

In spite of how I felt, I did my best to respond to Him through the application of four principles—obedience, generosity, humility, and forgiveness—all of them in as radical portions as I was able to offer, without yielding to the temporal consequences that might have fallen on me and with an eye toward completing the divine assignment sent my way. That was my approach then and it remains so today.

CHAPTER
33

Dad once told me that he had a recurring dream in which he attempted to give me a black stone. The stone had been passed from his grandfather to his father and then to him, but when he tried to give it to me, I refused. When he insisted, I opened my hand and showed him I already had a stone—a white one.

As he described the dream, I was reminded of a verse from Revelation. "I will also give that person a white stone with a new name written on it, known only to the one who receives it."[64] The black stone in Dad's dream represented a curse, one that he was trying to pass on to me and through me to his grandchildren. The white stone I held in my hand was symbolic of my life in Christ.

From a young age, I was determined to not be like my father, neither like him back then nor when had I grown up. As I thought about the future, I knew I wanted to be the best husband possible to my wife, should I be blessed to marry, which I was, and the best father to any children we might have.

As an adult, I learned from Scripture about generational curses. "I lay the sins of the parents upon their children and grandchildren; the entire family is affected—even children in the third and fourth generations."[65] My grandfather was abusive to his wife and to my father. My father was abusive to our mother, to me, and to my siblings. When I became a husband and father myself, I was grateful that the curse had been broken in my life and would not rule our marriage or be passed to our children.

✦ ✦ ✦

In the eyes of some I am an old man now, but I certainly don't feel like one. I'm as healthy and energetic as ever, filled with a vision for the future and excitement about seeing it come to pass. Thirty years ago, I felt quite differently. Back then, I really did feel like an old man. I was anxious to find affirmation from God and spent a lot of time rushing about from one thing to the next trying to earn His favor by the things I accomplished. A leftover from that generational curse my dad endured and under which I lived as a child, which left me exhausted and on the verge of an emotional collapse.

Now I know and understand that God's affirmation doesn't come from my accomplishments. Only from my obedience. My life in Christ is not about me doing all the good things I can think of and then asking God to bless that effort; rather, it's about hearing His voice and following His direction.

Not just the general direction He gives about living a Christian lifestyle, but the specific direction about where to go and what to do. Like the time He told me to go to Israel and meet with Menachem Begin and later, during that same trip, when He told me that I should call on Benzion Netanyahu to express my sympathy at the remembrance of his oldest son's death. Or when I went to New York to meet with Ahmadinejad, even though everything else I knew about the situation told me he would never see me.

Affirmation from God comes through obedience, and when I obey, I feel His pleasure. For me, each time I obey and step out in faith to execute those assignments, I hear the Holy Spirit say, "I'm proud of you, son. You did a good job!" That's the kind of response I never received from my biological father but which I've found in my heavenly Father many times over.

I didn't understand that years ago when I sat on the back steps of our building in New York and wept. Or when I sat on the back steps of our home in Texas and did the same. I was depressed and discouraged, fully convinced my effectiveness as a minister was over. I felt as barren as the desert, and God seemed more remote than ever. I still prayed, but the heavens were like brass, and my prayers seemed to bounce straight back at me without reaching anyone. All of which had a cascading emotional effect as condemnation and confusion from the Enemy mounted.

When the Enemy of your soul sidles up to you like that, suggesting that your ministry is over and that you're finished as a person, it's not because he has your best interests at heart. And it's not because you're his new best friend. He has one purpose and one purpose only—to destroy you. Scripture says he comes to "steal and kill and destroy."[66] That's his job and he does it well. I had to be reminded of that, and that Satan is a defeated foe.

Jesus came for the opposite effect. "I have come that they may have life, and that they may have *it* more abundantly."[67] As Paul told us in his epistle to the Ephesians, we really have been raised up with Christ and seated with him in the heavenly realms.[68] Living in an awareness of who we are in Christ takes time and attention. Time spent with Jesus and attention to what He says when we are with Him.

You can't know your friends, or spouse, or children without spending time with them. Time when you are genuinely devoted to only them. Time when you listen to what they have to say—really listen and not merely note the sound of their voice—followed by action designed to help them in the furtherance of their mission and calling in life.

It's the same with God. To hear His voice, you must spend time with Him. Listening—really listening—and allowing His voice to penetrate the clutter of your day. And when you hear from Him, you must do what He says, no matter how contrary that voice might be to the generally accepted wisdom of the day.

There were many key moments in my journey away from despair to victory. I have related many of those moments in the pages of this book. One of those moments came one morning when I picked up my Bible and read, "Being confident of this very thing, that He who has begun a good work in you will complete it until the day of Jesus Christ."[69] In that moment, the presence of the Holy Spirit surrounded me and I was reminded I must stand on the word God gave me and believed that He was still at work in my life. God wasn't finished with me then, and He's not finished with me now. He remains committed to completing the work He started in me.

Total release from depression and despair didn't come in that single moment, but the change in my direction did. The season of barrenness came to an end and I gradually learned to move forward again, this time focusing on listening for God's voice and acting in obedience to the things He directed me to do.

When I look back on the years we were in New York and then those first few years back in Texas, I see it now as a time when God refined my faith, honed my patience, and gave me the opportunity to sense Him reaching out to me through the darkness and emptiness that clouded my mind. As a result, I learned to listen more closely for the sound of His voice and to obey the things I heard.

Much of what I have heard from God has come through scripture, particular verses that He declared to me for my specific situation or a task that He wanted me to do. That was a change from what I expected. I expected Him to speak to me as He had that night in my bedroom when I was eleven. But I'm not eleven anymore, and instead He now speaks to me through the Scripture.

In conjunction with that, I have learned to speak the verses He gave me out loud. As a result, negative thoughts flee and I stop rehashing events of the past. Speaking the verses aloud becomes a form of meditation, a way to rehearse for the future, and a reminder to myself that I can become the person God made me to be. That I really can "do all things through Christ who strengthens me."[70]

American culture places very little interest on silence. You and I were trained and conditioned from an early age to fill every waking moment with sound, much of it little more than noise. Television, radio, computers, cell phones. We almost always have something playing in the background or at our fingertips.

Our spiritual lives reflect that perspective, too. We are prone to believe that when God is silent it means He has turned His back on us. If we do not sense His active presence, we feel alone, abandoned, and unloved. In reality, the opposite may be true.

We live in a very busy world. Our lives are awash in noise, some of it from without but much of it from within. Often, when it seems God is no longer present, He is simply waiting for us. Waiting for us to "Be still, and know that I am God."[71]

In my own life, I find that He speaks as powerfully as ever, but now I hear Him more often in the "still small voice," with which He spoke to Elijah long ago.[72] Not that I'm anything like Elijah, but that He always is as He was then. Defining Himself on His own terms. Interacting with us as He sees fit, not as our American cultural perspective might demand.

Often I think we are like little children—not so much hard of hearing as we are hard of listening. We hear, but we do not necessarily heed His warnings. Learning to hear God's voice from scripture—learning the way He expressed Himself to the men and women of old—teaches us how to distinguish the sound of His voice from our own and helps us avoid the deceptive whispers of the Enemy.

My journey to wholeness in Christ was painful, but it was not an unfamiliar path. I meet people all the time who feel that in order to get God's attention they must do more, work harder, talk louder, be smarter, but God tells us that in order to hear Him we must wait and seek and listen closely. Seeking first the Kingdom and His righteousness leads us to increased faith and less worry. Peace and worry cannot occupy the same space. One forces the other out. Instead of doing more, our prayer should be, "Help me to wait patiently for the very best You have for my life."

This is a truth we can live by as we continue through the twenty-first century. If God can get us to remain quiet in the Spirit, we will see His salvation. We will not allow our spiritual lives to be destroyed by the powerful forces that threaten to overwhelm us and render us helpless.

As a child I was fearful of my father, and that fear permeated every aspect of my life. I was shy and withdrawn. Anxiety, worry, and hurt dogged my every step. A spirit of rejection held me in its grip. I was unwanted and unloved—and I knew it. And then Jesus came to my rescue. I embraced Him and dedicated my life to His service. I learned that the Jesus about whom I had learned in Sunday school was as real as the air I breathed and as close as the skin on my back. He had called me "son," said He loved me and had a wonderful plan for my life.

When faced with adversity, we can do one of two things: we can accept it as our lot in life, or we can overcome it through the power of Christ and His Word. The moment I realized that the Enemy was out to destroy me, I did what God had told me to do. I got up and went—all the way to Israel. Doing God's will gave me the strength to overcome adversity. And then I began to worship Him, to praise Him, to exalt Him as my Creator. Praise dispelled the darkness and allowed the light of God's love to shine in and through me.

✦ ✦ ✦

A few years ago, I was in Dallas attending a conference. As I made my way across the lobby of the Fairmont Hotel two men walked by. As they passed me, one of them took hold of my jacket sleeve and began to shout, "Peace, peace, peace! Oh, seed of Israel, the hand of the Lord is on you. You will be a mighty witness to your people. Out of the pain of your cellar, out of the residue of your wounds, the Light has shined. Follow your favor. When the angel appeared to Mary, he called her 'highly favored.' You, too, are highly favored. You must respond as did Mary, 'Be it unto me according to Your Word.' That's how God wants you to respond today."

As suddenly as he had grabbed me, he let go and continued on his way. I followed after him and eventually cornered the man who was with him. "Who is that?" I asked, pointing to the man who had taken hold of my sleeve.

"That is Pastor John Osteen," he replied. "From Lakewood Church in Houston." John was the father of Joel Osteen, who most of us now see on television.[73]

After that initial encounter I talked with John often and we became good friends. He always ended our conversations with, "Mike, follow your favor."

The dictionary defines the word *favor* as meaning "provided with advantages; specially privileged." David wrote, "For You, O Lord, will bless the righteous; with favor You will surround him as with a shield."[74] What a blessing when I realized God wanted to give me special privileges! And not just me, but you, too. We all are righteous in Christ.

Although my childhood gave no hint of promise, God's favor has flowed through my life since then. Especially during the past thirty years. Not because of any work I have done, but solely by His grace and mercy. The only thing I *do* is believe and obey as best I can. I believe what He says to me, both by His spirit and by scripture, and do my best to obey His leading.

That same relationship of favor is readily available to you, too. That's what John Osteen was trying to tell me. If you walk according to God's leading, He will favor you.

Perhaps you feel you are not a particular favorite of anyone. I know how that feels. And you may not be the person others would choose to bless. Many times the world assesses our worth based on how much money we have, or how physically attractive we might be. God isn't like that. If you obey the leading God gives you and step out in faith to do His will, He will affirm you—and some of the most unlikely people will affirm you, too. God's favor supplants people, places, and circumstances. He will become for you "a shield about me, my glory, and the lifter of my head."[75] As I have tried to show in this book, I have learned to trust God, and though I have not always been perfect in that, His faithfulness has not waivered. He offers that same faithfulness to all of us.

CHAPTER
34

Over the past thirty years, I have come to realize that the key to living in a vital relationship with God rests in our response to Him. Radical obedience, generosity, humility, and forgiveness mean more than all the self-loathing and self-sacrifice we might force ourselves to make. Those qualities reflect the qualities of the Holy Spirit[76] and when they are evident in our life they magnify His image in us. They lift up the Lord and as He said, "If I am lifted up from the earth, [I] will draw all *peoples* to Myself,"[77] including us.

Drawing close to God teaches us to see with the eyes of our spirit, rather than with our natural mind. Not that we eschew reason altogether. Rather, in terms of our relationship with God we put reason in second place. As human reason takes a secondary place, the Holy Spirit is able to bring His plan and purpose to the forefront. Reason still plays a part. The things that He reveals through the Holy Spirit find confirmation, often through His Word, which requires reason to understand. But reason no longer drives the train. We no longer see the world through the lens of reason, but through the lens of the Holy Spirit.

The first chapters of the Gospel of Luke give us a glimpse into the early life of Jesus. And it is there we learn that, "Jesus grew in wisdom and stature, and in favor with God and man."[78] We find that same increase as we allow Him deeper and deeper access to our mind, our will, and our motivations as we learn to see the world through His eyes and allow His direction to become our motivation.

Scripture contains a record of the words spoken long ago by prophets, priests, and kings. By Jesus and by His disciples. What they saw and heard and experienced has been applied by the Holy Spirit to the lives of every succeeding generation. If we allow Him access to our lives, God will apply them to us as well. As His word becomes active in us, we will increase in favor with both God and man.

In my life, that has happened by the kind of radical response I mentioned above—the response of obedience, generosity, humility, and radical forgiveness. And when I say radical, I mean not merely responding with the minimum but with all that we have to give.

Radical forgiveness is a gift given to us by Jesus at Calvary. As the events of my life have shown, forgiveness can change a person. God's forgiveness changed me, and the forgiveness I extended to my father changed him. When we choose to forgive, we give an unearned and undeserved gift to two people who can't get that gift any other way. Those two people are the person who wronged us—and us. When we forgive someone, both of us are released from the wrong that stood between us.

And it's that way with the other elements of response that I've discovered. Radical humility means allowing God to dig deeply and constantly into my personality, rooting out not just the pride that confronts me in a given moment but the undiscovered areas of my personality as well. As the psalmist said, "Search me, O God, and know my heart! Try me and know my thoughts!"[79]

Radical generosity doesn't mean merely giving the tithe but going beyond financial gifts to lavishing opportunity, access, and acknowledgment on others. And radical obedience means doing the things God has told you to do, even when it seems silly or even crazy to your natural mind. Like when I sensed the Lord telling me to walk into the hotel in Saudi Arabia and say to the first person I met, "Can I go with you?" If I had not done that, I would have missed the opportunity to establish a relationship with the Kuwaiti royal family. I would have missed meeting the modern-day king of Nineveh—a relationship that led him to the Lord and made it possible for me to visit Iraqi Kurdistan ten years later.

You can probably recall dozens of similar incidents discussed in this book. Incidents that sounded ridiculous to the natural mind—in my case His command for me to stand on the sidewalk outside the hotel and wait for someone to pass by, which led to the opening in Uganda—but which had dramatic and eternal consequences. Not because I thought of them or dreamed them up, but because they came at the instigation of the Holy Spirit. If I had not responded to His voice with a radical, all-in response, I would have missed all that He had for me.

We cannot live in the presence of God while wallowing in discouragement and defeat. And seeking affirmation, in and of itself, is a waste of time and energy. I know—I've tried that and it doesn't work. I only found the sense of completion I really sought when I sought God for who He is. Himself and Himself alone. As I focused on that, He made His presence known to me by focusing my attention on those four areas—obedience, forgiveness, humility, and generosity.

It's always dangerous to systematize our personal experience with God and offer it as a plan for others to follow. God speaks to each of us in a unique way with a unique assignment. But I know this—those four key qualities the Holy Spirit spoke into my life are His character qualities, elements the apostle Paul described as "fruit of the Spirit." When we seek God, and seek Him with an ever-increasing and ever-deepening conviction in our hearts, His character will become more evident in our lives. And then we will find His affirmation.

Time and time again I have seen men and women who turned only to their spouses for affirmation. Others looked to their toys—boats, cars, clothes, jobs—or to their friends. People are obsessed with finding affirmation. They seek it of its own right and along the way get lost in a life of consumerism or promiscuity—looking for things or people to supply a sense of purpose and accomplishment that only God can give, and that only by seeking Him simply for who He is. Not for what He gives.

When we seek to grow in the image and favor of God, we find ourselves weaned from the affirmation of others. And we are not limited to a singular encounter with Him, but His presence gives us His light and life moment by moment, day by day. Bringing direction, empowerment, affirmation, mercy, grace, and purpose.

As I mentioned before, I was able to give my father the gift of radical forgiveness. Most of my siblings have been unable or unwilling to do that. They remain united to each other by a single thread—hatred for our father, and it has all but destroyed them. Having been abused by him and having chosen to respond in hatred, they have been trapped in a life that mirrors his. As a result, they have likewise become abusive, violent, and more. Rather than forgive they have chosen to blame, a choice that has left them bitter and broken.

God has given each of us gifts. Treasures of His image placed in us that can only be released by opening ourselves to His presence in our daily lives. It doesn't matter if we have been cast aside by others. It doesn't matter if we've been abused. The prophet Daniel said, "The people that do know their God shall be strong, and do exploits."[80] If you respond to Him with all your heart and all your being, your life will never be the same. "Have I not commanded you? Be strong and courageous. Do not be frightened, and do not be dismayed, for the Lord your God is with you wherever you go."[81]

✦ ✦ ✦

In the course of our work and ministry in Israel, we founded the Friends of Zion Heritage Center. One of its key functions is the operation of a museum located in Jerusalem. The museum tells the story of the modern state of Israel and showcases people—Jews and Christians alike—who helped establish the Jewish state, risked their lives and fortunes to protect and defend Jews from the Holocaust, and who have exhibited a commitment to "pray for the peace of Jerusalem."[82]

At its founding, the center established the Friend of Zion Award as a way of recognizing those who continue to exhibit a commitment to Israel. The initial award was presented to former US president George W. Bush. The center's international chairman and former

Israeli president, Shimon Peres, came to Dallas for the presentation ceremony, which was held at the George W. Bush Presidential Library on the campus of Southern Methodist University. The following year, we presented the award to Prince Albert II of Monaco. President Peres made that presentation as well.

Later that year, President Peres and I visited with Pope Francis at the Vatican. When we arrived, President Peres and the pope met alone. In that conversation, Peres told the pope about me, mentioning that I was named for my great-grandfather, Rabbi Mikel Katzenelson, who was a rabbi from Vishnyeva, Belarus, the same town as Peres and his family.

Pope Francis was interested in the account of my great-grandfather and the way the lives of our ancestors were intertwined—Peres' grandfather and my great-grandfather were best friends and died together when both Nazi soldiers and townspeople burned their synagogue to the ground.

After their private visit, President Peres and Pope Francis came out to the room where I was waiting. We had a picture of Abraham that we presented to him and as I handed it to him I said, "This is a picture of the first Holy Father."

He studied the picture a moment, then turned to two cardinals who accompanied him adding, "For two thousand years we have said that Peter was the first Holy Father. Now the Jews have come to set the record straight."

They laughed good-naturedly, then the pope turned to me and very softly said, "You are a Jewish man."

"Yes," I replied. "I am a Jew and a Christian."

"President Peres has told me the story of your great-grandfather. Can you tell me how you as a Jew came to faith in Jesus Christ?"

As succinctly as possible, I recounted the story you read in the earlier chapters of this book—how my father abused us, the night I thought I was going to die and cried out in agony, "Why was I born?" then Jesus appeared to me in my bedroom. As I shared that account I began to cry. Pope Francis began to cry, too, and so did Shimon Peres.

Later that evening over dinner Peres said to me, "I know why you were born."

"Why was that?"

"You could not defend one Jew—your mother—from an anti-Semite. But God gave you a nation of Jews to defend." I had heard this from the Lord, but it was great to have that word confirmed through him.

"You and I have become very close these past couple of years," he continued with a smile. "Like family."

"Yes," I said. "It felt that way to me and I have hoped it felt that way for you, too."

Peres explained, "Today I realized why I felt that way about you. I went to Israel because of my grandfather, Rabbi Metzner. Everything in my life has come about because of him. He was my hero. But your great-grandfather was the chief rabbi of the synagogue. They died together. Burned to death in the same synagogue—your great-grandfather and my grandfather." Then he looked at me and said, "You are truly family."

When I asked the question that night as an eleven-year-old, "Why was I born?" I didn't know it would take so long to find the answer. That question—the desperate cry of a desperate boy—provided God with an opening into my life and launched me on a journey. A lifetime of twists and turns.

That journey led me to an answer. Actually, it led me to many answers. The first answer came as soon as I asked that question, when Jesus appeared and told me He had a plan for my life. My question was, "Why was I born?" His answer was, "To fulfill the plan I have for you."

The next answer came as I battled through depression and despair and learned to seek God for Himself and Himself alone. Why was I born? To fulfill His plan. What was His plan? That I should worship Him with all my heart and live for Him in a life of radical obedience, free from depression and despair.

But what does that mean? On a daily basis. What does it mean to live a life of radical obedience? It means that I sit quietly when He says sit. I pack my bags and travel when He says go. And no matter how strange His command may sound to my mind, I do what He says.

And what has He said? That I who could not defend a single

Jew—my mother—will defend a nation of Jews—Israel. And that is what I have done and what I am doing. Some call me a Christian Zionist and use that term derisively. I accept it as a description of who I am and the person I was called to be. Building bridges between Jews and Christians. Reconciling them to each other as I have been reconciled in myself. A Christian Zionist. A defender of Israel. A man doing his best to hear God's voice and do the things He tells me to do. That's why I was born.

ENDNOTES

1. Like many immigrants in the early twentieth century, Schleman and Michla took Americanized versions of their names after they arrived in New York. Schleman became Samuel and Michla was known as Mollie. They chose new names for their sons, too. Nochem was renamed Nathan and Mottle became Max.

2. Bryce Hospital is the state of Alabama's psychiatric institution.

3. In the 1940s, military personnel were given "goofballs" during WWII in the South Pacific region to allow soldiers to tolerate the heat and humidity of daily working conditions. Goofballs were distributed to lower the respiratory system and blood pressure to combat the extreme conditions. Many soldiers returned with addictions that required several months of rehabilitation before discharge. http://en.wikipedia.org/wiki/Barbiturate; accessed November 2011.

4. Daniel 10:13, 10:21, 12:1; Jude 1:9; Revelation 12:7

5. J. Roswell Flower. Reared in the Methodist Church he later lost interest in Christianity but his mother was saved at a Pentecostal Revival. Her conversion led to his salvation and subsequent call to ministry. He was present at a meeting in Hot Springs, Arkansas, in 1914, at which the Assemblies of God denomination was formed. Flower was elected secretary and went on to serve the denomination in many key leadership roles, including general secretary.

   Other things that Dad did to us were, in retrospect, not quite so threatening as the beatings but still conveyed the shallowness of his concern for us.

   Most Saturdays, Dad awoke to a horrible hangover.

After sipping on a glass of tomato juice and downing a few aspirin tablets, he ate breakfast—usually eggs and bacon—then moved downstairs to the basement. A place he'd dubbed Bob's Bar. It was set up like one of the taverns in town, with an actual bar complete with shelves that were lined with bottles of liquor. When his friends came over, he'd serve as bartender, pouring drinks for them and regaling them with stories.

His friends loved the place, not just for the free drinks but because Dad also had a rifle range down there that he'd built to NRA specifications. It was lined with large barrels to contain any stray bullets and was rigged with a system of pulleys to retrieve the paper targets from the far end. It was quite a combination—booze and guns.

One day when I was ten or eleven he forced me to clean up the target area. The barrels were banded with metal, and raw electric lines dangled overhead near the water pipes. In winter, condensation formed on the pipes and sparks flew every time moisture dripped onto the wires. The combination of moisture and electricity frightened me, but I was also claustrophobic.

As I picked up the spent cartridges and shredded targets, one of the wires touched me. I felt a jolt of electricity shoot through my body and tried to escape. Dad just laughed at my fear. He wasn't at all concerned.

6. Childhelp.org; retrieved December 1, 2016.

7. Herbert Ward. Director of St. Jude's Ranch for Children, Boulder City, Nevada.

8. Even so, our dog tag numbers were sequential. Mine was RA112052. His was RA112051.

9. 1 Samuel 3:10, NIV

10. Daniel 10:9–11 NKJV

11. Two years after I left Korea, that spot on the mountain where I had prayed was purchased by Dr. David Yonggi Cho and became the Osanri Choi-Jashil Prayer and Fasting Mountain Facility owned by Yoido Full Gospel Church. Today over a million and a half people visit the site annually to fast and pray. Dr. Cho later told me I was perhaps the first person to pray on that mountain.

12. Sometime after that, while I was still living in Philadelphia and working at the army recruitment office, I was involved in an automobile accident. We notified the police and they sent an officer to the scene to write an accident report. When the officer checked the registration of my car he learned that it had been stolen. I tried to explain how I came to have the car but the officer arrested me anyway and took me to the police station for questioning. I called my commanding officer at the recruitment office and told him what happened. He came down and got me out, but I lost the car in the process.

13. Psalm 1:1–3 NIV

14. 1 Corinthians 2:9–10 NIV

15. Despite our less-than-ideal living conditions we had only one fight that year. Carolyn's poodle chewed the cover off my Thompson *Chain Reference Bible*. It sounds silly now and I laugh about it, but at the time I was not a happy camper.

16. Jeremiah 29:13

17. Matthew 21:21 NKJV

18. Matthew 5:23–24 NIV

19. Psalm 147:3 NKJV

20. Proverbs 15:33

21. As he began to weep, he told me he had not cried when his father died. Instead he had said, "I'm glad the old fool is dead."

22. Exodus 17:12

23. In 1986, he became the second sitting member of the United States Congress to fly in space, as a payload specialist on the Space Shuttle *Columbia*. http://en.wikipedia.org/wiki/Bill_Nelson; accessed June 2011.

24. Isaiah 53:5 NKJV

25. That scripture became my constant companion. I posted it in my car, in my office, on the mirror in my bathroom, on the refrigerator door. I made it into a card and put it in my wallet. I thought about it, meditated on it, and prayed it day after day.

26. Isaiah 40:31 NKJV

27. Twenty years later, I told Benjamin about my encounter with Mr. Begin. He replied with a grin, "I don't know if I should kick you or kiss you."

28. My good friend Ben Armstrong, executive director of National Religious Broadcasters, wrote of my relationship with the prime minister, "Mr. Begin genuinely loved Mike Evans. He was his friend."

29. The only thing Dad ever said about Mom's father was, "I met him, but she had rotten things to say about him. I think he was abusive from what I gathered. She told me things that I didn't want to hear in the first place. She'd come out with stuff that didn't sound so good."

30. Six people were killed by the 1993 attack and more than a thousand injured.

31. The Alfred P. Murrah Federal Building was destroyed on April 19, 1995, by a bomb designed and detonated by Timothy McVeigh. For his role in the attack, McVeigh was executed in 2001.

32. Snell was convicted of murdering the pawnshop owner and state trooper. He was executed on April 19, 1995.

33. The car's license plate bore the prefix 666, common among Israeli vehicles, but a little unsettling for the rest of us.

34. Hebrews 13:2 NKJV

35. Isaiah 58:14 NKJV

36. Isaiah 43:1–2 NKJV

37. Job 42:3 NIV

38. Second Chronicles 7:14 NIV

39. My paraphrase of Acts 3:6

40. Isaiah 41:10–12 NIV

41. Psalm 121:4 NIV

42. Isaiah 43:6 NKJV

43. William Shakespeare, *Hamlet Act 3, Scene 1*

44. Isaiah 60:1–4 NKJV

45. The site of the ancient city of Nineveh is located on the northern outskirts of Mosul.

46. 1 Samuel 15:22 NKJV

47. Isaiah 62:1–3 NKJV

48. Acts 16:9 NKJV

49. 1 John 4:4 KJV

50. Genesis 18

51. Philippians 4:19 NIV

52. Isaiah 40:28–31 NKJV

53. Oral Roberts was a Methodist–Pentecostal minister and a pioneer in the use of television. He began preaching at the age of twenty and remained active in ministry until his death at the age of 91 in 2009.

54. Benjamin L. Armstrong graduated from Nyack Missionary Training Institute in 1945 and went on to earn a BS, MA, and PhD from New York University. He did additional study at Princeton Theological Seminary and earned an MDiv from Union Theological Seminary. After pastoring a number of Presbyterian congregations he became the director of radio for Trans World Radio in 1958. From 1966 through 1989 he led the National Religious Broadcasters, conducting NRB conventions in Washington, D.C., that became the focal point of conservative Christian political involvement, especially during the Reagan years.

55. Isaiah 55:11 NLT

56. Jeremiah 33:3 NKJV

57. Mark 7:37 NKJV

58. Since then, I went on to publish more than forty titles that have been read by more than 28,000,000 people worldwide.

59. Joshua 1:5 NKJV

60. Joshua 1:3 NKJV

61. Revelation 3:8 NKJV

62. I also wrote two other books that contain several chapters detailing his insanity.

63. Revelation 2:17 NIV

64. Exodus 34:7 NLT

65. John 10:10 NIV

66. John 10:10 NKJV, the remainder of the verse cited in note 66 above.

67. Ephesians 2:6 NIV

68. Philippians 1:6 NKJV

69. Philippians 4:13 NKJV

70. Psalm 46:10 NKJV

71. 1 Kings 19:11–13 KJV

72. John Osteen founded Lakewood Church in 1959. He pastored there until his death in 1999.

73. Psalm 5:12 NKJV

74. Psalm 3:3 ESV

75. Galatians 5:22

76. John 12:32 NKJV

77. Luke 2:52 NIV

78. Psalm 139:23 ESV

79. Daniel 11:32 KJV

80. Joshua 1:9 ESV

81. Psalm 122:6 NIV

BOOKS BY: MIKE EVANS

Israel: America's Key to Survival

Save Jerusalem

The Return

Jerusalem D.C.

Purity and Peace of Mind

Who Cries for the Hurting?

Living Fear Free

I Shall Not Want

Let My People Go

Jerusalem Betrayed

Seven Years of Shaking: A Vision

The Nuclear Bomb of Islam

Jerusalem Prophecies

Pray For Peace of Jerusalem

America's War:
  The Beginning of the End

The Jerusalem Scroll

The Prayer of David

The Unanswered Prayers of Jesus

God Wrestling

The American Prophecies

Beyond Iraq: The Next Move

The Final Move beyond Iraq

Showdown with Nuclear Iran

Jimmy Carter: The Liberal Left
  and World Chaos

Atomic Iran

Cursed

Betrayed

The Light

Corrie's Reflections & Meditations

The Revolution

The Final Generation

Seven Days

The Locket

Persia: The Final Jihad

GAMECHANGER SERIES:

  GameChanger

  Samson Option

  The Four Horsemen

THE PROTOCOLS SERIES:

  The Protocols

  The Candidate

Jerusalem

The History of Christian Zionism

Countdown

Ten Boom: Betsie, Promise of God

Commanded Blessing

Born Again: 1948

Born Again: 1967

Presidents in Prophecy

Stand with Israel

Prayer, Power and Purpose

Turning Your Pain Into Gain

Christopher Columbus, Secret Jew

Living in the F.O.G.

Finding Favor with God

Finding Favor with Man

Unleashing God's Favor

The Jewish State: The Volunteers

See You in New York

Friends of Zion:
  Patterson & Wingate

The Columbus Code

The Temple

Satan, You Can't Have
  My Country!

Satan, You Can't Have Israel!

Lights in the Darkness

The Seven Feasts of Israel

Netanyahu

Jew-Hatred and the Church

The Visionaries

Why Was I Born?

Son, I Love You

COMING SOON:

Jerusalem DC (David's Capital)

Israel Reborn

TO PURCHASE, CONTACT: orders@timeworthybooks.com
P. O. BOX 30000, PHOENIX, AZ 85046

MICHAEL DAVID EVANS, the #1 *New York Times* bestselling author, is an award-winning journalist/Middle East analyst. Dr. Evans has appeared on hundreds of network television and radio shows including *Good Morning America, Crossfire* and *Nightline*, and *The Rush Limbaugh Show*, and on Fox Network, *CNN World News*, NBC, ABC, and CBS. His articles have been published in the *Wall Street Journal, USA Today, Washington Times, Jerusalem Post* and newspapers worldwide. More than twenty-five million copies of his books are in print, and he is the award-winning producer of nine documentaries based on his books.

Dr. Evans is considered one of the world's leading experts on Israel and the Middle East, and is one of the most sought-after speakers on that subject. He is the chairman of the board of the ten Boom Holocaust Museum in Haarlem, Holland, and is the founder of Israel's first Christian museum located in the Friends of Zion Heritage Center in Jerusalem.

Dr. Evans has authored a number of books including: *History of Christian Zionism, Showdown with Nuclear Iran, Atomic Iran, The Next Move Beyond Iraq, The Final Move Beyond Iraq*, and *Countdown*. His body of work also includes the novels *Seven Days, GameChanger, The Samson Option, The Four Horsemen, The Locket, Born Again: 1967*, and *The Columbus Code*.

✦ ✦ ✦

Michael David Evans is available to speak or for interviews.
Contact: EVENTS@drmichaeldevans.com.